ALIVE IN WORLD WAR TWO

The Cousins' Chronicle
1939 - 1945
commentary and memoir

Susan Barrett

Copyright © Susan Barrett 2016

For my sister Jane
and all our cousins, known and unknown

Introduction

Anyone who has ever gazed in dismay at a pile of possessions and wondered what to keep and what to throw away will sympathise with my late cousin Alice. In 1943 she was faced with a growing problem: the result of an idea she'd had at the beginning of the war. The monthly newsletters circulated among the scattered members of her extended family were piling up in her small Rye cottage. She asked the writers for their views: was what she'd christened the Cousins' Family Chronicle worth keeping?

Yes, they decided, it was. The Chronicle continued, every month without fail, until December 1945. Two thirds of the newsletters have survived.

My own involvement with the Cousins' Family Chronicle started with a question from my sister: "Did you know that a cousin of our father lives somewhere near here?" Jane was on a visit from her Surrey home to mine in East Devon. A cousin! *Here*? Our only first cousin lives in New York. He was brought up in Canada and was not part of our childhood at all. As children growing up in West Devon, we'd heard tell of distant relatives on my father's side, who lived far away. They were called Cousin Joe, Cousin Jack, Cousin Ivy, Cousin Grace and so on. They were no more real to us than the characters living between the covers of the musty-smelling books at the bottom of our toy cupboard. There was one exception: Cousin Alice. She used to visit us in Tavistock. She'd been entirely real – in the 1940s.

A living cousin, here in Hemyock? It was unbelievable. Alice would have long since died; she'd lived in Sussex; she'd never married. Our mother's family came from Surrey; our father's from Manchester. They only came to live in Devon because our father was appointed the commander of the Royal Engineers in Devonport a year before the war began. When the war ended, my mother insisted on staying put in their rented house. As the daughter of an army officer and the wife of another, she'd spent her life going from one outpost of the Empire to the next. It was only when Jane and I had left home that our parents moved away from Devon. My mother ended her years in the converted stables of her parents' Surrey home. In her wedding photograph taken on the lawn in 1919, the stables appear in the background. She'd come full circle.

While I've moved from Devon to London to Greece and back to Devon, Jane has been the settled one. She and her husband built a house in the corner of our grandmother's garden, near the stables, and they still live there fifty five years later. Jane has always kept in touch with members of the family, however distant. It was through one of these relations, a man much our age called John Werner, that she learnt that one of his daughters was living in my neighbourhood.

I'd collected Nicola Werner's Majolica pottery for some time, without ever suspecting we were related in any way. I should have guessed, though, from the surname. I'd heard in childhood of someone called Grace Werner, said to be my father's favourite cousin. I have a faint childhood memory of a gentle presence with a halo of soft hair.

Not long after this, John came to stay with Nicola. He brought with him a brown, leather suitcase filled with papers he thought might interest me. The case had two bright, gilt clasps, the sort that spring open on release. Inside were piles of papers covered in handwriting of different styles, bound into sheaves with coloured wool. "Family letters," said John, "exchanged during the Second World War. Your mother was one of the contributors."

I scrambled for my spectacles. The pages held the voices of people writing during a war I had lived through but hadn't understood. I wanted to read, and share, every last word. John lent me the suitcase. But I soon discovered what an immense task this would be. The handwriting, for a start – the confusion of names – the unknown relationships – the context of the war I had been too young to understand – above all, the sheer quantity of material – it was just *too much*.

I realised that, before it could all be easily read, it would have to be typed. This was a bigger and more tedious task than I had imagined. In the end, my sister and I, with the help of a typist, managed to produce a digital file of the handwritten letters. Printed out, they became a document of 200,000 words on 400 pages – a cumbersome object that weighs several pounds. Well before this, my interest in finding references to my mother's younger daughter had all but evaporated. A new desire had developed. I wanted to share with as many others as possible the wealth the suitcase contained: descriptions of the daily lives of members of an extended family dispersed by war, which they'd recorded monthly from 1939 to 1945.

This mammoth labour was the brainchild of my remembered cousin, Alice. At the outbreak of war, she'd invited four families, connected with her and each other by their common grandparents, to keep in touch by sending her newsletters each month. These she would bind into folders which could then be circulated around the same group of cousins before being returned to her. No-one imagined the project would last very long. The war would be over within a year, surely.

By the time Alice threaded red wool through the holes she'd skewered through the final month's letters, she calculated the total number of folders should have been 72. But not all the issues of her Chronicle had survived the war: the bombing, the U boats that sank Atlantic convoys, and the haphazard nature of wartime mail from cousins in different parts of the world – Canada, Africa, the Middle East, India and Burma, as well as France, England, Italy and Germany. In spite of this, John Werner's suitcase contained 50 folders of handwritten newsletters. The cousins' wartime lives lay in my hands.

Even after I'd read, transcribed, put together and printed the entire document, I was still bewildered by the names and the different relationships. I felt overwhelmed - but somehow responsible. The cousins had lived through six years of war and written monthly accounts of their experience, whenever and wherever they could, with no thought of a future readership. Today, the members of such a family might be communicating briefly and infrequently on Facebook, if at all. In those war years, they sat down each month with pen and paper and described at length what was happening in their individual lives. I vowed to bring their voices into the present, but in a less weighty, more digestible way. I took over Cousin Alice's role as editor, to create a new Chronicle relevant to the 21st century. The difficulties and tragedies they suffered could be viewed as nothing compared with the devastation and mass deaths experienced on the continent and elsewhere. Yet a parent who has lost a son is not consoled by the awareness that he or she isn't the only bereaved person in the world: three young men whose lives we follow in the early years of the Chronicle would not be alive at its conclusion.

The cousins were typical of the generation who responded to Churchill's eloquence when Britain defied Hitler: they were ordinary people, unknown, unhonoured and remarkable only for their resilience. Today, we are in the midst of a different kind of war, with no end in sight. This Chronicle is my salute to the cousins of the past for the way they did their best in their time and place, and an invocation of their spirit for our times. On the scale of human evolution, wherever and whenever we live, we are all cousins working out how best to live our lives in the conditions of our own times.

And like all monuments to honour the war dead - wherever those monuments are built, by whatever nation and in whatever century - the Chronicle raises the question that Koestler once asked Freud: why war?

ONE

Introducing Cousin Alice

On my seventh birthday in June 1945, Cousin Alice, who was by then 77, was staying with us at Markham, Tavistock, Devon. She patted the place beside her on the sofa. "Seven is a very important number," she told me. I sat down with trepidation. She seemed to me like a character from Grimms' Fairy Tales; gaunt, long-skirted, smelling faintly yellowed like linen kept too long in a drawer. Her hair was looped up in intriguing coils which needed large pins to keep them in place. "Now," she said, holding her ear trumpet between her ear and my mouth. The trumpet was nothing more than a cardboard tube, of the sort used to send rolls of paper through the post. "*Now*. Tell me why seven is such an important number." I can still hear my silence. Perhaps I did come up with something, even if not her comprehensive list: seven days of the week, seven horsemen of the Apocalypse, seven seas, seven heavens of delight…I could have added 'seven seconds of sheer fright'. I don't suppose she was really frightening. But she was different from the normal run of Markham visitors, and immensely ancient.

Alice was described as being s*tone* deaf. In the Chronicle she often mentions a visit to Dr Jobson, a hearing specialist. It can't have been easy for her but I understand that she overcame her handicap in remarkable style. I've learnt more about her from a book 'Fifty Years in Every Street', a history of Manchester University Settlement by M.D. Stocks, published in 1945, which she may well have brought, hot off the press, on her visit to us in June. I guess she would have called attention to it in a quietly proud way.

University settlements were centres where the educated could bring education to the uneducated. The idea sprang from a paper read in St. John's College, Cambridge, in 1883 by Samuel Barnett, an East End parson, entitled 'Settlements of University Men in Great Towns'. Inspired by his vision, Toynbee Hall in Whitechapel was the first to carry out the mission "*to open up a more accurate conception among the well-to-do classes of the stresses and strains of working-class life"*, to quote from the book.

Cousin Alice was closely involved with the University Settlement in Ancoats Hall, Manchester. She was one of the first graduates of the university, with an MA in history, and was Warden of the Settlement from 1898 to 1907. The objectives of the settlement, which had recently combined with the Manchester Art Museum, were *"to disseminate and nourish a healthy love of Nature and of the best in Art, Music, Literature and Science among the industrial population of Manchester."* The job of Warden was to put together a calendar of appropriate lectures and persuade those able to deliver them to come to Ancoats. In the pages of the Cousins' Family Chronicle, Alice is constantly meeting friends made during that period. She often mentions J.J. Mallon who in the Foreword to the History of the Settlement[1] gave a scintillating description of her:

> "Alice Crompton was an exceptional leader. She swept into Ancoats like a wind. Someone said that she brought hope like a relief column and reassurance like a grant-in-aid. She vibrated with energy and purpose and was loved for her sympathy and grace. She upreared a banner and called a crusade. And crusaders responded. From the University and the Manchester Guardian especially, gifted men were drawn to Ancoats: among others, Tout, Weiss, Chapman, Hartog, Powicke, Hardhouse, Ensor and Laurence Scott whose early death was a universal bereavement. T.C. Horsfall, a civic saint who founded the Art Museum, and taught us to loathe jerry builders, was already attached; so was Pilkington-Turner. ...
> ... Unlabelled by Social Science Courses, unsustained by trust funds or grants of public money, these Settlement workers taught what they knew and learned as they taught. And among them rose the darting flame-like personality of the first woman Warden: Alice Crompton. Had one not known for certain that she was a duly authenticated graduate of Owens College (which became Manchester University), it might have been suspected that some willowy pre-Raphaelite lady, inflamed with an explosive energy that was no part of her creator's ideal of feminine grace, had burst suddenly out of an Art Museum folio, and looping up dishevelled draperies, swept out into Ancoats to find among its living people a warmth and variety of companionship denied to the passive exhibits of the lecturer.

---

[1] *'Fifty Years in Every Street'*, by M.D. Stocks, Manchester University Press, 1945

> Many years later a Settlement worker of the nineteen-thirties – knowing Professor Alexander's good repute as a life-long feminist and an admirer of active intellectual women – asked him what Alice Crompton was like, in those far off Ancoats days. The old philosopher paused for a moment, smiling with his eyes as though recapturing a pleasing visual memory. Then – 'She was a most beautiful creature,' he said."

Although Cousin Alice had resigned as Warden in 1907 due to family circumstances – I don't know what these might have been – she was called back in 1924, when the Settlement was in crisis due to lack of funds and energy for maintenance. Professor J.L. Stocks reported that it was as though he'd been present as Aladdin rubbed his lamp. Alice, by now 57, swept in like a wind once again.

> "Miss Crompton's deafness, in some respects an impediment, had one advantage. It enabled her to say what she wished without interruption and, by retaining full control of her amplifying instrument, to exercise a kind of chairmanship over the resulting discussion. On the occasion of this first interview[2], she expounded at length her plan of reconstruction, embodying a public appeal and an indication of the persons and interests to be drawn into its orbit. This done, she handed the mouthpiece of her amplifier to Professor Stocks with a flashing smile, embodying the surrender of the eternal feminine to the leadership of the eternal masculine, and the words 'Now please, you must tell me exactly what you want me to do..'"[3]

I'm sad that I missed knowing her. To my seven year old self she and her ear trumpet were too intimidating. How do you shout a hesitant response down a cardboard tube? If I could go back and meet Alice, I might still be intimidated. She patrols the pages of the Chronicle like a benevolent but stern headmistress. The contributors often sound like nervous seven-year-olds in relation to her. Had they remembered to leave a margin? Were they late with their contributions? Was the paper they used of the right kind and size? And what would she have thought of my project of bringing her Cousins' Family Chronicle into the present, seventy five years after she began it?

---

[2] With Professor Stocks in 1924
[3] *'Fifty Years in Every Street'*, (Ibid))

As I tussled with the cousins' handwriting, I sympathised with Alice over the enormous task she'd taken on, corralling the various family members into sending her their contributions every month, on suitable paper of the prescribed dimensions. Here she is in August 1941:

> *"Note from Alice*
> *Many apologies for the late appearance of this number. I have been waiting in the hope of receiving two more contributions, which alas! have not turned up!*
> *(The margin difficulty still arises! The simplest plan is to fold each sheet as this one has been folded. Then the margin is indicated at the proper place on each side.)"*

The margins were necessary to leave room for Cousin Alice to pierce holes in the pages with a darning needle, then thread them together between card covers with different coloured wools. A month later she wrote:

> *"Note from Alice*
> *Will Cousins please try to despatch their notes on the 3rd day of the month after that to which the notes refer? Otherwise the news gets terribly stale before it goes on Circuit. And it is sometimes almost too late to send to Canada."*

The Chronicle had started in January 1940, headed Volume I No. 1, with contributions written in December. She introduced the last folder, Volume VI, No.12, December 1945, as follows:

> *"Editorial Notes*
> *This number is No. 72 in the whole series of C.F.C & completes its 6th year of issue. Would anyone else like to take on the not unpleasant task of Editorship? If so, I would willingly hand over the job, tho' ready to carry on if need be."*

No-one volunteered to take over the 'not unpleasant task'. The war was over and the hardships of peace were beginning. The cousins had had enough.

*

Some members of the Becker family c.1857

L to r back row: James Esther Leigh Alice (Jay) Arthur Victoria Tony (Schulz) Lydia

L to r front row: Evilana (von Hoffman), Hannibal Leigh, Edmund, Wilfred

Names as noted at the time.

Ernest Hannibal Becker from Thuringia, Saxony = Lydia Kay Leigh (d 1843)
b 1771, d 1852, chemical manufacturer, violinist   (Leigh>Egerton>Stanley>Clifford>Brandon>Henry VII)

Hannibal Leigh Becker (b 1803) = Mary Duncuft (b 1807)

Lydia	Mary	Bertha	Sophia	Esther	Ernest	Victoria	James	John	Frederic	Arthur	Edward	Wilfred	Charles	Louisa
1827	1828	1830 d 1832	1833 d 1834	1834	1835	1837	1838	1840	1842 d.1843	1843	1845	1850	1851	1854

Chronicle's main contributors: IRENE BECKER, (nee Watts, wife of Trevor Becker, son of Wilfred), ALICE CROMPTON (daughter of Victoria), IVY CROMPTON (wife of JACK CROMPTON, son of Victoria), GRACE WERNER and KATHLEEN SMITHELLS (granddaughters of Mary Becker and John HENDERSON), MOLLY EASTON (daughter of Louisa and Edmund WITHINGTON), MOLLY WITHINGTON (nee Phillips, wife of Richard Leigh Withington, son of Louisa); A E I BECKER (Aunt Cissie, mother of Trevor Becker and Lettice Williams); LETTICE WILLIAMS (daughter of Wilfred Becker, Senior)

Victoria Becker = John Crompton
Jack Crompton = Ivy (Errington)   Alice Crompton, Editor of CFC   Winifred
b 1873   (b 1867 d 1958)

Wilfred Becker = Alexandra   Louisa Becker = Edmund Withington
                A E I Becker known as Aunt Cissie   (Aunt Loo)
Trevor = Irene   Lettice = Williams   Richard = Mary   Mary = Len Easton
Wilfred, Mike, Cecily, Juliet   (Molly Withington)   (Molly Easton)
                                     Jane Susan (Barrett) Ted, Bob, Dickie

Mary Becker = John Henderson
Joe = (unknown)   Leigh   Joey
Grace   Kathleen (Canada)
         (m. Smithells)   Joey Henderson = Gladys
Grace = Henry Werner
Paul, Roger, Charles, John   Graham, Roy, Gordon, Josephine

TWO

Who were the cousins?

In the late 18th century Ernest Hannibal Becker, a manufacturing chemist, emigrated from Thuringia, an area of Prussia in the heart of present-day Germany. It's thought that he was escaping conscription. Certainly there was war at the time. Prussia was allied with Russia and Austria in fighting against France over Poland. Polish land was 'confiscated' three times in what were called the First, Second and Third Partitions of Poland. It's a wonder that Poland has managed to maintain nationhood. Its location has made it for centuries a kind of motorway intersection, a thoroughfare for warring armies tramping from west to east, north to south, and back again. Thuringia, a small duchy not far from its western boundaries, once the homeland of a Germanic tribe in the Roman Empire, now known by its tourist board as the Green Heart of Germany, must have endured a similar fate.

Whether Ernest was escaping conscription or not, he brought his formula for bleaching cotton to Manchester, the hub of the growing textile industry. He met and married Lydia Kay Leigh, a member of an old Lancashire family which traced a zigzag line back to Henry VII in a way that selected, for stepping-stones, mothers as well as fathers. When I learnt this titbit of information in my teens, I was suitably impressed – until I realised how many ancestors of all kinds I have, and how many hundreds, even thousands, of King Henry's descendants must be alive today. For a start, we each have four grandparents, eight great-grandparents, 16 great-great - and so on for many repetitions of great. The numbers are bewildering without even contemplating the cousins that multiply in every generation.

Ernest and Lydia were the parents of Hannibal Leigh and Mary Becker who had fifteen children. Looking at the dates of their births, I feel faint for Mary. They were born over a period of twenty-seven years, some with barely a year between them. The eldest child was Lydia, an activist for women's suffrage, well known at the time. She never married. Four of her siblings were the source of the cousins of the Chronicle: Mary, the second eldest of the 15 children, born in 1828; Victoria, Alice's mother, born in 1837; Wilfred born in 1850; and Louisa, the youngest, my grandmother, born in 1854.

The size of the family meant a large disparity in age between the eldest and the youngest. This puts generational levels out of kilter. Grace was the granddaughter of Mary and the grandmother of my cousin Nicola, my local friend and Majolica ware potter. Grace and my father were much the same age, but with a generation between them.[4]

Cousin Alice listed the offspring of the four Becker siblings in order of seniority on the cover of each of the Chronicle's folders. The first family belonged to Joe Henderson, the son of Mary who had married a John Henderson. In 1939 Joe was a widower living with his daughter Grace at 30 Brunswick Street, Manchester. Joe features in the Chronicle only as a walk-on part, never writing a contribution for himself. He is 'Father' in Grace's contributions, always ready to play backgammon when Cousin Alice comes to stay.

Grace was an enthusiastic contributor to the Chronicle, writing at length about her family. She and her husband, Henry Werner, had four sons, Paul, Roger, Charles and John: young men on the threshold of their lives. When war broke out, Roger was working on a tea plantation in Assam. Charles was an apprentice journalist. John, in his last year at school, wrote a few contributions. His interest in the Chronicle led to his inheriting the collection.

Sometimes Joe Henderson would go and stay with his other daughter, Kathleen. She wrote brief contributions in a large, round hand. She and her husband, Archie Smithells, had no children. They come across as a quiet couple who liked nothing better than a weekend walking in the Malvern Hills or the Lake District. A favourite place to stay was Newby Bridge. There's a photo of Kathleen, Grace and their father Joe fishing from a rowing boat on Lake Windermere.

---

[4] Grace and Richard were first cousins once removed. Grace and my sister and myself were second cousins. Whenever Nicola and I meet we try and work out how our own cousinly relationship should be described. Might it be second cousins twice removed?

Joe also had two sons: Leigh, who was married with children and living in British Columbia, and Joey, married to Gladys with four children: Graham, Josephine, Roy and Gordon. Roy and I met at Markham at the time of the Chronicle, he on a weekend's leave from his ship in Devonport, and I as a six-year-old enamoured by his sailor's collar. I was learning the Hornpipe in dancing class.

The second name and address on the folder belongs to Jack Crompton. Victoria Becker had married John Crompton and they had three children, Jack, Alice and Winifred. Winifred does not feature in the Chronicle. Perhaps she died young. Jack was the most faithful male contributor; no doubt he was in thrall to his fierce sister, Editor Alice. His wife, Ivy, had been married previously. As Ivy's handwriting was quite the hardest to decipher, it was some time before we had worked out the names of Ivy's children by her first marriage, both adults at the time of the Chronicle: George with a wife called Peggy, and Bobby who'd married an Australian called Pam. Bobby and Pam had six days together before he left for war. He was taken prisoner by the Japanese.

Jack and Ivy were much devoted to each other. I have no memory of meeting them but I do have a hazy recollection of visiting a magical mill house not far from Bath where Jane and I were at school. It must have been during a half-term visit when our mother stayed at the Lansdown Grove Hotel. Was my remembered scene Jack and Ivy's mill? A long, straight, level drive, running in tandem with a sky-reflecting stream on which ducks paddled, led towards a tranquil house, with a row of little, old, mellow stone-built cottages on the right: a peaceful, romantic scene, in a green landscape bathed in warm sunshine; a Valhalla glimpsed briefly during boarding school internment.

On first reading the Cousins' Chronicle, I made a note to find Jack and Ivy's house one day. I have now finally carried out the hunt. A teenage Valhalla has merged with today's reality. The mill's present inhabitants have even given me links directly back to Jack and Ivy. They bought the house from Ivy's son and daughter-in-law, Bobby and Pam Errington. Suddenly, names in the Chronicle become people. In 1945 Ivy described Pamela, her new daughter-in-law:

From Ivy Crompton
"Pam has the most beautiful manners and is very pleasant to have in the house. She is wonderfully appreciative of every small thing & is much more like we used to be in our youth than the moderns of today. That doesn't mean anything against the moderns ... but only an extra good mark for Pam. I hope she has enough "beans" to face life under modern and impecunious conditions, she is willowy & with the most lovely fair colouring but does not look awfully strong. They tear about, so I suppose she must be."

After the war, Ivy, as a widow, moved into one of the cottages in the drive. Jack had been killed when he fell from a poplar tree he was lopping.

The third name listed on the Chronicle's folders was that of Trevor Becker, the son of Wilfred, the thirteenth child of Hannibal Leigh and Mary Becker, the only male among the four siblings. Wilfred married Alexandra MacGowan who was known as Cissie. They had two children, Trevor and Lettice. In the Chronicle's pages, Lettice is living with Cissie, her mother, in Ringwood, both of them keen gardeners. Lettice has the surname Williams, but no Mr. Williams is mentioned. I have the idea, which I may have formed in childhood, that she was divorced, and there was something rather disreputable about this. She comes over in her newsletters as a vigorous eccentric. Her name is a corruption of Laetitia, meaning happiness. And I think she did spread happiness, in a haphazard, sometimes startling way.

In the pages of the Chronicle, Trevor's wife Irene gives Cissie the title of "Aunt". This confused me for a while. How could a mother-in-law be an aunt? But then, in our childhood, there were many aunts and uncles, most of them honorary. Trevor was my father's first cousin but we called him Uncle Trevor. Aunt Irene was my godmother. I have good memories of staying with the Beckers at number 70 Eccleston Square. Their four children – Mike, Wilfred, Cecily and Juliet – were considerably older and usually absent.

Cousin Alice listed the fourth branch of cousins on the Chronicle's folders under the name and address of my mother - Mrs R.L. Withington, Markham, Tavistock, Devon – even though she was not one of the Becker cousins. My father, on active duty, was given dispensation from contributing. His mother was Louisa, the youngest of the 15 Becker siblings. She married Edmund Withington and they had two children, Richard and Mary, known as Dick and Molly. Dick then went on to marry a Mary, also known as Molly. And Dick's sister Molly married a Canadian pilot just after the First World War. Thankfully, he was called Len. Molly and Len, living in Montreal, had three sons; Edward (Ted), Robert (Bob or Bobby) and – after quite a gap - Richard, (Dickie), who is, with Jane and myself, one of the three Chronicle-mentioned cousins still alive.

Grandmother Louisa, my aunt Molly Easton and my mother Molly Withington were all contributors. Louisa first wrote a contribution from Montreal for the April 1940 issue.

> *From Louisa Withingon, April 1940*
> "Don't know what to say! Am generally cheerfully employed in various ways and deeply interested in the young life going on around me. I keep doing my needlework which is a great interest. Of war work, can do none but it does not seem anything is needed. More Red Cross workers than work to be done. Bridge and crosswords great relaxations.
> I can't see I have any business in the Cousins Chronicle so will now retire."

No business in the Chronicle! Why did she think that? She was the only one of the four siblings, the source of the cousins, still alive. Reading her contribution, I want to urge her to write more. As the war progressed, she did. Like all the cousins, she found solace in reading, and writing for the monthly Chronicle.

What brings people together? What drives them apart? Love and hate are part of the same spectrum of emotions, the yin and yang of the same human need as a social animal. On any scale, from personal to national, the cohesion of 'us' implies, needs, even demands, exclusion of 'them'. We do this separation all the time and detach our indulgence from whatever is not me or us. But that's not my family – it's my husband's. That's not my dog; it's my neighbour's. That's not my town, county, country, ethnicity – at each division a feeling of difference can deepen into dangerous enmity. I remember in the Greek village, which was our home for a time, the boundary between the warring halves of a family was drawn through the middle of a single house. The dividing line went through the kitchen, one sister's family cooking, eating and washing up in one half, the other sister's doing the same in the remainder.

The Chronicle was created in the face of war. Without the war, the cousins would not have stayed in such close and loving touch.

*

The locations of the Chronicle's contributors 1939 – 1945

The cousins who contributed to the Chronicle were descendants of four siblings, the children of Hannibal Leigh and Mary Becker.: Mary (born 1828 named after her mother), Victoria (1837), Wilfred (1850) and Louisa (1854)

On the map, each branch has been given the appropriate initials.
MB = Mary Becker's descendants
VB = Victoria Becker's descendants
WB = Wilfred Becker's descendants
LB = Louisa Becker (a contributor) and her descendants

In Canada
MB: Leigh Henderson, Kelowna, British Columbia
LB: Louisa Withington, Montreal
    Molly (and Len Easton)
    Ted, Bobby, Dickie

The first contribution from Irene Becker

Barnston, Western Road, Bournemouth. Feb 1940

BECKER

All our family was gathered together at Bournemouth on January 6th which was our first united meeting since War began.

Trevor is now living in the upper part of No. 70 Eccleston Square, with one maid, our Irish Mary Roche who is now cook housemaid and housekeeper combined and very well and energetically she carries on too!

Smith our former general handyman is now serving his country as a full time policeman but he and his wife live in the basement at No. 70 and she answers the bells for us, which still seem to be quite numerous though our household has shrunk so much. Aunt Ciss' lower part of the house is all shut up as she is living at Ringwood with Lettice for the duration of the War. Her spacious studio bedroom at No. 70

The cover of the first folder of newsletters

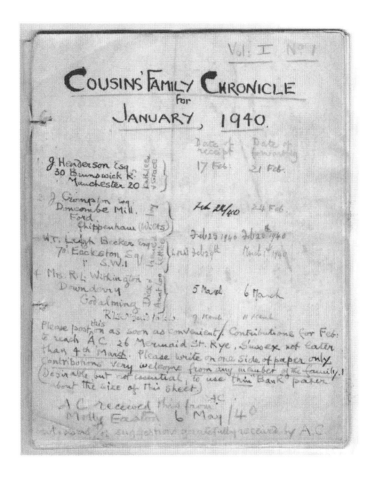

THREE

The first month's folder, January 1940

Cheerful letters from France

Cousin Alice instigated the Chronicle in the autumn of 1939 and the first folder of contributions, titled Volume 1, No. 1, was ready in January 1940. It took five months for the folder to complete the circuit, despite the way the cousins responded well to her commands, each taking only a few days to read the collection and send it on, meekly filling in the dates of receipt and despatch. The first contributor received January's CFC on 17th February 1940 and the last sent it back on 11th March from Canada. It arrived with Editor Alice on May 6th. The journey by sea across the Atlantic, to Canada and back, had taken eight weeks. The need for merchant shipping to form convoys as protection against attack by air and sea, both on the surface and under it, added to the time waiting in harbour before the slow and hazardous crossing. Some folders never made it.

Although Alice listed on the covers the four families of the Becker siblings in the order of seniority, the contributions within each folder were in alphabetical order: Becker (Irene and Lettice), Crompton, (Alice, Jack and Ivy) Henderson (Grace Werner, Kathleen Smithells), Withington (Molly W, Molly Easton, Louisa W.). From these names, it's clear it was the women of the families who kept the Chronicle going.

Irene was the most willing contributor of all, writing at length as she chased around the country looking after her scattered family. Her newsletter, the first in the first volume, I've transcribed faithfully, complete with capital letters and her strange way of giving the word 'together' a hyphen. I want to preserve as far as possible the character of the cousins and their times. There was something Forsyte Saga-like about the life of the Beckers that the war was disrupting.

From Irene Becker, February 1940
"Barnston, Western Road, Bournemouth.
All our family was gathered to-gether at Bournemouth on January 6th. which was our first united meeting since War began.

Trevor is now living in the upper part of No. 70 Eccleston Square, with one maid, our nice Mary Roche, who is now cook housemaid and housekeeper combined and very well and energetically she carries on too!

Smith our former general handyman is now serving his country as a full time policeman, but he and his wife live in the basement at No. 70 and she answers the bells for us, which still seem to be quite numerous though our house-hold has shrunk so much. Aunt Ciss's[5] lower part of the house is all shut up as she is living at Ringwood with Lettice for the duration of the War. Her spacious studio bedroom at No. 70 we find of untold use to keep our surplus furniture in, with her consent, as owing to the times we have let our garage flat which has hitherto been the home of the two boys for a year to a very nice young architect and his wife. They fell in love with it after much hunting for a smaller home than they had occupied in the more prosperous days of 'before the War'.

Mike has been serving, with a battery of gunners away in the country since Sept. 1st. and he seemed very happy in his new life except for the fact that his health hasn't been too good for some time; they passed him into the Army as fit for lines of communication only but happily the open air life seemed to suit him fairly well and he has grown fatter and larger altogether. He is now 6ft 1in and getting broad and square shouldered. However his throat has been rather a nuisance and the Authorities, after they had tried to cure him at Netly Hospital, decided that his general health wasn't fit for existing standards so he has been discharged altogether from the Army. He returned home to Eccleston Square soon after his New Year's leave. He brought Influenza back with him unfortunately with which he was pretty ill for about ten days. However he has practically recovered now and is going to start work in the City helping his father for a time with many areas of Work."

Sometimes Irene's handwriting makes it hard to tell whether she intends an upper case letter or not. The capital W may have been caused by a sudden, exuberant jerk of her pen rather than a wish to underline the importance of Trevor's occupation. Even now that I've read the entire Chronicle, I have little idea what Uncle Trevor did in the City. It may well have warranted a respectfully big W.

"Meanwhile Wilfred spent a fortnight of his Xmas holidays with us at Bournemouth where Cecilia[6], Juliet and the two maids are evacuated

---

[5] The mother of Trevor and Lettice. Irene always refers to her mother-in-law as Aunt Ciss, or Cissie, as the cousins of her generation did. Her first name was Alexandra. Ciss may have been a childhood corruption.

[6] Names of offspring throughout the Chronicle are variable. Cecily is

to my Mother's house for the time being. Trevor was down with us for Xmas and came again for the week end of January 6th to the 9th. He then returned to London by car and took Wilfred up with him for him to go on next day to stay with some school friends at Rufforth near York. Wilfred came back in ten days' time in the midst of an attack of Influenza. So I had a month's sojourn in London altogether delayed by the illness of the two boys whom I had to nurse back to health. Wilfred was at last able to return to Harrow over a fortnight late and I heard from him that he has been very busy since making up for lost time in Work. He has now just passed his seventeenth birthday and he will not have so much longer now to enjoy school with all its pleasures.

Cecilia is working as a student at Sandecotes School preparing for entrance to one of the Oxford Colleges which she hopes to obtain in the Autumn or early Spring. But the War may interrupt this course for her life I am afraid as her services will probably be required for War Work in the near future."

Ah. Two big Ws. Irene wouldn't have been alone in giving war work such upper case importance.

"Juliet is also going daily to the same school just two miles from where we are living at Bournemouth. She is very happy and thoroughly interested in work and play there. She has to be off at 8 o'clock in the morning as it is a boarding school really and most of the girls are older than she is; but she has a very good time all the same and both she and Cecilia had a very warm welcome there as it is my old school; my sisters and I used to travel backwards and forwards to Sandecotes term by term from Monmouthshire where we then lived thirty years ago now! Two of the present mistresses were girls there in my day and I have known the head mistress for some years also. It is altogether a very happy atmosphere there for the girls now and a joy to me and they are both getting on very well indeed.

I find my time very occupied spending my life between two houses with the family divided and very much regret to say that so far I have had a very little time for War Work though I am hoping to have some opportunity of doing something later on.

We were interested to see Graham Henderson[7] on January 20th when he came and spent a Saturday evening with Trevor and me during his last leave. He looked so well and was very cheery and gay spirited. Alice has been to see us but except for these two I am sorry I haven't

---

Cecilia; even Cicely, which is closer to how I remember her name being pronounced.

[7] Graham was the son of Joey Henderson, and two generation-rungs down from Trevor who was the first cousin of Graham's grandfather Joe.

come across any members of the much scattered family just lately. It is sad distances seem so much further in War Time, though it is just the time really when we would all appreciate a family foregathering were it even possible.
Irene H Becker"

As a young adult living in London, I would sometimes be invited to a meal with the Beckers at number 70 Eccleston Square. Uncle Trevor sat at one end of the enormous dining room table and Aunt Irene at the other. I can bring to mind now Uncle Trevor's way of making indecipherable noises, preludes to speech. It was as though what he was about to say rested somewhere between his plate of food and his throat. His eyes beneath his shaggy eyebrows were half-closed, there were rumbles and stirrings all about him, inside and out; his food would be moved about on the plate, his mouth would begin to form words, his napkin might mop at his lips, then with a harrumph he would begin. It made me think of the starting handle of an old car, perhaps the Austin that had been laid up in the war, its tyres removed; set on blocks inside the Markham garage, smelling of old leather.

The subject of Trevor's talk (hardly a conversation – we'd all be listeners) often came from an article he'd read in the Times. He would not talk of anything that had happened in his mysterious business in the City. I understood there was much more money available in his household than there was in my Withington home in Devon. There were a number of people looking after the Beckers. They came in and 'did' or maybe even had a room in the Mews at the back of the house. There was someone in the kitchen which was directly below the dining room, connected by the platform on which food was hauled up on ropes and dirty plates hauled down by the same invisible hands.

I'm sure Aunt Irene knew everything about the invisible helpers, and there was care, concern and even devotion exchanged between them. She was kind and gentle, a woman of her class and generation. "Yes, dear," she'd murmur if ever Uncle Trevor called for a response. I thought she could stand in, if need be, for the Queen Mother. One or two of her four grown-up children might be at the table. I understood that Cecily lived at home in a bedsitting room at the top of the house; she'd had at some point a nervous breakdown. Juliet, the youngest, was living on her own in a flat nearby. Later she became, on my marriage, our family solicitor. There was Lettice living in a flat made out of rooms somewhere on the left as you came in at the front door but she never appeared in the dining-room. There would be a lot of empty space around the mahogany table beneath the greyish-greenish glass of the domed skylight. The dining room was like a museum's atrium. To me, used to family meals at close-quarters in the Markham kitchen, Number 70 presented a strange mixture of thrill and unease.

Alice introduces Lettice, Trevor's sister, bracketed with Irene on the cover, and enters her contribution after Irene's, under the surname Williams, the never-mentioned husband. (Rather than divorced, Lettice might have been one of the thousands of First World War women who had lost their men). Lettice and her mother, Irene's "Aunt Ciss", were living in Ringwood.

From Lettice Williams, February 1940
"The Homestead, Coxstone Lane, Ringwood, Hants. 2 Feb: We have been so frosted up in the cold snap as to have been entirely waterless in all Departments for the past 2 weeks. We thawed out on 31 Jan ...... I go to the local Red X each week. We have cut out 600 yds. of striped flannelette for underpants, & my mind began to feel like a railway junction. I have been exalted to a seat on the Committee! I think chiefly because there was nobody else much to choose from! My chief culinary invention of the war up to now is curried parsnips. We hate parsnips really, but one got into the house somehow by accident & as I didn't want to waste it I thought we would not notice it was a parsnip if I curried the creature. Since then we have actually bought them for this dish & it is really awfully good. Try it when you get home. I cut the parsnips into neat squares and boil the dice in a little water for about 1 hour. They keep their shape when cooked. I put an apple into the curry and onions & some jam & sugar & nowadays I keep the rice water & use it to thicken the curry.

I do hope you understand that, as nothing of interest occurs ever to us here, it cannot possibly interest others. We know nobody other than a handful of villagers & have no car or means of getting about, & often for days together we hardly go over the doorstep & when Aunt Loo (*Lady Watt is going to live in Pat Reid's flat in Eccleston Square. A.C.*)[8] and Miss Laing leave Ringwood on Feb 28th we shall seldom speak to a creature. I hope you have better luck with other members of the family, but I expect everyone is terribly busy with extra jobs of a dull nature & feel like the French War Communique, 'Nothing to report'.

I devoutly hope my astrological books are correct in prognosticating the possible <u>demise</u> of Hitler this month or next – Satan will join the ranks of the unemployed when that happy event occurs! My friend Prince Sapiela writes me that three of his nephews have been murdered, & their estates in Poland confiscated, his brother, the Archbishop of Cracow, is a prisoner in his palace, & his sister of over 70 is lost. The old lady was turned out of her house, & must now be frozen to death, I imagine. All this perpetrated by the Germans. L.M.W."

Never trust astrology, we might tell Lettice, but how exotic to have a Polish prince as a correspondent. What shockingly grim news he sent from Poland. In England the cousins, like everyone else in the country, were moving about all over the place to avoid bombs but without any fear of being murdered or frozen to death.

It was cold enough, though, that first winter of the war.

Alice, besides acting as organiser of the Chronicle, adding little notes here and there, also included her own news.

<u>From Alice Crompton</u>

"After spending Xmas 1939 with Marjory Lees at Oldham, I was held up there by the extraordinarily severe weather. I could not have been detained in more comfortable quarters – central heating, endless hot water, & no burst pipes. I paid a 3 days visit to the Werner's – saw Grace's sons (all but Roger) – Charles v smart in his R.A.F. uniform. All looked very well, from Joe[9] to John. Joe & I had some backgammon – one of the favourite family games. Hearing later that Paul had been 11 hours in the train from Euston to Manchester, (heated fortunately, & with Dinner available) I felt thankful I had stayed in Oldham.

I was also glad to be planning this Family Chronicle in Lancashire near Foxdenton & Hollinwood, where some of our forbears lived &

---

[8] The Chronicle has two Aunt Loo's. Irene's mother, Louisa, Lady Watts, was one; the other was my grandmother Louisa Withington.

[9] Alice was referring to Grace's father Joe, her first cousin.

died. The gardens of Foxdenton Hall are most beautifully laid out & kept up, & are open to the public, who go there in great numbers."

Foxdenton Hall! I'd heard the name in childhood and knew the Beckers had lived there in the 19th century. I decided to hunt for Foxdenton, now engulfed by a Manchester suburb. The local council has closed the house – it's in too dilapidated a state to be safe - but the gardens, as in Alice's day, are still open to the public. While wandering around a duck pond, I picked up the wrapping from a loaf of sliced bread and dropped it in a litter bin with a nod to any Becker ghosts that might be watching.

On the ivy-clad side wall of the house is a plaque.

The family home of

LYDIA ERNESTINE BECKER

1827 – 1890

Suffragist, campaigner and political lobbyist,

Founder of the National Society

For Women's Suffrage

Women gained the full vote in 1928.

Cousin Alice, surely proud of her Aunt Lydia[10], was born in time to know her. She was 23 when Lydia died aged 63. There, beside the duck pond's green water, the uncaptured conversations between aunt and niece slip through my fingers. They would cover big subjects: Botany, Women's Rights, Evolution, Egyptology, all to be introduced with upper case letters. I found at the back of the house a large, smoothly-mown, green lawn, edged by clipped bushes, framed by trees.

---

[10] Lydia, born in 1827, was the eldest of the 15 children of Hannibal Leigh and Mary Becker. She was a pioneer in the campaign for women's suffrage and wrote many articles for the journal of the society she founded. As a botanist, she corresponded with Charles Darwin.

Surely, the growing family of Hannibal Leigh and Mary Becker played croquet on it. I see in my mind's eye the large oil painting that hung on a wall of the drawing room of Trevor and Irene's London house. Two young girls, aged around eight and six, dressed in pale blue and silvery dresses, stand together in a garden, holding hands. They are Lydia Becker and her younger sister who had the same name as her mother. People said I looked like Mary which pleased me. But I would be proud to be just like plain, clever Lydia.[11]

Alice ends her contribution with a note about Jack and Ivy. I feel I know the Cromptons better now I've found and visited Doncombe Mill.

Note from Alice

"There has been a good deal of coming and going at Doncombe Mill and George Errington's little daughters, Caroline and Daphne (about the same ages as Jane and Susan) spend much time there with their nurse, their mother joining them at intervals. Jack keeps well. They have laid up their car, but get lifts from friends, or hire, or use buses. Buster (the spaniel they had from Dick, when he went to Hong Kong) is flourishing and enjoys 2 days shooting a week with Jack."

The next contribution under the name Henderson comes from Grace Werner.

From Grace Werner, January 1940

"Father goes a small walk each day & has kept very fit all through this very cold weather. He gets bridge as often as we can get him a four. He reads a lot & listens to the wireless - & what perhaps is most important sleeps very well all night. Henry is hard at work at the Town Hall from 8.30am to 5.45pm & then A.R.P. 8pm to 9.15pm three nights a week.

---

[11] This is as I remember it. Irene, writing in February 1945, said this: "Susie so reminds me of the little Becker sisters – Aunt Lydia and Aunt Mary – in the 'after Romney' painting that Aunt Ciss has. It was always in her drawing room and is now in safety at Earl's Barton I am glad to say. I can't quite remember which little sister Susie is most like, but I think it is Aunt Mary. It will be interesting to compare them altogether some day soon, when it and we all can meet in London once more."

Paul still at George Kent's – but working from M/c at the moment. Roger still on his tea garden in Khoomtin, Assam – he hopes to get a commission in a Cavalry Regiment which might bring him back here – but it is all very vague – His five years out in Assam is up in October 1941 & his leave is due. Charles is still at Cambridge – St. John's College in the R.A.F. He wondered if they are getting them ready for Canada, as they have been inoculating them for everything this last month. They are only able to get 15lbs of coal a day: it just lights the fire at 5pm & then burns out. So they have all been bitterly cold, with the result that many of them are in the sick room. Charles has come through with only a slight cold.

John is back at school, Trent College, Long Eaton, & very happy. Joey still hopes to be called back into the army.[12] He is with Gladys at Brerton Hall, Sandback, where their small daughters' school has been moved to. Their boys, Roy & Gordon, are at Trent College. Graham, the eldest boy, is at Aldershot at the Cadet School. G.W."

In early 1940 when Grace wrote about her sons and nephews, Charles was the only one who had joined up. Roger in Assam was hoping to get a commission in a cavalry regiment. He must have felt that such a regiment might provide the same excitement as his recent tiger hunt.

Letter from Roger
"I've had quite a lot of luck at Shikar recently, bagging my first tiger or rather tigress. I enclose some snaps. She's not amazingly large but about average for a female. I got her with Pop's shot gun which wasn't bad going. She appeared in a village about 2 ¼ miles from my bungalow in broad daylight and killed a cow and 4 goats in about a minute taking one goat off into the jungle and leaving the rest. I went down as soon as I heard and had small "chung" built in a nearby tree and started sitting up about 4.30 p.m. The tree was full of red ants and by 8.30 I was pretty cold and miserable with cramp in both legs. However I decided to hang on for a bit more and a few minutes later, I heard something jump on my right and land on the path below my tree. There was hardly any moon and all I could see was a dim dark shape moving along the path. I don't think I ever saw anything so wonderful as that tigress as I shone my torch. She was standing with one paw on a goat, with her tail twitching; just as I was about to fire she turned and looked up at me. I fired and couldn't see anything for smoke. The next thing I knew was dozens of vultures trying to settle on me. They had been feeding on the dead cow and were frightened by my shot. In trying to see what had happened to the tigress, I

---

[12] Joey, Grace's brother

dropped my torch. I spent the next ten minutes fighting a mental battle over my longing to get back to my bungalow and a fire and the thought of a wounded tigress crouching in the undergrowth waiting for me. Anyway I beat a hasty retreat for home and next morning went back to find the tigress 30 yards from my "chung" stone dead. After this there was a triumphal procession back to my bungalow surrounded by cheering villagers. We had to stop at every village, and let the village maidens come out to have a look at it, and give me salaams and presents. I was all the time trying to look "The Big White Hunter" and all the time feeling self-conscious and very uncomfortable. I am just off for another week's training with the Assam Valley Light Horse, which I hear is going to be very stiff. We do 3 days a week training. I am getting better at Polo, and have been quite in demand for matches and tournaments; it's been very nice but terribly expensive. I shall have to go very carefully for a bit if I want to keep square, especially as I may be called up any month now."

It sounds as though the recruits in Asia were thinking in terms of the First World War. While Roger was training with the Assam Valley Light Horse, my father had been posted from York, to Aldershot and then to France. With a surname starting with a W, my mother comes last in the first month's folder.

From Molly Withington

"News for the Family Chronicle. <u>January 1940, Downderry, Godalming</u>

This month we had once more to migrate. Dick left York on the 1st to report at Aldershot. I came down with him in the car, leaving my sister-in-law (who was staying with us) in charge of the house and family [13]. We stayed a week at Downderry while Dick was busy collecting his staff and kit. I returned to York on the 8th & Dick went across to France on the 10th, he is Chief Engineer (Works) on South L.of C.[14] I had a busy week myself settling up all our affairs & packing up – we have left the things we had collected up there in store. The furniture was hired so no trouble about that. One wonders when we shall have a home all together again! I came down here on Jan. 18th with the children, nurse, & the large black dog! Though rather an invasion we are preferable to the 4 noisy schoolboys that

---

[13] My uncle Dicky's first wife, Mary, who was something of an invalid and would die young.
[14] Lines of Communication. These were the delivery routes between supply depots and the fighting forces. The interception of these L. of C. by the Germans led to the army being cut off in Dunkirk.

were billeted here till Christmas time! Jane & Susan are well & jolly, & have quite settled down here. Jane goes to a dancing class once a week at a school on this hill. Dick writes cheerful letters from B.E.F[15].

We don't know where he is: he seems to have an extensive area. His H.Q. are in a chateau, & the Comte & his family occupy one wing; there is central heating but no bathroom!

It has been intensely cold in France as reported in the papers. Dick has met a lot of old friends & acquaintances during his tour of his Area.

News from Montreal. I have had two letters from Mother written soon after Christmas. They are all well & busy at various activities. Teddy is in the O.T.C.[16] of the university. Dickie sings in the Choir & is very keen! Teddy & Bobby are very keen skiers & went up to the Laurentians for a week after Christmas & had a grand time. M.R.W."

As my mother reported, my father had met 'a lot of old friends and acquaintances' in France. He was back on familiar ground. He'd fought all through the First World War and been awarded a Military Cross for an act of bravery in the face of enemy fire. What did he think about fighting the Germans yet again? He never spoke of either war.

My need to follow broadcast news began at the school we called the R.S. Its full title was more of an embarrassing mouthful: The Royal School for Daughters of Officers of the Army. It had been founded in the aftermath of the Crimean War to help educate the daughters of those killed and wounded, besides those of soldiers serving overseas. In my time at the school, from 1949 to1956, there was a weekly slot set aside for discussing the news. When I began working on the Chronicle, I started to record terrorist actions in the world beyond my study. I made a note of the thirty-eight holidaymakers lying on a beach in Tunisia, who were shot dead in a hail of bullets. The beach umbrellas remained undisturbed. A few days later we were reminded of the London bombings known as 7/7. It was the 10th anniversary of that event. Fifty-two people had been killed and over 700 injured, most of them young people on their way to work. The news, reporting on memorial ceremonies in St Paul's and Hyde Park, included an interview with a survivor.

---

[15] British Expeditionary Force
[16] Officers Training Corps

Her mother had rung her as soon as she'd learnt what had happened, out of her mind with worry. One of the bombs had exploded on a number 30 bus passing through Tavistock Square, her daughter's normal route to work. When she heard her daughter was alive, she said "Sugar, I'm coming at once." The endearment adds greater poignancy, love and hate sharing the same time frame.

This is war, 21st century style.

*

Roger Werner with tigress, Assam 1940

Roger Werner

FOUR

The Phoney War

Doing their bit

The cousins' contributions for the next few months echo the uncertain state of the country since the previous September. It was a puzzling time. The playground bully had been challenged, but neither the challengers nor the bully were ready to fight. The leaders of France and Britain had declared war on Germany as a matter of principle after the invasion of Poland but were reluctant to provoke invasion of their own countries. They could not agree on strategy. Stalin had made a pact with Hitler to allow each other's territorial ambitions on the continent but this was not known at the time. Other nations were hedging their bets, hoping to maintain neutrality. Memories of the First World War were still too fresh.

The country was like a disturbed ant nest. People were travelling hither and thither for all the manifold reasons connected with the war. One and a half million women and children were evacuated. Bomb shelters were built; curtains were made up in thick, black cloth to stop any chink of light escaping into the night. Socks and scarves were knitted for servicemen, blackout curtains were sewn and, very strangely as seen in the Chronicle, *pants*. Lettice writes:

> From Lettice Williams
> "Our Red Cross pants were sent off completed – 385 pairs and about 3 hours work per pair. We now await our new stuff and are wondering what garment we shall be making. I see E.F. Benson is dead.[17] I remember you (that is, A.C.) pointing him out to me in Rye. I met him at dinner once, as a bride, and I believe he took me in to dinner."

385 pairs of pants! I see piles of baggy knickers, incongruously associated in the same breath with E.F. Benson. I wonder where they were sent and who was to wear them.

---

[17] He lived at Lamb House, around the corner from Alice. Henry James was a previous owner.

Meanwhile the rest of the Becker family was knitting away feverishly, as Irene reports from Bournemouth.

From Irene Becker
"The whole household including the children and the maids has been knitting and knitting during any spare time they have. Juliet has nearly completed two long thick scarves, one for the Army first and now another for the Navy.
Bournemouth is gay and always full of people and - except for soldiers everywhere - one wouldn't realise there was a war at all. But there are a great many soldiers training everywhere, and we are aroused each morning at 6.30 by the musical notes of Reveille from the nearest contingent, which lives in a large house just across the road from here.
Trevor and Michael were here last week-end and we all went along to Lilliput Quay on Poole Harbour to say good-bye to Mr. Knight the proprietor and boatman there who has just been called up for the Naval Reserve; he has always looked after our boats for us and we still have our sailing dinghy and the rowing boat at this yard. The boys hope to have an occasional sail if they can in the holidays – 'the Powers that be' permitting of course! We wished him good luck and success on his beat as he has gone off to an unknown destination to help guard our coasts. Mrs Knight and the children are left to live in the family boat now moored just inside and close to the Lilliput pier, and to carry on whatever small yachting trade there may be available when summer comes – if at all."

On the cover of this volume, Trevor noted under the column for date of receipt '*Unknown, got mixed up with Wilfred's school bill of similar appearance. T.L.B.*' Wilfred was in the sanatorium at Harrow, 'rather bored with life' and suffering from German measles. The infection got its name not through any xenophobic feelings but because the rubella virus was first described by German physicians in 1814.

Meanwhile Cousin Alice continued her train journeys, crisscrossing the country to visit members of the family and friends made in her Settlement days.

From Alice Crompton
"Until 7 Feb I continued the visit to Marjory Lees at Oldham which I began on 21 Dec but which was interrupted by going to Blackpool, Llandudno and Manchester. I was lucky in having so hospitable a hostess, who would not let me think of leaving till the severity of the weather had abated. On 7 Feb I went to 70 Eccleston Sq and had the usual extremely kind welcome from Trevor and Irene, both of whom

were well, tho' T had had flu or a v. bad cold. I saw Ivy 2 or 3 times, as she was up in London on a variety of business and was staying in a Bayswater flat with her sister Mrs Fletcher.

On 12 Feb I went to High Wycombe to the Ensors for a week and there, high up on the Chilterns, snow fell heavily again on 16th and 17th, but had gone by 19th. I went to Oxford one day to see the Miss Sidgwicks and Mrs. V.L. Stocks, travelling with Mr. Ensor who is pro tem. filling Sir Arthur Salter's Chair in Oxford, while Sir A. is in office. On 19th I went to stay with Prof and Mrs Weiss at Merrow, and had arranged to go to Godalming on 20th to see Molly and the children, and Col. and Mrs Phillips. A cold, however, kept me indoors so Molly v. kindly drove over in the aft. and had tea with Mrs. Weiss and me, looking radiantly well and bright.

On 22nd I went back to London, dining at 70 Eccleston Sq that night, and going back to Rye next day. After my absence of 10 weeks and a day, my cottage felt surprisingly warm and dry, thanks to my good charwoman.

There have been many deaths in Rye this winter amongst the old people. Six of my acquaintances have gone. Mr. E.F. Benson will be greatly missed. He was very fond of Rye and is buried here."

Margaret, a sister of E.F. Benson, was described as an Egyptologist. If she ever visited her brother Fred in Rye and met Alice, the two would certainly have tangled delightedly over the pharaohs. In fictional 'Tilling', closely based on Rye, Benson made fun of its citizens. Cousin Alice was not a dinner party hostess nor a bridge addict, but she might have been satirised as a 'blue stocking', which is what clever women were called at the time. I grew up with the idea that it was best not to be a blue stocking. On the other hand, cooking and sewing were not part of the model held out for me. My mother didn't learn to cook until after the war. As for sewing ...

From Molly Withington
"I have been working at the local Red Cross Supply Depot. As I am such a poor hand with a needle, it is rather a penance but I've made a beautiful pink dressing jacket for a Finn! Featherstitching and all!"

Although I find it hard to visualise my mother sewing , let alone *feather-stitching*, I can see her being keen to help the war effort; to 'do her bit', as the expression was. But why make a dressing jacket, usually worn in her pre-War world when sitting up in bed, waiting for early morning tea to be brought by a maid? How a Finn would respond to such a garment in the spring of 1940 is hard to fathom. What they needed and were not getting from Britain or France was military support against the Russians. The troops that were grudgingly mustered, more as a token gesture than as a solid commitment, had still not arrived when the Finns gave in to Russia on March 12th.

Yet of course in emergencies, as in natural disasters or the refugee crisis today, ordinary citizens want to do something, anything, to help – and the collection of boxes of toys, clothes and blankets is a tangible and more personal method than sending dull and anonymous money.

My father, as related in the first month's folder, was in France with the British Expeditionary Force. The conditions don't sound in the least bit warlike.

> "Dick writes frequently and cheerfully from his H.Q. and sent some snapshots of himself with the grandchildren of the Comte who owns the chateau. They are about the same age as Jane and Susan. Dick is hoping to get 5 days leave in April. The Comte gave an afternoon Bridge party one Sunday in Dick's honour – tea and very rich cakes were followed by glasses of port and then they sat down to Bridge!"

Dick was a reluctant bridge player. He would 'make up a four' but would much rather be outdoors, shooting snipe on Dartmoor or fishing for trout in its rivers. Fortunately, as far as his in-laws were concerned, he was also a player of outdoors sports like tennis and golf. He played hockey for the army. My mother's family assessed people on their ability to play games. Her brother Dicky's first wife, also a Mary[18], did not play bridge or any sort of sport. She was something of an invalid and died young. But Uncle Dicky's second wife Elizabeth, welcomed into the family with enthusiasm, was a brilliant bridge and golf player. She and Dicky met at the bridge table and often played together, winning tournaments. Elizabeth, by far the younger, died aged 93 in 2015. I packed up their many silver trophies to send to my nephew in Scotland, the one with

---

[18] There seems to be a family law that a Richard should be called Dick, Dicky or Dickie and should have a mother, a sister or a wife called Mary or Molly. Likewise, if you are a male Henderson, then your first name should start with a J as in John, Joseph, Joe or Joey.

the Austrian wife whose father fought the Russians in the Second World War.

When my mother was writing her contribution in February 1940, her brother Dicky Phillips was a young man who, having graduated from Oxford as an economist, had enlisted in the Army at the outbreak of war.

From Molly Withington
"My brother and his wife will be coming to stay for nearly 3 weeks on the 9th. He has passed his exams and will shortly be gazetted 2nd Lieut. R.A. He goes to Larkhill for a course next."

There was anxiety over this at Downderry, mixed with approval. My mother's father, Tom Phillips known as Pop, was a retired Royal Artillery colonel. He and Hilda, my grandmother known as Mop, had spent a lifetime in various parts of the Empire. It was right that their youngest son Dicky should join up and fight, and as a gunner. But they had already lost their first son, Tommy, when he was a naval midshipman stationed in Malta shortly after the end of World War One. He had died of diphtheria, far from home.

It can't have been easy for this generation to listen to the younger members of the family, on the brink of adulthood or in its early reaches, who were longing to leave home and get going in the war. On March 2nd, Grace Werner included a contribution written in pencil by her third son, Charles.

Letter from Charles Werner
"After being at Cambridge since December 6, the only development is that from being an Aircraftman 2nd class, I have just been promoted to a Leading Aircraftman! The only advantage apart from the wearing of a 'Propeller' on the sleeve is that one gets 5/- a day instead of 2/-. All of this is, of course, quite incidental towards my becoming a pilot. After six months of continuous service – rewarded by 8 days leave – I'm as still as far away from actually going up in an aeroplane as ever – which is strange considering that I joined up as 'a pilot for immediate training'. However at Cambridge we are learning a new thing which will no doubt be useful to us later on. We are presumably officer cadets as we have been informed that when we get to our next station we will be made 'members of the Officers' mess'. It is all very well but one would like to know what it is like to be up in the air. Meanwhile one endures life in this the second 'Bore' War."

Boring! Boring! The frequent complaint of teenagers in every time and place. Charles had joined up as soon as war had been declared, even though it meant giving up his job as a young reporter on Glasgow's Sunday Post. He wrote again in March 1940.

Letter from Charles Werner
"Since my last contribution – in pencil – my life has suffered little change for I am still at Cambridge. My only move has been an internal posting to another squadron, formerly billeted at S. John's College. I am now living in a suite of rooms in the new Mermaid Court at Clare College. Thus 'forty years on' history has repeated itself and in the old hall I find myself sitting on the same bench at the same oak table as my father used when he was an undergraduate. His were perhaps happier times but one doesn't take life in the RAF too seriously and one can enjoy the river and many other of the amenities of Varsity life. We had an RAF night in the bumping races early in March (I was not a member) and they gained several bumps aided by a cox and a coach from the Trinity Hall boat club. It was the first time I had seen these races and I found it rather a novel experience.

A couple of weeks ago I went to the dinner of the Cambridge Old Mancunians Association and found that there were many old friends there who remembered me on the field of sport if not for my scholastic achievements. By way of keeping my hand in at my old profession I am, with the aid of two other airmen ex-gentlemen of the press, starting a Wing magazine but it is so far in a very embryo stage. When the weather gets warmer I hope to be able to swim in the Cam if not to emulate the feats of my father who had the distinction of being Captain of the Cambridge University Swimming Club. Finally I might add that though I now have a magnificent set of Flying Kit I have not yet had the privilege of going up in an aeroplane!
C.L.H.Werner 967878 Pilot U/T Clare College, Cambridge."

In contrast with the younger generation of cousins, my father cannot have been so keen for the war to change from being Phoney to Real. This was the second time he had been in France to fight.

This is my mother's contribution in March 1940.

From Molly Withington
"Downderry, Godalming <u>March news from the Withington family</u>
The only event of importance this month was the return of the warrior from B.E.F[19]. on the 29th! for only 4 days' leave which went like a

---

[19] British Expeditionary Force

flash. Dick looked well and was cheerful though not particularly optimistic about a short war. He is impressed with the spirit of the French and says the Entente is much more pronounced than in the last war in every way. He is very comfortably housed in this 15th century chateau and the H.Q. have now got a hut in the ground as the Mess, with an anteroom and kitchen and a shower bath as well – the latter necessary as the Chateau has no bathroom. Dick was delighted with his daughters and they with him. Susan has produced 2 eye teeth lately and has just learnt to walk up and down stairs unaided. This accomplishment she finds so entrancing that she seems to spend a good deal of time indoors, on the stairs! Jane is growing so fast she has been promoted to a skirt and jumper on Sundays which gives her intense pleasure.

Somehow or other we have all managed to avoid flu and German measles germs which have been rampant in this neighbourhood, though we had colds.

We shall soon be thinking of our next move, our tenant leaves Markham on the 15th May."

I have no recollection of my two-year self, entranced by my mastery of the Downderry staircase. What I do remember, from visits in later childhood, is the ritual of my grandmother's morning descent of the stairs. After her wartime accident during the blackout, one leg was considerably shorter than the other and she wore a shoe with a substantially built-up heel. She could move about very slowly on two sticks, bringing her right foot to join her left before she took the next step. We'd hear her go clump, ker-clump, clump, ker-clump, along the bedroom landing towards the head of the stairs. She'd had her early morning tea with thinly cut brown bread and butter brought up those stairs by Lily. She'd had her breakfast, too, delivered in the same way. Now Lily would call out, "Madam is coming down!" And we would all have to hide. Mop hated to be watched. Once she was down the precipitous stairs and past the inlaid, rosewood, pedestal table which would have seated eight had it not been in the hall, and into the dining room where the Cosy stove was lit, the All Clear would be sounded. Mop and Pop were now seated either side of the fire, ready for the day.

Now that I have visited Doncombe Mill, I can better form a picture of Jack and Ivy Crompton. They were quintessential country dwellers. In the Chronicle, Jack is always reporting on his work in the garden and the millstream. He takes pot shots at pigeons, magpies, rabbits and squirrels from his bedroom window, and likes nothing better than a day out with a gun and a dog. He has as distinctive a style of expression as his wife Ivy but their handwriting is worlds apart. Ivy's words tail off in indeterminate squiggles in her hurry to say everything, while Jack's words march solidly from the start of a line to its end, every letter in each word evenly paced and clearly legible. Jack must have provided a steady anchor to Ivy's flights of fancy. Here he is describing a walk with Buster, the springer spaniel they had taken over from my parents when my father was posted to Hong Kong not long before the war.

From Jack Crompton
"The story of an incident which shows that the countryside is not quite as peaceful as one supposes.
Buster and I were walking back from a morning's rabbiting. I cut across the fields to a farmyard preparing to come out on the other side and rejoin the road further on. When in the farmyard I noticed a couple of cows in the field beyond through which I intended to go and as all farm animals evince the greatest interest and possible animosity to Buster I got round the wall into another field and called him to heel. Some pigs came charging at us but I didn't think much of it and kept on towards them. However they weren't deterred and I had to use the butt of my gun to keep them off. Unfortunately I slipped and fell flat on my back. The next thing I knew was a pig's jaw closing on my shin. I got a shrewd blow on its jaw with the gun butt. Then it tried the other leg and I gave it another one. All the time I was trying to use the gun with enough force to keep the pig off, but not enough to smash the stock. I was also wondering when I was going to feel the second pig on my head. It was somewhere behind me but Buster was keeping it occupied. I got to my feet in a lull and whilst the pigs stood off for a minute we both jumped back over the wall. Just then the farmer appeared. I said, 'Did you see that?' but he hadn't. I told him what had happened. He said he had never known of such a thing before. The sows however had litters tho the little ones were not with them at the time. It was partly that and partly Buster. The farmer and I had some chat and he asked, 'Have you been foxhunting?' !!! with a gun and a spaniel!!! It seems, however, according to Minnie, that foxes are now being shot, tho that is the first I've heard of it. Anyway, I proceeded on my way home little the worse, tho my legs were bruised and sore with a couple of small wounds on them. I dealt with them with iodine when I got home and am none the worse. In spite of my endeavours to save the gun, I find it is badly damaged. The stock is broken beyond repair and the lock, I fear, badly

damaged. The whole thing was rather ludicrous and I must have looked foolish lying on my back with 2 pigs gnawing at me. It might have been rather beastly had old Buster not dealt with the other pig.

No need to go to Assam to get big game hunting. J.C."

Guns were important. So were dogs. I have a photograph of my mother with a fox terrier in a rowing boat on Lake Windermere.[20] The boat might have belonged to Kathleen and Archie Smithells. She wouldn't have wanted to give up Buster, the springer spaniel, on going to Hong Kong. Later, in Devon, a black Labrador called Sam joined the household, the first in a line of dogs that included a second Buster.

Markham provided my mother with her first settled home. As a child, she'd been parked with her grandparents in Holloway Hill House, Godalming, while her father, Pop, served abroad, in India and Bermuda. She'd married Dick Withington in June 1919 when she was 18. For the next twenty years, she had moved with him around England and to India and Hong Kong. Jane was born in Hong Kong in 1936. My mother's March news ended 'We shall soon be thinking of our next move, our tenant leaves Markham on the 15th May.'

The house must have been sublet. My parents had rented Markham on the edge of the moor on the outskirts of Tavistock when my father was appointed the commander of the Royal Engineers in Devonport in 1937. I was born in a Plymouth nursing home in 1938 and then taken back to Markham for a brief period before the family moved to York for a new posting. When my father joined the British Expeditionary Force, my mother went to stay with her parents at Downderry before moving back to Markham where she'd be until Jane and I left home.

Dick was 'very much impressed with the spirit of the French', so my mother wrote – a view unlike that of the Duke of Gloucester who had been sent over to France to gauge the state of affairs. The Duke travelled over 4,000 miles and reported back that little had been done by anyone to prepare for war[21]. His brother, the ex-King and his wife, now the Duke and Duchess of Windsor, were shimmying up to Hitler in Berlin.

---

[20] See photo on p. 294

In this first year of the war there was a great deal of ambivalence. There were right-wingers who secretly and not so secretly admired what a fascist dictator could achieve. There were left-wingers who set their sights on communism. My uncle, Dicky, reading economics at Oxford during the 30s, was a quiet but ardent socialist. Even as a child, I understood that his views were regarded by my grandparents with a mixture of tolerance – he was, after all, their only surviving son – and apprehension. If a Times leader was discussed in the dining room after breakfast, before everyone fell on the crossword, the conversation had a smouldering quality, barely contained. The ambience got linked in my mind with the business of lighting tobacco-filled pipes. 'Tom, watch what you're doing!' my grandmother would interrupt sharply, referring to the burning spill Pop held in his hand between the Cosy stove and his pipe.

In April news from Godalming, my mother included a cutting from the Daily Mail, which gives a different picture to the one provided by the Duke of Gloucester.

> ***Superb Engineering Feat by B.E.F.***
> *A great triumph of military engineering organisation, carried out by the B.E.F. in France in face of appalling difficulties was announced today.*
> *Tens of thousands of men, working through one of the worst winters on record, have brought the supply system for the ever-growing army to a point further than was reached in the last war after nearly two years.*
> *Fighting against the phenomenal autumn rains, and two months of bitter frost which sheeted the ground with ice at many points, they have accomplished the following gigantic task:*
> *Laid many a mile of full-gauge railway track, with material entirely brought from Britain;*
> *Established a petrol-canning plant with a capacity of hundreds of tons a day;*
> *Prepared a number of dumps of petrol in tins which would cover tens of square miles in all, if placed in one spot;*
> *Laid concrete equal to 70 miles of the very wide Great Western-road, just outside London;*
> *Imported many locomotives and trucks from Britain;*
> *Completed camps for thousands of men;*
> *Laid water supply systems;*

---

[21] London Review of Books, July 30th 2015

Constructed giant bakeries, capable of producing vast quantities of bread per day.

...Every man of the Army of over 300,000 will be kept supplied every day with food, clothing and ammunition.

As massive preparations were taking place across the Channel, the younger cousins were gearing up for the war. In the same month's folder, April 1940, Grace gave news of her four sons.

From Grace Werner
"We have heard from Roger. He is now at Bombay – working for a commission. He was given four days in which to settle up his affairs on the Tea Garden and get off. He seems happier now he is really in the army and going to do his bit.
Charles is still at Cambridge but may be moved any time now. He has passed all his exams there well – much to his relief – those that failed have been pushed out into the Army. He expects now to start to fly (how I hate the thought of it). There is just a chance that he might be sent to Canada. It would be wonderful if he got there and was anywhere near Leigh and Aunt Loo[22].
Paul is trying hard to get into the RAF but so far has failed. John has gone proudly back to school with a pair of Wilfred Becker's white flannel trousers. It means a lot to have a well cut pair – he had been using a pair that had been passed down from Paul. We, John and I, had a lovely eight days at Ford thanks to Jack and Ivy – the woods were so beautiful with the daffodils and primroses just starting – by now everything must look lovely. Roy Henderson[23] has made a wonderful recovery from his cerebro meningitis and may go back to school at half-term. He is off to Blackpool with his Father and Mother and we who have been there all know that the air is a wonderful tonic. Our house at Wilmslow is still empty – John and I had many trips over on the bicycles and picked flowers and sat in the garden during the holidays. It was great fun.
We have filled the vegetable garden with potatoes, cabbages, cauliflowers etc. I only hope we shall be able to collect them when they are ready. As we seem to have started to put in snapshots I enclose one that I know will interest Aunt Loo. Father and Miss

---

[22] This "Aunt Loo" is Louisa Withington in Montreal. Leigh Henderson, in British Columbia, is Grace's brother and son of Joe Henderson.
[23] Roy is Joe's grandson, and the son of Joey. Roy is still at school but later on he will be in the Navy and visit us at Markham when he's stationed in Devonport.

Lane, Charles and Paul with a friend. They were taken with a small 5/- camera of John's given to him by Kathleen.

I made a very good pie for a cold supper last Sunday. It consisted of sausage meat and hard boiled eggs (cut up) in a puff pastry case. It was certainly very tasty. If one could add ham or bacon it would be even nicer. I am afraid Charles's contribution will have to follow on later. It ought to have arrived last week-end.
G.W."

The cousins were getting into the swing of the CFC. Molly Easton wrote on 16th April from Canada.

From Molly Easton
"This will be all about the Boys! They fill our world. Len and I are well and happy and quite definitely on the shelf! It is so amusing when I think back, I remember feeling that middle-aged people were so ignorant and stuffy in their ideas, and now I am on the other side of the picture and can afford to laugh at adolescent conceit although I don't let them know it!

Ted has a steady 'girl' – a very lively and attractive youngster called Elsie. Ted has become much more mellow and more tolerant since Elsie came along. It has done him good. He does love to take her out in the car. It was a huge thrill when he was able to get a driving licence. He has stopped growing at 5ft 10 but Bob is going ahead, he is 6ft now and broad in proportion so I feel sure he is going to be as big as his father. He is 16 ½ now and grows out of all his clothes with lightning and disastrous rapidity! Dickie[24] is too far behind to come in for cast offs so the local rummage sales benefit considerably – it's about the only possible destination for Bob's things when he's done with them. He (Bob) has a girl too, a very vivacious brunette called Jean. It is funny when they both want to telephone to their loved ones, and each take about three quarters of an hour to say six words, there is a regular fight for possession of the phone! Ted is through his lectures for the year, has exams this week and then hopes to get a job. He's thinking of going in for metallurgy but it may be mechanical engineering after all. He wants to get a job at the Marconi Radio factory which is only 10 minutes walk from home. He hopes the University will not find him a job out of town. He loves his home and his Elsie and weekends in the Laurentians and what he calls 'binges' which consist of driving out to a hot dog stand about 3 miles away where they have coca cola (a noxious but innocuous drink) and dance. He doesn't smoke or drink and would rather have a chocolate bar than anything else – thank goodness.

---

[24] Richard Easton was named after his mother's brother, my father Richard Withington, and known in the family as Dickie.

He has passed his Officers Training Corps exams, and now nothing more is to be done until he is through college which will not be for two years, so I pray that he will never have to go to war.

I'm afraid I am taking up too much space in the Chronicle but I must just say a word about Dickie. He is the typical young brother to the boys – they tease him and send him on errands and in return he bothers them to death but they all get along fairly well really. Dickie is in Grade 1 at school and can read and write fairly well and do 'number work' too. He is the best scholar and best behaver in the class – so he says! He belongs to a club called the 'Red Star Rangers' composed of 5 tough, dirty little mischievous boys. When I ask him what the club is for he says it is too 'serious' to tell me about!"

Alice added the note that she had received from Molly Easton on May 6th.

From Molly Easton
"Dear Cousin Alice
Just a line to tell you how much I like your idea of the Cousins Chronicle and how very interesting it is specially for us in Canada, we are so dependent on the post for news. I hope I have not been too profuse but when I get on the subject of the boys I never know when to stop!
We are just emerging from winter now, the snow is gone and crocuses are showing in sheltered spots. Perhaps summer will come in a rush. We never have any spring.
Much love, and good luck to the Cousins Chronicle. Long may it flourish! Yours lovingly, Molly"

The Chronicle was reminding the cousins of their common forebears. Molly Easton's contribution is followed by one from Kathleen Smithells. Typically, it is brief.

From Kathleen Smithells
"I am enclosing this cutting about Altham as I am sure it will be of interest to the family. Father had it sent to him so I said I would enclose it this month."

Pasted onto the page is the cutting from Accrington Observer & Times, dated Saturday 20.4.40.

It is interesting to note that Lydia Becker, pioneer of Women's Suffrage, had a long and close association with Altham, but there is no memorial in Altham Church to the remarkable woman. Lydia Becker, the eldest of the fifteen children of Hannibal Leigh Becker and his wife whose maiden name was Mary Duncuft, was born in

Manchester in 1827 (her name appears in the Reformers memorial in Kensal Green Cemetery, London), but the family removed to the Old Sparth House at Clayton-le-Moors when Lydia was three years old. About two years later Mr Becker built Moorside House, Altham, and the family took up residence there. Mrs Clara Haworth (nee Halham), by the way, has resided for many years in the Old Becker homestead, Moorside House. Mrs Haworth and her sister inherited the estate at Altham.

The Becker family attended Altham Church and Mr Becker was actively connected with the church management. On a brass tablet which commemorates the restoration of the church in 1857 his name appears as one of the churchwardens. Lydia Becker, whose noble character and magnificent work for the emancipation of women made her world-famous, should be commemorated at Altham, where so many years of her extraordinarily useful life were spent. She was editor of the "Women's Suffrage Journal". The last issue she edited became her memorial number for she died before it was published. It contained a photograph of the women's suffrage pioneer.

Altham lies north of Manchester. The place must have held good childhood memories for grandmother Louisa, for she named her married home in Guildford 'Altham'. Foxdenton Hall did not exert quite the same tug on the Becker heartstrings. Hannibal had rented it from the Radclyffe family, and never owned it himself.

By the summer of 1940 family ties were increasingly valued, particularly by the members of the family far from home: Roger in Assam, Molly Easton and Louisa Withington in Canada. As time went on and the war showed no sign of ending, more outlying cousins would want to take part.

*

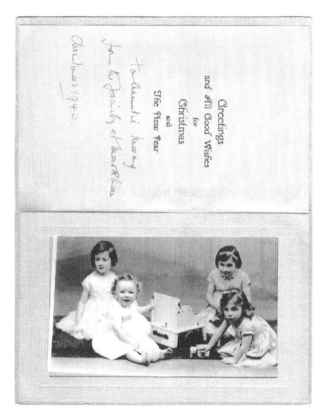

Antonia and Nicolas Mellersh, Jane and Susan Withington,
Christmas 1940

Grace Werner with Roger, Charles and Paul, 1930s before John was born

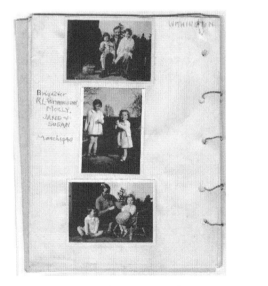

Dick, Molly, Jane and Susan, Downderry, 1940

FIVE

The Fall of France – 1940

Refugees, evacuees, and empty London streets

By the time Cousin Alice was threading red wool through the punched holes of the cousins' June newsletters, the war had taken on a terrible reality. Now much closer to home, it was no longer a phoney or a 'bore' war, as Charles and others had described it. Since Hitler had invaded Poland, Finland had been taken over by Stalin, despite ferocious defensive battles fought by the Finns. Norway was the next nation to collapse in the face of German attacks. France and Britain, with limited resources at this stage, were half-hearted in their attempts to defend a country so far away, when they knew they would be next in Hitler's sights. Once Norway lay in Wehrmacht hands, Germany began a major advance through Holland and Belgium and into France. On May 10th a defiant Winston Churchill became prime minister, replacing Neville Chamberlain who had favoured compromise and appeasement. Hitler's army moved fast along a sixty mile front intent on cutting off the British and French armies in Belgium. Not all the details of the disastrous defeats that led to the collapse of France were reported in the British press and radio. The cousins, listening anxiously to every news bulletin, would not have known the extent of the mass migration of people away from the advancing Germans: later it was estimated that about eight million people left their homes and moved west and south. Paris was deserted. The British army was evacuated from the beaches of Dunkirk.

Irene Becker describes the time, as she and her family experienced it.

From Irene Becker. June 1940
"It is difficult to know what to say in the way of family news this mid-June morning from No 70 Eccleston Square. So much seems to have happened since last I wrote in March or rather early April. London looks just the same but the atmosphere is quite different. Not many people anywhere and all who are about busy, and bent on their jobs. The streets are quite empty and very few cars to impede one's progress; the vast spaces in Piccadilly and Oxford and Victoria Streets

make it all seem so much larger than before and Bond Street seems quite a wide thoroughfare down which the busses hurtle along at top speed. There is, even so, always plenty of opportunity for the few pedestrians to cross at leisure. It appears to be rather like a perpetual Sunday now - in this large half-empty West End at any rate.

Down our way we have a great many Belgian refugees. A great use for the many deserted and empty houses. Their bright coloured frocks and the children's voices bring quite a cheery note to the otherwise half deserted Square. Trevor and I offered to house two and now we have a couple who as it happens turned up quite unexpectedly from Antwerp a few weeks ago, and are now living in part of the house for the time being. They are not quite refugees in the way we had expected as sent by the Westminster C.C. but as Trevor knew the husband, Kenneth Spafford, years ago in Derbyshire we were very glad to have him and his Belgian wife who had to leave their home deserted with all it contained.

It was a great pleasure and a joy to me to be able to get everything ready for them and feel that our half deserted house was being of some use to people who were in need of one. We moved our surplus stuff into one of Aunt Ciss's rooms and Trevor was able to give up a day to help us with the arranging and heaving up and down. Mike's health is still none too good which is a pity as he is unable to do any material war work at the moment. However he was able to help me to collect the equipment for our boat which was requisitioned by the Admiralty and had to be launched and prepared to put to sea while Trevor was away in the North on one of his periodical peregrinations on business. We had all the bedding and internal paraphernalia kept in dry storage at the house so it was quite a business hunting it all out and listing it up to save the time of more urgently busy folk than we.

I am hoping to get down to Harrow and see Wilfred on Sunday as it may be my last opportunity now and he is leaving school at the end of this term; he is now seventeen and a half and nearly old enough for war-work.

Cecily too is expecting to get a job before long as she has almost finished her work for the Oxford entrance now. What sort of Oxford it is going to be after the War remains to be seen!

But we are all hoping to be able to help collectively with some sort of agricultural work in the Summer Holidays. I feel with the harvesting the farmers will be glad of any amount of help this year from young and old alike. I expect as far as we are concerned it will probably be in Hampshire.

It has been interesting seeing all the soldiers - English and French - who returned from Dunkirk and learning all the stories of such wonderful bravery and spirit against the heavy odds. The Bournemouth Steamers, which we knew so well on the water last summer, all went to Dunkirk to do their bit in helping to bring our Warriors home and at least two of them returned to Bournemouth Pier laden with Frenchmen - tired and torn .....who were very glad to be quickly housed, fed and refitted with clothes by the local people. They returned much refreshed to their own country and the spirit of camaraderie between them and our people was a real joy to see. I was glad to feel the little Bournemouth Steamers were able to return safe and intact as they seem quite old friends to us, who knew them so well last summer when they used to pass us on their way to their day trips and jolt us up with their wash as we lay at anchor. Many the minor spills of food I've had when, busy in the galley, I was unexpectedly overtaken by the wash of the Bournemouth Queen or Princess Elizabeth!

Strange happy days to look back to now!

I saw Lettice and Aunt Ciss last Saturday when we all joined forces and met in an outing and picnic to celebrate a long postponed meeting. They seemed very well and Lettice is very busy continuously making pyjamas, shirts and all sorts of garments about three days a week for the Red Cross. Aunt Ciss is growing a marvellous garden of vegetables, as well as her beautiful little flower garden which really is looking lovely - like an old world embroidered picture!

Trevor and I have quietly spent our silver wedding together this week as we felt it was no time for festivities though we did secretly rejoice we had actually lived twenty-five years together, or rather mostly together with sundry breaks in the way of the last war and a trip to Peru etc; and that at the end of it we were perfectly happy in so far as our inner life was concerned, confident of the future in the knowledge that nothing can deprive us of the life we have had and that whatever may lie ahead, if we are allowed so much more time together, it will all be of intrinsic and enduring value to us in the infinite world.

We are hoping to be able to have a family gathering of all the cousins some day in more auspicious circumstances.

Irene Becker"

It sounds as though the Beckers' yacht must have been requisitioned for the evacuation from France, although Irene doesn't say so explicitly. No doubt she was mindful of the rules of censorship. Something that didn't need the censor is the secret rejoicing in 25 years' of marriage, and their devotion to each other and to their four children and the extended family. A gathering of all the cousins at number 70 would have been a great event. But neither Irene nor anyone else could possibly imagine when she wrote her contribution how long it would be before 'more auspicious circumstances' arrived.

A letter from Charles Werner to his mother follows, pasted into the Chronicle by Alice. In June 1940 he was feeling, with only a few reservations, 'very, very lucky'.

Letter from Charles Werner
"Tuesday 5/6/40   967878 PILOT U/T
R.A.F.
K6 Clare College
Cambridge

Dear Mum
I still don't quite know what to think about my coming trip but then I never did like being jolted out of my normal way of life and I suppose that once I settle down again I shall be quite happy. After all it is rather a big undertaking to get used to all at once, rather like finishing one chapter of one's life and starting afresh with another.
But the new chapter holds so many possibilities, new experiences, adventure and a chance to see the world. What more could anyone ask for a perfect training for one who wants to write for a career. No I must admit that I am very very lucky though one can't help feeling the wrench all the same. Yet in these days life can't be free from 'wrenches' no matter where one goes and it might be so very much worse, when one thinks of what other people have had to go through.
Of the hazards of the journey I have no fear. The Mary still seems to be very much master of the seas and I have no doubt that we won't go unprotected! I don't suppose it will be by any means a pleasure cruise as from your experiences in the last war you will know better than I but that we will get there in the end I am quite confident.
Only eight of us are going from Cambridge and on the whole they seem to be a pretty decent crowd, there will probably be some more from the other Wings and I may meet some of the old Padgate crowd. The last remnants of the Feltwell fellows are going to their Flying Schools on Monday so I shall be the last to leave. Anyway I should be able to spend at least some part of next week at home if I am allowed another four days as I think is almost certain.
I had a letter today from Frank Kelsey. He has now done nearly four hours flying in an aeroplane. He says that for the first few times he found that he had little or no appetite for meals afterwards. Now though, he says he can actually face food an hour or so after landing!! So that's cheering. He says that they are throwing out so many on the slightest pretext that he sees no hope - especially as whenever he gets up in the air he can never find the aerodrome again and invariably tries to land in the wrong field! He thinks he'll join the Tank Corps and when he's failed his exams in that and has been thrown out he'll try the Artillery, by the time he's thrown out of that he's hoping the war will be over! It really is very hard to serve one's country these days but as Frank says 'at least we have tried to do something'. It's rather a pity that the fellows at the top haven't tried a bit more since last September but there we are.
Must carry on now with my 'Editorial' duties but will let you know as soon as there is any more news.

Much love
Charles
P.S. I sent John some sweets."

Sweets! I could tell you exactly at which Tavistock shop counter I stood with Jane when sweets came off the ration. We were bewildered. It's strange to realise today that we really didn't know how to buy sweets. We'd never learnt. John Werner being older would have remembered sweets from the days before the war. In fact, they weren't rationed until 1942.[25] It was just at school they'd have been in short supply. He would have been thrilled to receive Charles' parcel.

Their aunt Kathleen's newsletter comes next in the June 1940 folder. The more I read Kathleen's contributions the more I warm to her pessimistic hopefulness - or is it hopeful pessimism.

From Kathleen Smithells
"June 3rd
I seem to have very little to report this month. Only that Manchester is getting its full share of refugees. I am giving as many afternoons, packing up clothes, as I am needed. Our house is being painted on the outside, as we had booked it before all this started.
It may give people fresh courage when they see it being done.
I hope the men will not kill all my beans and lettuces, I have planted them in the beds, they look to be doing quite well. It is good to hear of Aunt Loo's recovery - she must have been very ill.
I wish the Werners' problem of whether to go back to the Wilmslow house was solved."

On the cover of the folder, Grace and Kathleen are linked together under Joe Henderson's name at 30 Brunswick Road, Manchester 20. It's possible that Grace was living there due to Henry Werner's need to be near work. But the city would not have been the best place to be. Grace talks of the possibility of moving back to an earlier home, in her contribution for June.

From Grace Werner
"Charles is still in England - he expects to sail in about two weeks

---

[25] Sweets came off the ration in 1948 but for only a few months. The end of rationing of sweets, eggs, cream, butter, cheese, margarine and cooking fat didn't happen until 1953, and meat a year later.

time for darkest Africa. I am very thankful to feel he will be away from whatever we may be going to get here. Paul has again been turned down for any kind of military service - he must go on with his work at Kents they say for the present. I feel sorry for him but am very thankful myself. Roger is still going on with his training in Bombay. Henry has got an engineering job at Warrington and starts on June 10th. I think he may have to go into rooms otherwise he will get tired out with the travelling. So we may - Father and I - go back to Wilmslow. Our house there is empty and as we have to keep the garden up it is costing quite a lot and we are getting no benefit from it. I am afraid Father will feel rather cut off from his friends and we shall not find it easy without a car, me with a bicycle and John in the holidays, but it is certainly a little safer there than here. Kathleen and Archie may be glad to join us there. We shall have to make up our minds within the next few days. We were all here overjoyed to hear of Aunt Loo's recovery.[26] Molly must be thankful too - in fact both Mollys. We shall all be glad to hear news of Dick - he has been very much in our thoughts these last few weeks. Father keeps wonderfully well, if somewhat depressed at times, and can one wonder. I have been toying with the idea of sending John out to Leigh in Canada and have got as far as writing to Leigh on the subject. It's difficult to know what to do for the best. My two girl P.G's[27] may be off at any time. The one in the B.B.C. expects they will be moved if things get hot here and the other one would stay at her home near Fleetwood if there should be trouble here. I am afraid this is a dull instalment as I feel I have little of interest to write this time.
G.W."

It could hardly be a dull instalment at such a crucial time. Thousands of parents were worrying over the same difficult decision: whether to send children away to unknown safety or keep them close in possible danger. Besides a government scheme which sent nearly three thousand children to Commonwealth countries, there were hundreds of private arrangements. For the cousins, there was the possibility of sending their younger children to Leigh in British Columbia or to the Eastons in Montreal. The Chronicle kept the Canadian branches of the family constantly in mind. The health of 'Aunt Loo' in Montreal was of particular concern.

---

[26] Louisa, born in 1854, was 86. Her illness, not mentioned in the selected extracts, had concerned the family.
[27] Paying Guests. With the pressure on accommodation, many households offered spare rooms and meals for payment.

From Ivy Crompton
"I expect the CFC will be only a thin leaflet this month but I send a small contribution for what it is worth. I suppose one of my chief sources of thankfulness this month is the news that dear Aunt Loo is restored again. We always feel happy to think that this Chronicle must give her great pleasure, bless her. George went off last Monday week to France but of course we have no news and don't know where he is exactly. Jack has offered himself for work (engineering) at the 2 adjacent aerodromes and is joining the L.D.V.[28] I am working daily at the Food Office in Chippenham, very dull but I suppose essential work. One doesn't feel much heart to write at length this awful month so I append my Minnie's views with which I agree wholeheartedly.
'Wicks is very meek earted about the war, e says it ought not to ave appeared and no more it never didn't ought, did it mum?'"

Minnie, the Cromptons' cook, sounds like a Dickens creation. There was a long tradition in the family for preserving, verbatim, idiosyncratic pronouncements like this.

Jack, besides joined the Local Defence Volunteers, was involved with what today we'd call re-cycling, but in those days was termed salvage. Jack gave the word capital letters.

From Jack Crompton
"I had an interesting meeting ... about SALVAGE but it is a difficult thing to arrange over an area such as ours, consisting mainly of very small villages or hardly that, with considerable distances between. It was decided at present to deal only with paper, and to make a start with 4 or 5 of the larger villages and see how it goes. If successful it can be extended. Before we can move, however, it has to come before the Council so, in a way, my hands are tied till then. As to paper, any and all sorts, cardboard etc all is good. Where there are great quantities I believe it helps to have it sorted into grades, but it's not needed here."

Alice wrote from Rye. Its position on the south coast, not far from Dover, put it in the front line of the fast-unfolding events, though Alice remained unalarmed.

From Alice Crompton
"I have been quietly in Rye all May - a most lovely month in this countryside: Primroses abounded and lambs. (There are more sheep to the acre on Romney Marshes near Rye than anywhere else in England). The hawthorn was finer and fuller than I can remember.

---

[28] Local Defence Volunteers

> For the Whitweek holiday I had an interesting friend from London, Mrs Beer, who sits on Alien Tribunals and Trade Boards, and has done much work for Refugees. After Whitweek I was to have visited the Loesches at Heathfield. But just then Holland was invaded and I thought I might receive refugees in my cottage and/or otherwise be useful, so I stayed at home.
> I joined Women's Voluntary Service here months ago, and lately have been v. busy filling up the new Ration Cards. On 8 June a canteen for the Forces was opened by W.V.S and I have twice been there 6.30 - 10 pm as a washer up. About 170 men turn up. I have been lettering Menu Cards and notices for the Canteen. Rye seems pretty full of troops, and there are numbers of evacuated London children here. I am having 8 or 10 of them to tea soon. I was twice asked to conduct these from one school to another at which they have dinner.
> Last week I was grieved to see in the 'Sunday Times' that Sir Arnold Wilson M.P. was missing. He learned to fly recently and passed all tests as bomber and observer at the age of about 55. I wrote at once to one of the two of his sisters who have stayed with me here. She says there is still a faint hope he is a prisoner, as he was flying over Germany."

The career of Arnold Talbot Wilson is interesting in the light of current events. He started his career as an army officer serving in India with the Sikh Pioneer Regiment before transferring to the Middle East to protect the work of the D'Arcy oil company. In 1907 he was in charge of the Turko-Persian frontier commission. The expression 'drawing lines in the sand' comes to mind. As acting civil commissioner for Mesopotamia he worked to establish an efficient administration giving fair treatment and political representation to the many ethnic and religious communities – Arabs, Kurds, Persians, Islamic Shiites and Sunnis, Christians and Jews. After the first world war Britain was given the mandate by the League of Nations over the country now called by its Arabic name of Iraq, rather than its Greek name meaning 'between the rivers'. Riots broke out among the rival factions against British rule. These were 'violently repressed' by Wilson's administration. Around 10,000 people were killed. So many variations of 'them', so many different kinds of 'us'…

My mother's father was of the same vintage and schooling. They may even have been at Clifton at the same time, and later in India. They served the Empire according to their own lights. Wilson served again, this time in the RAF in the Second World War. He lost his life, shot down over Germany on May 31ˢᵗ 1940.

My mother's contribution ends June's folder.

From Molly Withington
"The Withington contribution is late this month, I am so sorry. We moved back to Devonshire on the 20th, I motored down in the Standard with the dog as company and spent the weekend with a friend and near neighbour so that I could get everything unpacked and ready before Nannie brought Jane and Susan down by train. We found everything in good order and Tavistock seems comparatively peaceful, though we have many troops back from Flanders resting here at present and there are quite a lot of R.E. in the town, too, now. Jane and Susan are very well and seem delighted to be back, with their sandpit and their swing, and to see their old toys again. My family has increased during the last few days! After some hurried telephone messages my cousin George Mellersh sent his two children and their Nurse down here on Friday last from Sussex. Antonia is 3 and a half and gets on very well with Jane, and Nicolas is a lovely baby of 8 months, and they are both very good indeed.
I am very glad to be able to give a good report of Mother's health. I had a cable from Molly on the 9th May to say her condition was improving daily, which was a great relief.
I have been getting letters rather irregularly from Dick since the invasion of Belgium, naturally, but he is perfectly well and I hope safe and sound. My brother is also in good form, his R.A. Base Depot was moved back and as far as we know he is still at the Base.
I have been putting in some hours' clerical work on several days lately at the local Food Offices, issuing the New Ration Books. This is such a very large Rural Area. I am also pretty busy in the house as I have only one daily maid from 9 - 6 so I cook the breakfast."[29]

My mother wrote this, I believe, just before Dunkirk. I am baffled by her measured tone, the mildness of her anxiety. *Dick is perfectly well and I hope safe and sound.* Where was he? The folder, titled Vol. I No. 5, contained the collection of May's newsletters, which circulated round the cousins in June although Irene had written her newsletter, included in this folder, in mid-June, after Dunkirk. My father, I know, left France from St. Malo, but on what date? I turn to Max Hastings.

---

[29] So she did cook. My memory is of her learning after the war, taking a saucepan of white sauce to the telephone to ask a friend how to get rid of the lumps.

"The conquest of France and the Low Countries cost Germany almost 43,000 killed, 117,000 wounded; France lost around 50,000 dead, Britain 11,000; the Germans took 1.5 million prisoners. The British were granted one further miraculous deliverance, a second Dunkirk. After the BEF's escape, Churchill made the fine moral but reckless military decision to send more troops to France, to stiffen the resolve of its government. In June, two ill-equipped divisions were shipped to join the residual British forces on the Continent ... After the armistice, because the Germans were overwhelmingly preoccupied elsewhere, it proved possible to evacuate almost 200,000 men from the north-western French ports to England, with the loss of only a few thousand. Churchill was fortunate thus to be spared the consequences of a folly.[30]"

My mother's contribution in the next month's folder fills in the personal details.

From Molly Withington
"News for June
Dick got back from France on the 18th, he crossed in one of the last ships to leave St. Malo. It was, of course, crammed full of troops, but as a senior officer, he got a berth. I had a 'phone call from London the day before from one of his staff to say Dick would soon be arriving, which saved me some anxiety. We were also very anxious about my brother as no news was received from him for many days. However, he turned up at Southampton safe and sound and was sent to Cheshire, then Ascot, from there he got 48 hours leave and he is now under orders for 'abroad' – destination unknown. Dick arrived here by the same train as my cousin's wife, Rachel Mellersh, with her cook and her cat, and masses of luggage! So we **are** a houseful! Dick looked very much better for the leave, as he was very tired and strained. He has now gone to the 11th Corps as Chief Engineer. The Headquarters are near Bishops Stortford. I have only had a hurried note from him, it is a very large 'Area' and he will have a lot of travelling to do.
Tavistock has been in the midst of 'alarms', if not excursions, lately, as we had 8 air raid warnings in six days last week. The raids were over Plymouth, nothing very drastic up to date, we understand, but I definitely do not like to go far from home, because of the children. All four have slept through the night alarms, and we haven't disturbed them, as there seemed nothing anywhere in this vicinity, and it's so bad for their nervous systems to be disturbed. I find it rather difficult not to be irritable! Though this has proved to be anything but a 'peaceful spot', we have an excellent 'hidey hole' under the stairs

---

[30] Max Hastings, *All Hell Let Loose*, HarperPress 2012, p. 72. Thanks for his permission to quote from this immensely valuable book.

about 4 steps down, and I really don't think the Germans will come here in malice, but merely offshoots from a raiding party on Plymouth. There are a lot of troops in the town, though the R.E [31]. have left. We had a small sherry party for some of the R.E. Officers while Dick was here.

Susie was 2 on the 24th and we had a nice little party for her, about 24 people for tea. It was so lucky Dick should be home for it, he found Susan very much advanced in the 2 ½ months since he had seen her, as she is now very talkative. Of course she wants to do everything Jane does."

The gate to Markham from Down Road led to three flights of steps bordered by hawthorn trees that flowered pink in May. My first memory of my father is seeing an unknown man push open the gate and start up the steps. My mother and I had come out of the house – she must have been watching and waiting for this moment. I was horrified to see the stranger, dressed most unusually, bound up the steps to join us on the redbrick platform in front of our blue front door. I watched aghast as the man seized my mother in his arms. It was not just outrageous, it was dangerous. He had a moustache like Hitler's. I may have embroidered that memory in later years but the main outline was seared too deeply to ever forget. Whether this happened at the time of my second birthday and the 'nice little party for 24', I doubt. It's generally held that true memories can't be formed until the age of three. Although I call this my first memory of my father it is not strictly my father who I am remembering. The man with the moustache came and went for brief visits. It was only after the war that he became 'Daddy', a truly loved fixture. Up to my 7th birthday, made so memorable by Cousin Alice as I described in the Introduction, his importance as father came from the cine films he'd made and my mother's often-repeated anecdotes.

One of these stories featured a neighbour, Lady Godfrey, who rang the police to report that a man, thought to be Colonel Withington, had been seen flying a kite on Whitchurch Down. Our garden gate opened onto this stretch of moorland. He could have been signalling to the Germans, said Lady Godfrey. It shouldn't be allowed. The family reacted with delight and savoured the story for re-telling over the years.

---

[31] Royal Engineers

Beside the brief invasion of Markham by the Hitler lookalike, another event formed an indelible memory. In the room that was called the Nursery, we were gathered together in the middle of the night, sitting on the two beds either side of the chest of drawers below the blackout-curtained window. Someone drew the curtain aside and said "That's Plymouth burning." There was a huge red glow in the sky over the moor. I felt my Nanny's lap becoming slowly, hotly, deeply awash. I was ashamed beyond belief. I'd behaved like a baby in front of the cousins who were living with us.

Cooks and nannies abounded in the household. How was it my mother had to cook breakfast because she had, as she explained, only a daily maid from 9 - 6? In the kitchen, approached (if you were brave) through a dark inner hall enclosed between two doors and hung about with rubber-smelling mackintoshes, there reigned two stout women. One was Mrs Grey, the cook the invading Mellersh cousins had brought with them. The other was our own Bessie. Whether there was ever any disagreement about what and how to cook, nothing was heard through the two closed doors.

Much more in our orbit were the nannies. There was Nanny Mellersh for whom we held no affection at all; rather, deep suspicion. We weren't going to obey *her* orders. At the epicentre of our universe was our own dear Nannie – the ie in the way my mother spelt her name holding the whole weight of my remembered love for her. She had pale blue eyes and a soft Irish voice. She was small and bird-like. The top of her head barely reached my mother's shoulders. When eventually she left us to go to another family, I was dumbfounded. It was unbelievable that Nannie did not belong to us; by us, of course I meant Me. Only when it was proven beyond doubt that she had left for good did I weep bitterly. The next time I cried in this way was during the first three weeks at boarding school. The koala bear who shared my pillow was sodden.

In June 1940 we were a household of 10 people. How we all fitted in is a mystery. Markham had four bedrooms, a boxroom (full of fascinating trunks stamped with labels and exotic addresses), and a dressing room. There must have been some strange doublings-up. Cooks in one room, nannies in another, children in a third, and a room for each mother? I suspect my mother, a giver and lover of parties, enjoyed the company and the general hooha.

It was news to me to read, at the end of her June contribution to the Chronicle, that she had thought of taking Jane and me to Canada; or rather my father did.

> *From Molly Withington*
> "Dick, after suggestions from my mother, rather toyed with the idea of sending me and the children out to Canada, but it seems very difficult, in fact impossible, from a financial point of view, except for State-aided schools, or for children who can go to rich relations or friends."

The same dilemma was being faced by Irene Becker and Grace Werner. Irene wrote at length about the decision the Becker family was facing. Trevor thought Irene should take Juliet, leaving the three older children in England. Irene was not at all at ease with this idea.

> *From Irene Becker*
> "We decided to have a family conclave on the matter. I adjourned to Bournemouth to talk it all over with Mike and Cecily who were both there then and Trevor collected Wilfred from school meanwhile so that he should be included in the discussion. Anyway Trevor thought with the war and the affairs of Europe in this present state a public school was perhaps not the best place for a boy who has reached the age of 17. The atmosphere could not in any case be conducive to working for exams, especially if his home was likely to be broken up and half his family possibly migrating to Canada.
> The result of our many deliberations was that all the older members of the family unitedly decided that Juliet ought to go to Canada but not alone and that she ought not to have to choose for herself in such a matter. The only possible course was for me to go and take her if it could be arranged.
> Many mothers we know and don't know here are all flocking to Canada and now the Government Scheme for the evacuation of the children is beginning to operate there seems to be a general rush. At least so we discovered when we tried for passport and exit permit. Trevor had taken the precaution of booking the passage early on for sailing on July 3rd, which is now today but I haven't a passport yet nor has the exit permit been granted! We had to relinquish our berths for the 3rd and under new regulations are unable to book a passage without the exit permit to hand. In order to get this permit granted one has to make financial arrangements with one's friends in Canada since the emigration must entail no export of capital whatsover and by the time this is done and the permit granted there probably will not be

a passage to be had for ages. So on the face of things it looks as though Juliet and I will not get to Canada for some time if at all!

However it is in some ways a relief to me for I didn't much like the idea of breaking up my home and leaving most of my family behind especially in these difficult days. Probably the Government would prefer people sent their children abroad under their own public scheme and auspices which seem to be adequate and quite a sound arrangement. In many ways private emigrations possibly add to confusion of the Public Scheme and as everyone in this country has the chance of entering their children to go under this arrangement no doubt the Authorities consider private enterprise in the matter merely a nuisance.

From my point of view Juliet is almost nine, old enough to appreciate what it means to leave her entire family for what to her seems a very long time, though she doesn't yet realize it will be longer than a whole summer holiday; she is too young to properly appreciate what she is fleeing from and whither. It is all very difficult as I have had two offers from friends, whom I could really trust to take her with them and their own children provided I was able to finance her, but she isn't at all inclined to go without me unless I say she has to. I am inclined to agree with my older children that the decision ought not to be left to her.

I hope all this isn't very boring to the Cousins but I am afraid it is a topic so uppermost in all our minds at the moment that it is difficult meanwhile to concentrate on anything else.

If ever we should get to Canada I am expecting to join up with a friend who is also going and we hope to be able to live together to share and also lessen expense. I should go first to Montreal and very much look forward to meeting Aunt Loo and Mollie and family, should our trip ultimately materialize, though we had thought of going to Ottawa to live as we hear it is less expensive than Montreal. However if anyone has any views on the matter to offer it will be interesting to hear them and I should be most grateful for advice.

I was most interested to hear what Grace had to say about her idea of sending John to Canada. Of course having a brother there[32] will no doubt be a great help and in the case of a boy of John's age I expect he would be quite happy to go under the Government auspices. It is sure to be the best managed means of travelling there, provided there is a home to receive the child in at the other end. But I feel it is very hard for Grace to have to think of giving up three of her boys to go so far in different directions, India, Africa and America. It really seems like the uttermost parts of the earth!"

Irene and Juliet never went to Canada, nor did John Werner. Years later Juliet became our solicitor. John, still a

---

[32] Leigh Henderson, Grace's brother

schoolboy in 1940, writes a contribution for the July folder. The family had moved back to Wilmslow.

> *From John Werner*
> "One of our biggest excitements has been our removing out to Sunnyside again. The worst part of my holidays was starting with measles the day I arrived back from school, but how much better to have it at home than at school. The night we arrived here Cousin Ivy wired to say that Sam Small, a black kitten from Cousin Alice's Tony, was on its way. So I hastily rang up my father, from the cottage at the end of the lane, to ask him if he would meet Sam at London Road station, M/C.[33] So off he went and returned without the kitten having waited two hours! The next morning as Paul and I were going down to Wilmslow on our bikes I went on and did the shopping while Paul went to the Parcels Office and asked if there was a cat for "Werner", he was handed a basket and set off at top speed for home. Although the poor little chap had spent the whole of one day and a night in a closed basket he was not in the least upset, he might have taken journeys every day. Imagine our horror when next day in the pouring rain, he wandered off! I put a notice on the gate – LOST A SMALL BLACK KITTEN WITH WHITE SPOT. Imagine our joy when a woman with some children returned Sam at about 7 pm. They had found him caught in the hedge down the lane crying. Since then he has stayed around the house, the farthest he dare venture is raspberry bushes in the kitchen garden. So ends, or perhaps begins the story of SAM SMALL.
> p.s Sam Small and Scamp (my dog) are the greatest of friends. Sam is biting the dog's tail at this moment."

John wrote that on September 9th. The story of Sam Small had started in Cousin Alice's contribution for June.

> *From Alice Crompton*
> "On Sat 22 June I left Rye for Doncombe a step to which Jack and Ivy had long been urging me. I am indeed fortunate to have such a lovely place to come to, and such an extremely kind welcome from its owners. There are plenty of small jobs for me to do, so I don't feel myself wholly a 'bouche inutile'. I can help Jack with his National Savings work and, to a lesser extent, Ivy with her work party. And the garden offers endless scope, tho so far I've done nothing beyond the very 'cushy' job of cutting off dead flowers.
> Before I left Rye I had become fairly busy, helping at a Canteen for H.M. Forces, started by the Womens Voluntary Service, where I washed up from 7 to 10 pm, once or twice a week, and lettered ornate

---

[33] Manchester. The family often used this abbreviation.

Menu cards. Also I house to house canvassed for a Salvage scheme, also initiated by the W.V.S.
The Meeting in aid of the Melanesian Mission, which was planned last winter, came off on 18 June, and was quite satisfactory considering everything. The audience numbered 51, and all were interested in the talk given by an unconventional young clergyman on furlough from the South Sea Islands.
Rye has for some time been in a Defence Area, and, the day after I left, the London children who have been there about 9 months, were sent away to Wales.
I had quite an exciting journey to Doncombe. No one would take my cat in Rye, so (Jack and Ivy cheerfully permitting) I brought her with me, in a huge basket. This I carried in one hand, in the other a bag containing the H.L. Becker silver tea service. Also my handbag, and gas mask and a little knapsack with my lunch, and ¼ lb raw liver and ½ pt milk to sustain Tony, (cat). Also 5 pieces of luggage in the van, as it seemed best to bring both summer and winter clothes. I managed very successfully and comfortably, tho' it was a Saturday, and crowds of troops were everywhere. On 30 June 4 kittens arrived for Tony. The gardener took away 3 almost at once and left a little black Tom. George Errington has a great gift for naming animals, and when he came to tea in the aft. I consulted him. He suggested about 5 good names from which I selected 'Sam Small'. George told us of a trooper in his regiment (10th Hussars) – a black man from Africa. He and another British soldier were taken prisoner by 5 Germans. Sam Small, the black man, had no weapons, but he seized his companion's revolver and killed 3 Germans. The other 2 G's ran away."

George Errington was Ivy's son by a previous marriage. I notice that I have become partisan about the cousins, viewing those with Becker DNA as Us, and anyone else as Them. The Erringtons are nothing to do with Us, however gifted and glamorous and worthy of our love and admiration they may be. Squashing these divisive thoughts, I will let Ivy talk of her family.

From Ivy Crompton
"The chief item of interest for us this month was a visit from Peggy and George, the first since the latter returned from France. They stayed close at hand with friends as we had full house but came to see us daily. George was involved in an accident in the blowing up of a bridge just before our troops all returned, he had a collar bone and rib broken and his lung pierced, it all healed splendidly however and I have never see him look so hard and fit, also he was in great spirits and very confident, he is of the opinion of which I have heard so many that as man to man the Germans are completely outclassed as

fighters on land and sea and in the air. He holds the view which also seems pretty general that we are better without the French, we at least know how we stand and cannot be 'carted' again, he opines.

We have planes over us nightly, but very high and almost inaudible and all the household sleeps calmly. Alice seems comfortably settled and her cat family is a great addition. The LDV's are rolling up and I am thankful to say a little equipment. I think it may be extremely hazardous later and I feel sorry Jack 'cooked' his age as I think it is far more suited to younger men, but Jack is mad keen.[34]

I am sure our sympathies all go out to Irene and the awful decision she had to make but perhaps now she need not make it and I expect her family will rejoice if in the end she is unable to go to Canada. One can't help feeling what a blessing that Aunt Loo went when she did and has been saved from so much.

I have not succeeded in finding a settled job, a bit of haymaking seems rather inadequate somehow and no hospital work seems wanted locally and things are so little changed here, it is difficult at times to believe in it all now that the anxiety for one's own belongings is lifted. Drought has been bad and crops rather disappointing I fancy and apple crops in this part of the world almost nonexistent. Jack is having good success with village War Savings and I have started a working party for the village women which they seem to like very well. All these things seem rather like a new game at present, which I suppose is a great mercy. We very much hope Alice will be happy here but fear she will miss her many activities in Rye."

While Ivy's son George Errington returned safely from France, Charles Werner, the third of Grace Werner's four sons, set sail for South Africa. The shared Becker DNA makes me feel warmly towards him, although we never met. Hannibal Leigh and Mary Becker are our mutual forebears. Grace wrote after she and Henry had said goodbye to him.

From Grace Werner
"Charles has sailed – he left Southampton on June 19th and should be more than halfway now to Southern Rhodesia. It is hard to say good bye when one does not know these days how long it is for - or even if we shall be here when he returns. One tries not to think this way, but now and again it comes over you and you cannot drive your thoughts away. I spent a happy weekend with John at Trent College during June and found him well and happy. They have been having many air raid warnings and been up four nights out of seven - now it has been decided to leave them in bed until they hear something really is

---

[34] After Dunkirk it was generally felt that the Germans would invade and the Local Defence Volunteers would be our front line.

happening. I think most of the parents feel that the risk is worthwhile as the boys were finding it hard work to keep awake during the daytime. Leigh and Helen have written asking me to send John to them. But as we find we can only take £10.0.0. out of the country we do not feel it would be right to give Leigh the burden of another child to feed and care for. Also if Japan comes in against us will Canada be much better than here? We have spent two nights in our cellar - quite comfortable, with an electric stove and kettle, barley sugar, chocolate and biscuits. Some easy chairs and a camp bed - but one does feel a bit the worse for wear next day.

Henry is hard at work at Risley near Warrington. Works Monday to Sunday getting a half day Saturday, and one whole weekend in four. He likes the work, but it's a long day - up at 6.30 and he gets back at 8.30 pm. Anyway he's thankful to have it. It will mean him giving up his A.R.P[35]. work, which is a pity he had worked hard at it and felt his lot were very well trained for any emergency. The knowledge will not be wasted, he can always use it if necessary in his own home. Roger seems very happy at the Cadet School at Bombay. It will be ages before I shall hear from Roger or Charles - now the air mails are off. I hope that Charles will be able to cable when he arrives. Paul is now in better rooms a little way out of Luton and seems much happier. He has joined the Local Defence Corps and seems to enjoy it. So far he has not had to be up at night and has slept through the Air Raids. Father won't get out of bed, he puts the clothes over his head and goes to sleep again - very wise I think. I wish Henry would let me do the same, but he won't. As we sleep right at the top of the house and he says it is not at all safe up there. There is a large 'To Let' notice outside this house. We still have the Wilmslow house empty and feel we must move back there and we cannot keep this going if that house is empty. We may divide it up into flats and live in one ourselves. This was Trevor's bright idea and we are now waiting to see what it would cost. My excitement this month is the fact that I took over a small class of children age 4 - 8 years in a tiny private school near here. One of the mistresses was ill and they are very badly hit by the war and could not really afford to pay anyone. So I was glad to help them out. They are old friends of Winnie Crompton and I have always liked them both - I mean the Miss Parkers who ran the school. I did it for two weeks and may be called upon again if the school stays open for the holidays. They were dear little children and I really quite enjoyed it. I am now expecting to be called up for canteen work in the Y.M.C.A. so many days a week. I shall still be able to manage this from Wilmslow. We had a visit from Trevor which we all enjoyed and we heard first hand of his family up to that date. That I think is all I have to tell of the month of June."

---

[35] Air Raid Precautions. Henry would have been an ARP warden, trained to deal with the aftermath of bombing raids.

Below this letter there is a note from Alice. *"Grace kindly let us see the appended letters from Charles. A.C."*

<u>Letter from Charles</u>:
"967878   Pilot u/t
R.A.F
J.7
Clare College
Cambridge
Sunday 16/6/40

Dear Mum
Well it's done at last, two great kit bags and my suitcase, piled against the wall. labelled and all complete. Somehow it wasn't quite such an unpleasant task after all, I had thought that packing everything up would have made me a bit sick at heart but it doesn't seem to have done so at all. It must be that I have not the slightest qualms about the trip and in my heart I am quite confident that it won't be long before I am back with you all again and we'll have a lot to talk about then, not that we are a talkative family for it is when faced with something like this that I realize how very very lucky I am in having such a family and such a real home to come back too. We've certainly had our fair share of ups and downs and we've weathered them all and I have no doubt that we can weather this spot of bother also. I think you were marvellous at the train and I was so glad that you did come to see me off, it won't be so long before you are coming to meet me when I return in a few months time.
I see on the 'Confidential letter' that we are to be 'on loan to the Southern Rhodesia government for special duties'! I don't quite know what this means but apparently they will be some sort of Flying Duties. If I remain an L.A.C[36]. I get an extra 4d a day, Colonial Pay which won't exactly make me a millionaire but I also get an extra 2/- a day Flying pay which isn't so bad. Anyway I hope that it won't be long before I get my commission or at least my Sergeants Stripes. The arrangements are just as I told you in my letter yesterday. We leave here on Tuesday morning for Uxbridge and will be sailing on Thursday, all being well.
I have been trying to get hold of some address out there for you to write to but so far I can't find out anything. I'm phoning tomorrow night so perhaps I will know something by then if not I'll have to cable it to you.
I wonder how you and Hilary[37] got on at Wilmslow. I hope you had a good time. This having to go away has made me realize what Hilary

---

[36] Leading Aircraftman
[37] Hilary was a girl friend.

means to me and I realize I am very fond of her. She has a great warm heart and I know she thinks a lot of you.
Well I must post this now. I'll be writing again before I leave and I expect there will be at least one outgoing mail on the ship so you'll be hearing from me. I shall be quite happy and shall only worry if you are worrying - so you mustn't!
So for now
Much love
Charles"

The next day he wrote again, and Cousin Alice attached his second letter to the pages of the June folder. News of the fall of France must have arrived overnight at the barracks.

Letter from Charles Werner
"967878 Pilot u/t
R.A.F
17/6/40 Monday
Dear Mum
Well what a to do! It is difficult to know what to think about things now. So far there has been no change in our plans and we are to leave for Uxbridge in the morning but surely they will keep us back now - if they think of it in time. The whole idea of going out there seems rather futile now - surely it would be better to give us a rifle to defend our own coasts. Still we shall just have to see what happens.
I'm relying on you to keep safe and sound if I have to go away so don't let me down! We certainly live in strange times and we've just got to keep hoping for the best that's all.
I'll let you know any developments tomorrow.
Much love, Charles"

We know from his mother Grace's contribution that he and his contingent did get away. They set sail for Rhodesia two days after he wrote that last letter. There they had intensive pilot training in German-free skies. Two of the Werners' four sons were now serving. It's easy to understand why the family was not keen on sending the youngest son, John, to Grace's brother, Leigh Henderson, in Canada.

Molly Easton, long settled in Canada, is more confident about the safety of her three sons. She included with her newsletter extracts from the letters of the eldest, Ted, who had left home but not yet for war.

From Molly Easton
"June 1st, 1940

Nothing much to report. We have a rush on Red Cross work, the whole community is banded together and we have a room in the High School and each branch has a day to go and work. The Anglicans have a day, the United Church another, the Catholics, Baptists, Community Club and I.O.D.E[38]. all have their days and woe betide any one who goes on the wrong day and so gives credit to some other organization - ! Very petty but human!

Mother is quite well again after being very seriously ill for 3 weeks – it is marvellous to see her herself again, enjoying her bridge and bezique in her usual style. Bob is working hard for his matriculation exams which start in 3 weeks. Ted has gone to the wilds to work in a gold mine. I will copy bits of his letters which I think most interesting – it is certainly a new life for him and will do him a world of good physically. I hated to see him go off for 4 months – the first time he's left home – but I am lucky he wasn't going off to war.

We are not going away this summer, but will make ourselves happy at home; although we shall miss our beautiful Lake Louisa, it is much more comfortable with electric light, stove, hot water and the frigidaire!

Letters from Ted Easton

Extracts from Ted's letters from Central Patricia Gold Mines – 130 miles from the nearest railway – in Northern Ontario.

"May 22nd Got off the train at 6.45 am took off in the plane at 9 a.m. I was never so sick in my life – that plane bumped around like a row boat at sea only worse – we were buffeted all over the place. I kept reaching for "vomitones" which are an outsize in paper cups – a bunch of them were placed within easy reach and I threw them out of the window after using them."

A plane with open windows! We in the 21st century register astonishment.

"I am still feeling slightly groggy and to my undoubtedly jaundiced eye the village of Central Patricia looks to be a dump. I repeat, an unmitigated dump. It consists of a group of nice-looking well preserved buildings that house the mine and bunk houses, besides which are a series of long hovels. The whole thing is placed in a clearing surrounded by scrubby poplars at the side of a fairly decent creek.

I have a bed in a bunk house. There are three other beds there.

---

[38] I.O.D.E. is an organization founded in 1900 by Margaret Polson Murray of Montreal to promote patriotism and charitable work among Canadian women. It is still active in 21st century. The initials stand for the Imperial Order Daughters of the Empire.

May 23rd. They put me to work today. I am 'on surface' which so far has meant heaving around 500lb barrels of lime, 200lb boxes of nails, great sacks of potatoes, onions and rice, and so on. The food is very good. We rise at 6.00 am working 9 hours ending at 5.00 pm. I am very tired and it has rained all day.

May 24th. I feel better today, eating and sleeping better, and the sun came out. One of my room mates left today – he borrowed an iron to press his travelling pants, and left a note on my bed, saying that he had burnt his pants and borrowed my grey flannels to travel in! Today I was a Carpenter and spent the whole day hammering nails. I am beginning to feel stronger already.

May 26th. This working business is really something. I am beginning to feel a new man, eating and sleeping the way men were originally intended. Yesterday I helped the teamster. This consisted in cleaning up around the mine buildings. We collected stumps from the site of some new buildings, shovelled rubbish behind the hotel (beer parlour, barber shop and bank!) picked up waste lumber etc. Some of it was quite hard work – I find I am better at carrying and lifting heavy loads than at shovelling. Last night an English fellow took me out for a trip in his canoe. We went a couple of miles down the river and stopped off en route to explore some abandoned prospecting camps. In one of them I found a Penguin edition of 'As You Like It' which I appropriated.

The village of Central Patricia is the most amazing place – it is completely self contained except for two power lines. All the heavy equipment and food supplies are brought up by scow from Hudson, 150 miles, with three portages over which are laid tracks. There is a winch at each end and the loaded scows are just hauled up onto trucks and across the portages, they are unloaded at Doghole Bay at the foot of Rat Rapids and brought 25 miles by truck. The magnitude of the work which must have been done amazes me.

The men with whom I have come into contact so far have been uniformly good eggs, be they Polack or English, and I enjoy very much working with them. They all look down on the Indians who are a scrubby dirty bunch. The squaws all favour the colour red, and go in for red clothes in a big way. They seem to wear three or four red dresses of varying lengths red scarves and red kerchiefs on their heads. They are quite shy and when you speak to them they just burst out laughing. The teamster I worked with could speak a few words of Indian and we met a couple of squaws over at the dump. When we spoke to them and they didn't understand they'd laugh to beat the band and I found it quite infectious!
They hang around the cookhouse to get the garbage which they go through and take what they want back to camp in small brown paper

bags."

Ted sounds so full of life. I register, for the first time, the loss of two of our three first cousins. It would have been good to know them.

Even in Volume 1 of 1940, it's clear that the Cousins' Family Chronicle was helping the feeling of solidarity among the contributors as the war intensified. It had become the means for requesting and exchanging advice, comparing and sharing experience, and providing support and encouragement. Kathleen Smithells, not usually the most eloquent of contributors, wrote a sentence that captures for me the cousins' loving concern for each other.

"Such anxious times are these, and one's heart just aches for Mothers."

*

FOUR

The Battle of Britain, Summer 1940

Dive bombers, alarms, and flying lessons in South Africa

Through the open window came the rumbling sound of a man's voice. I'd woken to find myself drifting in a familiar, comforting river of important, incomprehensible words. I knew this was The News, the important midday event for the grown-ups. I'd climbed up into the old pram and fallen deliciously to sleep in the warm, summer sunshine. I was too old for such a pram but I could still fit into it. It was more comfortable than another favourite hideaway: the third shelf of the airing cupboard among bathing costumes and towels. Much later, my eyrie was a high branch of the conifer at the far corner of the house. I listened to the family calling. 'Where's Susie?'

The pram, one of those big-wheeled, well-sprung affairs called baby carriages, was stowed away on the verandah. The open window belonged to the dining room. It must have been the One o'clock News. Lunch was ready. I could smell something delicious. *Where's Susie?*

There can have been few households which didn't tune in to listen to the news and, on special occasions, to hear Churchill speak. In a way, Churchill defeated Germany for us through his exceptional gift for language. He wrote and delivered speeches in the cadences of Shakespeare and the King James' Bible, inspiring the nation to withstand the blitzkrieg of Hitler. He gave a glowing purpose to what had been seen by many as useless resistance now that France had fallen. This is Winston Churchill speaking in the House of Commons on June 18th 1940.

"What General Weygand called the battle of France is over. I expect that the battle of Britain is about to begin. Upon this battle depends the survival of Christian civilisation. Upon it depends our own British life, and the long continuity of our institutions and our empire. The whole might and fury of the enemy must very soon be turned on us. Hitler knows that he has to break us in this island or lose the war. If we can stand up to him, all Europe may be free and the life of the world move

forward into broad, sunlit uplands. But if we fail, then the whole world, including the United States, will sink into the abyss of a new Dark Age, made more sinister, and perhaps more protracted, by the lights of perverted science. Let us, therefore, brace ourselves to our duties and so bear ourselves that, if the British Empire and the Commonwealth last for a thousand years, men will still say, 'This was their finest hour.'"

Of course with present day cynicism we can look on this speech as so much hot air thrown in the face of the future. But even if 'broad, sunlit uplands' are the stuff of never-realised fantasy, the speech did the job it was intended to do at the time. People rallied, as the bombs started falling.

What would Europe be like today if we had succumbed to the Nazis? Should one not resist invaders? Is it better to allow ideas with which one doesn't agree subsume one's own? On all levels, personal, national and global, should we defend what we consider good, rather than give way to what we consider evil, if the cost is violence and killing? Will humankind ever solve this dilemma? Barrel-bombing areas held by Islamic State may succeed in ridding the areas of Isis but in the process causes even more devastation and loss of life, besides creating more hatred.

Cissie wrote to Cousin Alice from Ringwood on July 20th. There's a note added to this contribution from John Werner who was reading it as an adult many years later. In this note he explains that the Beckers *'acquired the Ringwood cottage for Lettice and Trevor's aged mother to escape anticipated bombing in London.'* Not much of an escape, as it turned out ….

<u>From Cissie (A.E.I. Becker)</u>
"The Homestead, July 20th
Thank you very much for your letter on the 16th. I am writing with transfer paper underneath as have so many letters to answer and not much time with the daily round to write things over again to different people! Lettice's idea, and a good one.
We had two air raid warnings yesterday, and the day before no warning but 3 terrific explosions which I saw – German dive bomber in Mrs Jagoe's lane 2 miles away – such a noise! I was coming from the kitchen to the front door of the cottage when I heard a loud noise and I looked up to see 3 fountains of smoke and debris each as high and as wide as a huge *(illegible)*. It was very alarming and made my

heart go fast! No real damage was done. It was chased past this house, machine gunned over Bisterne and, I'm glad to say, brought down in flames at Christchurch over the water. The most sirens we have had in one day was 3, not counting the nights of raids, for which the sirens don't get let off!! We had our shelter finished on Sat. last at 1.o'clock. Slept that night and the next in it. It was wet (very) on Monday, and when we made for bed at 11.30 pm to our dismay the place was awash – bedding, blankets, our quilts, pillows, bolsters etc, all were sopping!

This sort of thing all makes extra work – a sort of curse on this place as nothing seems ever straight forward. We had cleared up all the mess of the air raid shelter in 2 days and felt all satisfied and lovely! All the work on the shelter was wheeled through the house – concrete, dirt, bricks, sand, cement, and white mortar dust in **every room** so it took 2 days **hard** at it to get it right. We slept upstairs that night but at 7.30 next morning I rang up the builder and 4 more men were on the job with all the aforesaid material again that day and all the dirt **back**! Plus all the heavy lugging of mattresses and all the other stuff on the lawn and on the line to dry! 2 days of this drying business! Well we are back in the shelter and sleeping and just wonder what the next downpour will do again! We have a long shelf and Lettice put her bedding up there (an upper bunk) and I lay below. Easier than both having mattresses on the floor. But we feel like rabbits scuttling so constantly into our shelter hole when the sirens squeal – I have always been sorry for rabbits….

We are going to spend today at Barnston but have to ring up the B'mouth police to see if we may go.

The garden produce is coming along nicely now bush marrows are splendidly prolific and cut young we like them v. much. The scarlet runners we are having now and we dug up one potato root but shall leave them a week longer to get the most out of them. I never have seen better carrots and **such** a good shape – a lot of the Cos lettuce found their way to some pigs as we can't cope with them as they were too long growing in the dry weather and were bitter. The maize is pushing out its cobs and the tomatoes are fruiting nicely but are still green. The 2 rows of sweet peas keep a good smell in this room and the mignonette keeps company – as I write the smell is delicious – the garden is **beyond words** – a real dream of billowing bloom – really remarkable – many passers say they have **never** seen its like before and **I** never have. Of course the season has brought the phlox and other flowers that bloom with them all out with earlier things and the roses all out together. The phlox are in **great** bushes. The garden looks like a corn field well up, but instead of corn all **different** colours the same height, phlox predominating at the moment. The jackmanii is hanging by the hundred, purple flowers over the phlox nearly at the top of the garage wall and looks fine with the phlox below in a mound.

Irene took Juliet to Winchester to stay with the Stevensons on Thursday – more or less permanently I imagine and Dorothy (maid) in attendance. Irene called here on her way back – but it was late and we wanted her to get home before anything like real dark and Mrs Watts rang up in distress for fear of real darkness. We gave her 2 scrambled eggs, some wine and some pudding and would not let her stay so we can chat today which we could not on Thursday. We took the Red Cross stuff to Lady Malmesbury at Heron Court last week – she was out but I was glad to see the house –'hard up' was the impression – v. badly kept drive and front to house and not an imposing mansion – I believe very old in parts."

I feel for Juliet Becker and her attendant Dorothy. You could hardly compare eight-year-old Juliet with the wandering Lear, or Dorothy with the Fool, but there is something of the blasted heath about them. They've been sent away from Eccleston Square to Granny Watts, Irene's mother, in Bournemouth. Next they teeter on the brink of Canada. Then off they go to live with a Mrs Stevenson and her daughter near Winchester. Juliet's school in Bournemouth had closed, not just for the holidays but for the duration of the war. Juliet was to share a governess with the Stevenson daughter. This was not going to be a success and soon Juliet and Dorothy would join Mike and Wilf in a flat above Barclay's Bank in Glossop.

This was where Trevor owned a boot factory, in which both Mike and Wilfred had begun working. Perhaps bootmaking was considered war work. Or the boots might have been made in a regulation pattern for the Army. Cecily was in Glossop too, cramming for Oxford. In September 1940 Irene writes:

From Irene Becker
"We went up to Glossop last Friday to see the boys and Cecily who is there with them and for Trevor to do some business. It was quite a pleasant change to have some peaceful nights – for although there were aeroplanes overhead and sirens each night, they didn't drop any bombs or worry us at all. ..They are all very happy together and appear to be quite enjoying themselves both at work and doing their own housekeeping and cooking. They are very busy though, and Cecily is hard at work cramming up for her entrance exam for Oxford – Somerville or Lady Margaret Hall, which two colleges are holding a joint examination on September 18th to the 20th. This exam can be taken anywhere with a recognised supervisor so though we had made arrangements for Cecily to take it at her old school, St Paul's Girls'

School in London, Trevor and I came to the conclusion she would be wiser to stay in Derbyshire and sit for the exam there as with all the renewed bombing we have been having since Sept 1st in London she would have had little peace to concentrate on her work here….

Whether the College life will be going on as usual during the Autumn remains to be seen! Trevor says all the girls will be needed by then for war work but Cecily says if only she can pass in and get an entrance to one of the colleges she is quite ready to take up any job then for which she may be required. She has worked very hard to get an entrance to College which at Oxford is very difficult these days and having obtained her entrance she hopes to be able to resume her studies again after the War interruption. She has been determined on this course for well over a year now and neither Trevor's advice nor persuasion from anyone can turn her away now, since she made up her mind. So I do hope she attains her objective this time.

But she is very busy studying and can only give a short time each day to household jobs. When I was there I cooked and helped them generally, and made blackout curtains more secure in the intervals but now that Trevor and I have returned to London, they will have to look after themselves.

Mike does most of the cooking when Cecily is too busy and they have scrap meals or occasionally go out in the town for one if they haven't time at all. I was lucky to find them a very good charwoman who comes in every morning for two hours and makes their beds, sweeps and washes up for them so it is really quite easy. Cecily is quite a good little cook and Mike knows a certain amount. I have left them Aunt Ciss's receipt [39] book and Boulestin's Evening Standard cookery book so they ought to manage quite comfortably."

I fly at once to Amazon to learn about this book. 'Simple French Cooking for English Homes' by Xavier Boulestin was first published in June 1923 and was, I'm told, an immediate success. So those of us who thought we were tremendously *avant-garde* as we followed French ways of cooking in the 1960s, were only re-kindling the previous generation's pre-war interest, not breaking new ground. *Plats du Jour* by Elizabeth David, given to me in our first year of marriage, still has its place in our kitchen.

Back to Irene:

"The flat is quite tiny; only two bedrooms, a sitting room, kitchenette, bathroom and a cloakroom. But though the bedrooms are small they each hold a camp bed or lilo on the floor at a push besides the

---

[39] The word 'receipt' was often used instead of 'recipe'.

permanent single bed in each. When Cecily is there Wilf sleeps in the sitting room on a marvellous settee bed we found at Lewis's Ltd in Manchester which is a double settee in the day time and simply pulls out at night into a four foot wide bed which really can hold two people if necessary with all the bedclothes on it ready made!! So convenient and its pillow sits on the outside in the daytime as a cushion in a cretonne cover to match the curtains!

Wilf is by far the tidiest member of the family and always puts his personal belongings away so we find him the best possible occupant of the sitting room by night. He usually is the last to go to bed (of the young folks - not counting Trevor of course!) and he has to get up in the morning to go to work so it all works out very well. Wilf is not so interested in cooking as the other two though he is very good at lending a hand in clearing up and washing up etc when time permits, but he is far the best at any carpentering jobs, repairing electrical stuff, plugs, etc, so between them they manage to keep the flat going quite well and very comfortably.

Trevor and I came back yesterday to London as he has a business appointment in Northampton at 2 o'clock where we left about five o'clock and got in without event in time to have our dinner before the usual nightly raid began at 9.15 last night."

I had reason to find out more about Northampton last year when our granddaughter started at the university. In the past it was a manufacturing centre, particularly for footwear and leather. The Barratt Boot and Shoe factory was established here in a grand building that looks (from the website's photograph) more like a Victorian railway hotel. Trevor's business appointment was probably connected with the boots made in his factory in Manchester. Earls Barton, a village not far from Northampton, was also known for boot manufacturing and Irene's mother, I know from the Chronicle, would be moving there in early 1941. But to return to Irene writing in the summer of 1940:

"I had been not a little anxious to see our home and how the maids and people here were faring after the terrific bombings there had been in London over last weekend. We had a good deal of difficulty in getting through to No 70 to find out any news but managed to do so on Tuesday, via a telephone call to Trevor's office and a return wire after they had telephoned here, saying all was well there which was a great relief to me. As we were getting out of the car at No 70 at 7 o'clock last night, we found streams of people walking along the square with their mattresses, bedding of all sorts in their arms, on their backs and in perambulators - all going along to the large air-raid shelter near by, which is a marvellous place and holds 1200 people underground. They all queue up, apparently, commencing about 6 o'clock, ready for the night where they sleep until the all clear signal blows - at dawn usually. We have had many houses destroyed in the streets round here, though so far this Square is intact, and a good deal of property damaged sporadically all over London, though driving through last evening from north to s.west there appears to be no difference whatever; it all looks much as ever, and makes one realize that London will take a good deal of destroying taking it all round – though of course if they continue at their present rate of bombing for two years, there may be a good deal less of it left standing!!

We have a very good shelter in the basement here – a re-inforced passage with heavy wooden pillars with a double exit and room enough inside for six people to recline on the floor for sleep. There are also two safe rooms for more space inbetween the worst bombings – one at the front with the windows all doubly protected and the Smiths bedroom at the back with windows also protected and heavily boarded outside. We should be quite safe short of a direct hit from H.E. shells like the one which destroyed a part of Buckingham Palace on Tuesday. We have three separate exits to our basement altogether, two gas cookers and two primus stoves in case of emergency.

Altogether there are eight of us to shelter when all at home. The two maids, the two Smiths (he being a policeman is out eight hours in every 24) the two Pratley's (the tenants of our garage flat, who come in here as they have no protection in the flat), and Trevor and myself when at home. So far we divide up between the rooms when warnings are on and heavy firing or bombs dropping about. Trevor and I slept on lilos in Aunt Ciss's dining room last night - on the ground floor with shuttered windows - and were very comfortable. We never undress at night until the all clear goes so we are ready for any emergency.

Mary our house parlourmaid says they were all expecting to be hit at any time on Saturday and Sunday nights – the planes came down very low and there were many bombs dropped quite close here. Since then we have had some new very powerful A.A. guns and the deafening roar of these has given everyone confidence. You can hardly hear the planes now. The all-clear went about six o'clock this morning and I had a peaceful three hours in bed when I had my breakfast and dressed and Trevor went off to the City. Another warning has been on since 10 o'clock and it is now past one so I am writing this in the basement. I did some jobs upstairs to start with but after Trevor left there were some whistling bombs and very heavy firing and the maids refused to let me stay up even on the first floor! I never worry really as, luckily for us, we are well shuttered in this house up to the 2nd floor - so there isn't much danger of broken glass splinters which after all does most of the damage in air-raids! We have a stirrup pump, three baths of water and lots of buckets handy for incendiary bombs, so are well prepared.

I am very glad the drought here has broken at last after about eight weeks without rain; it rained heavily during the night and has been continuing very well all the morning so I hope it means the general break up of the weather, which is really about due - and may make Hitler's ideas of Invasion fade out if he knows the landings on our coast in stormy weather will be anything but easy, and may likely cost him the loss of a large army.

As there has been so much time since I returned to London taken up with 'Warnings on', I haven't had any opportunity to go out and see the damage done about here.

Many streets are barred as there are still a number of time bombs about, and buildings damaged. Trevor had to go by bus to his office this morning, which I am afraid will take him much longer; but in the heavy rain it was no time for bicycling a long way, especially not knowing beforehand which streets would be closed and which side of the river he would have to go, so he started off on foot with a mac and umbrella! Many houses and buildings, I hear, are destroyed - particularly private property - but this hasn't done the Germans any good as there were no military objectives. There was a big fire in the City at the weekend which lit up the sky and I am afraid helped them to find some targets. But that wasn't visible from here last night so I expect it is all over. I am sorry this has been so long but I happened to have the time for once in the air-raid shelter hence this rambling! I forgot to say before that Wilfred has joined the Home Guard."

Wilfred had just passed his 17th birthday at the start of the Chronicle and was still at school. Now he's in Glossop, working at his father's boot factory. The question of how long the war might last must have haunted the minds of all the parents. Of the younger generation of cousins, several were either serving or on the brink of being called up. Charles Werner was on a Flying Course in Rhodesia. In a letter written from the Meikles Hotel in Salisbury in July, he said he was feeling 'very cut off from the war at the moment and it's wretched to think of what must be going on at home.' Grace forwarded a number of his letters to Cousin Alice for the Chronicle.:

Letters from Charles, July/August 1940
"My 'War Effort' still continues and I'm now quite a veteran of some 11 hours flying, and I'm getting quite used to the idea of 'taking the air' every day; the more one does the more fascinating it becomes, and I'm quite keen about it all now, and dread the idea of being 'grounded', I've got to the stage now when I'm just on the verge of making my first flight alone....yesterday the conditions were not good

enough. The trouble out here is that the heat in the middle of the day makes it very very 'bumpy' and the plane rocks about like a ship in a storm wh. makes it rather hard to control for a beginner. I think we must hand a lot of credit to my instructor, Flying Officer Baker, if he does make a flyer out of me! By sheer dogged persistence he has cured one by one all my careless faults – and if he says to me 'Right – up you go by yourself' I'll know that I shall be quite safe for he leaves nothing at all to chance. Denis Clive and Peter Grinson have both done their solos already, and I'm determined not to get left behind. .I find that one can't stay up late and fly next morning, and most nights I'm asleep by 9 o'clock. We have endless notes to copy out also, wh: keep us pretty busy. To relieve the monotony of the food here, we go into town, now and then, to have our usual 1/6 at Mother Keeley's. Mother K. is a very kind hearted person, and seems to have adopted us all, and her little restaurant is a rendezvous for us and she's always willing to darn socks or mend uniforms or help in any way. She is really just typical of the people out here, whose hospitality never ceases to amaze us...One could go to a dance practically every night and be quite welcome whether one bought a ticket or not. I've never once had to walk into town for one always gets a lift almost immediately....I've been asked out somewhere every weekend and this weekend Mr Taylor is taking myself, Peter, Denis, and another fellow out to his sister-in-law's place in the country for this afternoon and evening. Really I am incredibly lucky to be here, and last Sunday after playing tennis out at some people's place called Ellsworth Plantation, we sat on the lawn drinking our 'Sundowners' and watching the sunset and listening to the gramophone; it was all so peaceful and so like the days before the war at home that it seemed quite unreal...

.Last night I saw the picture 'This Man is News' again and the sight of a newspaper office made me very nostalgic for the old life. It is still winter here, and admittedly quite cold at night and first thing in the morning, but it is already pretty hot at midday, and, as we are still wearing our blue uniforms, we feel it rather....The rains start in November.

Monday evening (5 Aug)

.....at 7,50 this morn my worthy instructor, trying to be casual, climbed out of my plane, put his thumbs up to encourage me and said 'Off you go'. And, sure enough, off I went - all alone by my little self! I had a moment's misgiving as I climbed up over the trees and noticed the empty cockpit in front, but after that I was far too busy to worry. I miscalculated my first landing and had to open the throttle and take off again...As I started off on the second round after failing my first landing, and not at all sure that I cd make it at the 2nd attempt, I did not feel v. happy. But this time I made it and we bumped to a standstill.....We had a great time yesterday out in the country playing tennis, and afterwards sipping Sundowners around a great log fire and then a colossal dinner, all in v. good company and v. enjoyable.....

Sun 11 Aug; 1940   No. 25 E.F.T.S. (R.A.F) Belvedere, Salisbury.
Lying in bed relaxing this morning....one can go to bed and stay in bed any time one is off duty, and no-one worries....Perhaps it is the altitude, perhaps the strain of so much flying, but we all feel the same and find that at all hours, bed is a very desirable place! But don't think from this that I've got sleepy sickness or anything. I'm fitter than I've ever been and really quite active when there's anything doing ......It really is incredible that I am really here 6,000 miles away from home in the middle of Africa, that I'm part of a grim war and that this Flying, which is so light hearted and enjoyable, has behind it such a stern purpose, yet one just cannot realize that side of it, and it's all like being at school again - with grand companions all sharing the same thrills and adventures and, if necessary, when the time comes, the same risks......

On Friday our Course threw a Dance at the Salisbury Club. We all bought Double tickets and then sent out mass invitations to all the local wenches. They rallied round very well and there were partners and to spare for all.   Each of us treated our individual flying instructors and they came along in force....As a result I have two weekend invitations (one for a Leopard hunt!) and an invitation to a Sundowner party.

Since my first solo flight last Mon., I have got quite used to flying on my own, and it is a great feeling to know that one can take a machine off the ground and put it down again at will and with reasonable certainty. It is a great experience, too, to be able to fly away completely on one's own and say to oneself 'Where shall we explore today? Shall we go up and look at the clouds, or climb some mountains, or follow the railway line, or chase the buck across the Veldt?' And then to glide down to the aerodrome, lower and lower, judging the distance, easing the 'stick' gently back until both wheels and the tail skids touch the ground together, and one rolls along to a stop. It is something to have found there is still adventure in the world today, and I am thankful for it."

Charles makes it easy to understand his thrill in flying; in fact, his descriptions are so graphic that I feel queasy. Not an adventure I'd be thankful for. But, knowing what was to come, I'm glad he enjoyed these months so much. Meanwhile, his brother Roger was firmly on the ground at an army officers' training school in Bombay. He wrote home to Grace a letter she sent on to Cousin Alice for the Chronicle.

Letter from Roger, August 1940
"We have at last had our postings and now know our regiments. I am going to 2/4th Gurkha Rifles (Prince of Wales' Own) and will be going to Bakloh for further training with them. I cancelled my

application for Cavalry. I'm sorry in a way, but I expect I should have found things v. tight from the cash point of view. However I shall have to give up my polo and keep no ponies, which is a bit of a jar. I feel rather a worm being stuck here and not being able to do anything much to help things. I only hope I get a chance of getting away from India and doing something of more obvious use. I get a little leave before joining my regiment, part of which I shall spend in Bombay buying kit and having a final beat up with Macfarlane before we have to become too 'pukka' to enjoy life."

After reading these letters from the Werner brothers, I feel sorry for the cousins working in the boot factory.

The first skirmishes in the Battle of Britain had begun over the Channel in July. The German air force attacked coastal convoys, then turned their attention to airfields and radar stations. Nowhere on the south coast was safe. On August 12th Ventnor radar station on the Isle of Wight was put out of action. Six days later bombs fell on Rye. Cousin Alice was on her travels in the north of England at the time.

She reported in the September issue:

From Alice Crompton, September 11th 1940
"Since 9th August, when I left Miss Dale's (63 Eccleston Square), I have been paying a round of visits in the North and am now at Grace Werner's (Wilmslow). Didsbury (Kathleen Smithells), Bispham (Miss E. Johnson), Ulverston (Mrs Tout), Coniston (Miss Sharples, a cousin of Marjory Lees), Arkholme (Rev. A. and Nita Woodhouse), and Kirkby Lonsdale (Annie Stowell) have been my places of sojourn. The weather has been beautiful all the time and everywhere – less sun, perhaps, at Bispham, but the winds were West and we had the usual fine seas of Blackpool. There are masses of troops on the Fylde coast, they seemed to be mostly R.A.F. men under training. Many of the big Blackpool hotels have been commandeered for Civil Servants from London.
I have been grieved to hear that Rye was badly bombed on 18th Aug – a row of cottages near Mermaid St. was hit and 3 people killed. At Lamb House the beautiful 'Garden Room' where Henry James, and, later, E.F.Benson used to write was shattered. Rye Harbour, Camber and Winchelsea Beach have been compulsorily evacuated by all the civilian inhabitants."

She'd received two letters from Cissie in Ringwood and copied extracts to include in the Chronicle:-

From Cissie

"(13 Sep) We have endless raids here, 3 or 4 some days and many at night, but we seem to have more Jerrys over the nights that no sirens go. We have had explosive and incendiary bombs quite close – ½ mile and the incendiaries only 3 or 4 hundred yds away.
(15 Sept) About tea time yesterday you will be sorry to hear what happened to the Erringtons (Ivy's in laws). The siren went and Lettice saw a Jerry circling round over our own heads so we dashed into the shelter. We had scarcely shut the door than a series of Bombs were heard not far away – it shook our shelter wall – on emerging we learnt that the Erringtons' house 'Old Stacks' on the outskirts of Ringwood about ¾ mile away from here was razed to the ground by 2 direct hits. Mercifully the inmates were in the garden and only minor casualties – the debris had been shot right into the skin of the face and scalp of an elderly lady inmate, and the cook's hands were cut. Unexploded time bombs peppered their meadows and the road is closed till they explode."

Cousin Alice copied some of the letters and extracts by hand. It took time and patience. I copy extracts to include in this present day Chronicle with the press of a few keys on the keyboard. It still takes time but in a different way. Mine is spent teasing out the context and detail of the cousins' letters. Who were the 'inmates' of the house 'Old Stacks'? Had the in-laws' house become some kind of institution whose residents would be known as inmates? Or was Cissie referring to the Erringtons, Ivy's ex-parents-in-law, in an 'I'll make you smile' kind of way. But *debris shot into the scalp of an elderly lady inmate* – ! You can break into a smile at the way it's expressed, though not at the actual hit and hurt. Making light of things was the way people managed.

There is a definite flavour of enjoyment in the cousins' newsletters. People's lives in peacetime can become boring for long stretches of time. Is that some of the why of war? Quarrels between individuals and wars between nations can stir the blood, get the adrenalin flowing, create change. It was the war that brought people together. It made the cousins value their relationship. A common enemy creates cohesion on a personal level as well as national and international.

The Second World War ended with the two most destructive acts of all time: the dropping of atomic bombs on Hiroshima and Nagasaki. Out of this came peace, which can be said to have lasted until the present, until you remember the endless wars on a smaller scale, ethnic cleansing, mass murder and terrorism.

I'm writing this on August 14th 2015, the 70th anniversary of VJ day: Victory in Japan. Could there have been another way to make Japan accept defeat? How can one defend against aggression without resorting to aggression oneself? Does Daoism have the answer in martial arts? The word 'martial' combines two Chinese words: stop and battle.

In 1945 the dropping of the two bombs was justified by the refusal of the Japanese to accept defeat until after such a cataclysm. Neither would they admit to any war crimes. Decades passed before the emperor formally presented an apology. In the news today the present emperor of Japan is reported as saying that he and his nation have said sorry often enough for the atrocities they committed in the war. It is time to forget and move on, he says. He wouldn't admit that his country had fought a war of aggression, which had started with skirmishes in China from 1931 onwards as Japan sought to access China's resources. Nations, like individuals, seldom see themselves as being at fault.

Have we apologised for using atomic weapons on their civilian population? Was the Japanese military's refusal to accept defeat vindication enough to use such means to persuade them? Have we said sorry for the blanket bombing of German cities, or begged forgiveness by the people on whose backs we built the British Empire? For the slave trade? How far back should a nation go with apologies, which do nothing to remedy past injustices.

I don't believe that any nation or any individual has a corner in small misdeeds or outright evil. The potential is present in us all, as well as the potential for kind acts and astounding altruism. We each respond according to our genetic capabilities and the circumstances in which we find ourselves. In extremis, people can commit atrocious deeds. We are lucky if we are never tested, either as victims or perpetrators. In terms of human evolution, are we working slowly and haphazardly towards the time when there is true global peace or is such a state impossible?

FIVE

The Blitz begins – 1940

Explosions, Sirens, Shelters

In the summer of 1940 Hitler was preparing for the invasion of Britain. The bombardment of the south coast intensified. On August 15th 1940 there was a particularly ferocious engagement. Wave after wave of Luftwaffe bombers approached over the Channel, to be repeatedly attacked by Hurricanes and Spitfires scrambling fast from Biggin Hill and other airfields along the south coast. By the end of the day 75 German planes had been shot down. The British lost 30 planes and 17 pilots. It was estimated that one in five of the pilots who fought in the Battle of Britain lost their lives.

Pilots and planes had to be replaced fast on both sides. The Luftwaffe was the greater force but British factories produced single-engined fighters faster than the German factories could replace planes. Over the course of the summer's battles, 544 Fighter Command pilots were killed. In Bomber Command 801 men lost their lives while dropping bombs over Germany, with a further 200 taken prisoner. But the Luftwaffe lost 2,698 highly skilled airmen.[40]

The defence put up by the British air force, the scale of Britain's industrial resources, and the resilience of the civilian population, persuaded the German generals to give up any idea of invasion, even if the natural obstacles to invasion of an island could be overcome. Borders between nations on the continent are little more than imaginary lines on a map, compared with Britain's boundary in the encircling seas. On September 17th Hitler called off Operation Sealion, though the change of tactics wasn't immediately apparent to the British. They still expected the Germans on their shores at any moment; dogfights continued; night raids and bombing intensified. The Blitz had started.

Several contributions for October were written in shelters at night to the sound of sirens, planes, and explosions. Irene

---

[40] All facts and figures from Max Hastings, '*All Hell Let Loose*' p.90

writes in an unusually breathless way. Her words pile up with hardly a stop, reflecting the strains of life in London during the Blitz.

From Irene Becker, October 9th 1940
"Here Trevor and I are once more in our underground shelter at No 70 Eccleston Square...bereft of our family for which I personally cannot but be thankful, though I do miss them all after so many years of a full household! However we might well be worse off in this great suffering city with its crowds of homeless people whose children are fast disappearing now to country homes where possible; in this great evacuation the mothers are nearly all going too and in many cases fathers and grannies and aunts as well; whole families migrating together, hating to be parted especially after the great shocks which have happened; it is a calamity to lose home and worldly goods but to be separated from the remnants of the family, after having kept alive and safe from the terrible upheaval of the bombing would be the very last straw for these poor bereft Londoners. But where in the country they will all find homes, especially the whole families, who refuse to be parted, is a problem indeed. Trevor and I have just returned from the North (he on business and I with him to see the family), via Oxford, and wherever we went we found it full of people - refugees or evacuees as they were mostly erroneously called! Small towns, villages, east towns – anywhere within possible reach of London and the large cities full to overflowing. In one large town we found there were literally hundreds of Londoners, whole families together living in a huge cinema and ice rink with the kindly local committees working hard to feed them and collect clothing.
At Glossop, just as we were leaving, Miss Newton the Head mistress of the Grammar School there, who had been so kind to Cecilia in helping her over her exam for getting into Oxford, asked if I could possibly take to London some parcels of clothing, which the children of the Glossop Grammar School had collected for the poor and homeless in the bombed areas. I was delighted and we filled up the back of the car completely with at least a hundred parcels and bundles of children's clothes all ready sorted into different age requirements. Trevor was rather surprised when he saw his car with no room inside for our luggage but he took it in good part in so good a cause and just said "Old woman, you must leave your own clothes and

luggage behind; happily I have nothing to take but my papers and night shift!" So this was all we took ourselves, except our bedding for the night – 2 lilos a small pillow, 2 rugs and the bellows in Trevor's Army Valise."

Old woman! And bellows packed in the army suitcase! Lots to exclaim at in this letter. I remember bellows were essential for getting a fire going. Was wartime firewood always too freshly-cut and damp to light easily?

"We always take our bedding about with us now since it is almost impossible to get beds in any places in civilised areas! However we generally manage to get a comfortable floor on someone's sitting room with the addition of washing accommodation in the morning, so really we are just as happy this way as if we were often in the best hotel and probably a long way from where we might want to be.

We were very cosy the other night at Oxford when we went to see Cecilia who has just got a vacancy at Somerville College to begin this term on Oct 11th;. We slept on the top floor of a dear little house just opposite the College gates and she was able to run in, in the morning while we were having breakfast. She is so delighted to be able to begin her College life at last, even though the atmosphere is not the same as in pre-war days and there may be a curtailment of university life even for young women before long. However in the meantime she is very busy settling into her room and finding her way about before the beginning of term. Quite a number of students and most of the staff were already assembled there, as many - like Cecily - have had to leave London homes on account of the bombing or having time bombs dropped outside their homes, waiting to explode. She came back with us here for two nights to collect her books and some furniture which (I hope) is leaving tomorrow by the carrier.

Juliet is no longer happy in her country home with the Stevensons in Hampshire; she is terribly homesick, hates the feeling of being so far away from all her family and is quite worried when she hears people talk of the London bombings, so I am taking her away shortly to stay at Glossop for a time."

I breathe a sigh of relief for Juliet. She will be with her brothers in Glossop and will see her parents more regularly.

"A kindly doctor's wife there who happens to live up the road a few doors from the boys' flat has offered to take in Juliet and Nannie for a few weeks until I can find further accommodation for them. They will sleep at Mrs Malloch's and can spend the day at the flat. It will cheer her up to be near the boys even if she cannot see us all the time. I hope to get up there as often as I can without deserting Trevor too much. It is impossible to describe the sense of peace and quiet there, in being able to go to bed properly even for a few nights in the country.

We feel reasonably safe in our basement here but the continuous noise is terrific at times. A great bomb has just been dropped somewhere near us – Trevor thinks about 300 or 400 yards probably. We heard a tremendous whizz and waited in intense excitement a few seconds for the great explosion which when it came shook our walls and windows and blew the curtains right out into the room, even behind our massive wooden shutter barricades! There have been some fires too tonight but so far not too near us happily.

I forgot to say in continuation of the earlier account of our bringing the consignment of children's clothes from Glossop Grammar Schools that, needless to say, they never got as far as London. At one large town we found hundreds of poor homeless London families parked out in large halls and cinemas – 'little London' the local inhabitants called the district where they had found refuge! So we handed over the neat little bundles to the Police Aid Distress Fund Committee feeling they would be in a good position to discover the really needy ones. I am going to write to Miss Newton at Glossop and tell her the news to hand on to the children. Next time I happen to go that way I shall try and find out how the parcels were received.

We have just heard the midnight news which is usually our signal for going to bed in our shelter and as it seems a bit quiet now perhaps the night will improve! London is marvellous really and considering the gruelling it has been having these last five weeks, except in certain places looks very little different to its usual timeworn city appearance! A house gone here and there, a large store and some streets and blocks of flats badly hit in certain areas but, taking it all round, I know we shall survive a great deal more and a long time yet!

I forgot to say the boys are very fit. Mike is improving very much in the keen North air and Wilfred is so interested in his work; he is now in the Home Guard and very keen; he goes out every Saturday night on guard from 8 pm until 5 am and is very glad to have that night as it is the one morning he doesn't have to get up early for work.

Alice came over from Oldham to see us one day, when we had quite a large gathering for lunch - 8 of us, in all, in the tiny flat! However we all had room to sit round the table and managed in comfort."

In the October folder, Cousin Alice describes this visit to the Beckers in Glossop, but first she apologises for the late appearance of the September issue. She was on her travels, had had a cold, and besides *'the last of the contributions did not reach me until 19th.'* The job of corralling the cousins must have taken up much time.

From Alice Crompton
"On 21 Sept. I had a very jolly visit to the Becker flat at Glossop, wh. is easily reached by train from Oldham (via Guide Bridge). I was delighted with the flat and with the cheery camaraderie of the 3 young folk. We all had lunch together at a Restaurant, and then, on the way to Whitfield Vicarage (where I used to stay in my young days with the Wards), we were diverted by the Fair, with a multitude of side shows, including animal freaks (patronized by Cecily and Wilfred) the largest St Bernard dog in the world (also visited by C. and W.) and tiny motor cars whizzing and bumping everlastingly in which Wilfred took me for a joy ride! Michael and Cecilia looked on, somewhat stately and aloof!"

The Dodg'ems! Cousin Alice in a bumper car! I'm trying to visualise this.

"I was very sorry to leave Wilmslow on 13 Sep after a most happy 9 days visit. The house and garden are charming and I had pleasant walks and talks with Grace, and lots of backgammon with Joe[41]. I was pleased to see again my kitten, whose portrait adorned our last number. But it should have been named not SAM but SAL Small (short for Sarah)!
I got over to Kathleen's for the afternoon on 19 Sep: and had a peep at Grace there. As usual Kathleen's house looked v. pretty, and she gave me a delicious tea.
The record of my fairly exciting experiences when I left Oldham for London must wait for our October number.
(I expect to return to Doncombe on Tues 29 Oct. till which date I am c/o R.C.K Ensor Esq., Sands, High Wycombe, Bucks.   A.C.

N.B. Will everyone please try to let me have their contributions by the 3rd of each month? Otherwise the months overlap bewilderingly."

Cousin Alice seems to assume that all animals are male until they produce kittens. She christened her cat Tony. Tony produced kittens, one of which was named Sam, which in turn produced more kittens.

The Ensors she stayed with frequently were, like nearly all the people she visited around England, old friends from her days as Warden of the Manchester University Settlement. Ensor is noted somewhere else in the Chronicle as being 'Scrutator', a columnist on the Sunday Times. A walk and talk, as Alice had enjoyed with Grace and no doubt all her

---

[41] The father of Grace and Kathleen

friends, is one of my favourite occupations. Would I have enjoyed a walk and talk with Alice, or would I have been put so much on my mettle that I would have been as silent as I was aged 7 at the end of her ear trumpet? I hope we would get on like a house on fire, with no need for Irene's bellows.

And yes, the Chronicle's dates are bewildering. I am not even certain if the month on the folder's cover refers to the month it is circulating, or to the month of the events which the contributors are describing. Alice might think I'm being slow. I'm sure she walked, talked and thought fast, as well as carefully. Even at this distance of time and space, I realise I'm still in awe of Alice.

I have now checked and she has supplied the answer. On the cover of the folder labelled October is her contribution describing that month.

> *From Alice Crompton*
> "The first half of October found me still with Marjory Lees in Oldham, enjoying daily almost unbroken sunshine. Chrysanthemums and dahlias abounded in the gardens round about, as was the case in Manchester too. German planes often come over by night, and the sirens sounded, but we never felt it necessary to repair to the cellars, which are very spacious and clean and warm. Local opinion holds that the Germans want the Cotton mills for themselves and therefore avoid damaging them. I had a delightful second visit to the Glossop flat and made the 8th at lunch in the little kitchen, as the Directors of the Boot Factory were having a meeting in the dining room. Trevor and Irene of course ran the meal most skilfully and comfortably. I was again greatly struck and delighted by Mike looking so much stronger. On 10 Oct. I was over at my old Settlement in Ancoats where I met the new charming young Warden Miss Sheila McKay. Ancoats has greatly changed since my day there – 31 years since I left - as a great deal of slum or semi-slum property has been demolished (on purpose, not by enemy action) and the air is perceptibly fresher. Many of the people have moved out to a new Municipal Housing Estate in Gorton, where the Settlement is going to start a Branch for Community Welfare activities.
> I left Oldham on 14 Oct. for Eccleston Sq. as I had to pay my quarterly visit to Dr Jobson (aurist)[42]. My journey to Guildford to see him was my first (and a very typical) experience of London transport difficulties in war time. At 9 am I left Eccleston Sq. for the Army and Navy Stores, and for the Food Offices hard by – about 10 minutes

---

[42] Hearing specialist

walk from Trevor's. At each place I was at once sent down to the basement, as the sirens had sounded. In neither case were we detained long, and I'd finished my jobs and was ready to go to Guildford by 9.45. Three omnibuses for Waterloo passed me – all full. So I thought I'd go by train and tube to Waterloo and walked on the tiny distance to St James Park Station. No trains running Eastward! I hailed a taxi and drove to Waterloo. No trains running out of Waterloo! I then consulted another taxi man about Green Line buses to Guildford. No one knew anything about them. How much would it cost to drive to Guildford? Thirty shillings. That stumped me. The driver then suggested driving me to Wimbledon, where he thought I could certainly get a train. How much? 10 sh. So I closed with that as time was getting on and my appointment was for 2.30. The train I got at Wimbledon was packed like a sardine tin with troops, evacuees Mothers and babes and travellers like myself. All turned out at Woking, and a protracted wait there, so that it was 2.30 pm when I reached Guildford and I had to take a taxi up to the Dr. not wishing to arrive breathless. The rest of the day was highly successful. I arrived on the stroke at the Astolat Café where I had invited Prof. and Mrs Weiss, and Mrs Bergel (Nelly Gumpert that was) to tea at 3.30. We had a very cheery time together and I got a train back to Vauxhall Bridge Station which landed me at No. 70 exactly at 6.30 – their war time dinner hour.

Trevor and Irene had been at Ringwood and brought back cheerful accounts of A.E.I.B.(Aunt Cissie) and Lettice.

The nights at 70 were a strange experience. On Tues 15th Trevor, Irene, Mr and Mrs Bratley (tenants of the little flat) and I all slept in our clothes on 4 camp beds and a sofa in the basement. About 2 a.m. they roused me out of a deep sleep as they thought the upper part of the house might be damaged, bombs falling very near. Trevor and Irene and Mr B. went to reconnoitre and reported no damage to No 70 but a big fire blazing near the river. They took me to the drawing room window to see it – a huge lurid glow in the sky near the Tate Gallery. I think they said it was a Furniture Repository that was aflame.

Next day I went off to the Ensors at High Wycombe – not sorry to be in a more peaceful scene again. But I found, in going about in London for 2 days, that it seemed only here and there that great damage was visible. The worst thing I saw was St Thomas' Hospital, the middle part of which was just a skeleton.

The beech woods in Bucks were gorgeous in their tawny autumn tints and there has been a marvellous crop of plums and apples. The Women's Institute of which Mrs Ensor is President made over 4000 lbs of jam and jelly, using a ton of sugar, which they applied for and got from the Food Ministry.

One day Mrs Ensor and I went to Oxford and lunched with her husband in Corpus Christi College of which he is a Fellow. To meet us was Mrs C.E. Montague, (daughter of C.P. Scott of Manchester

Guardian) whom I had not seen for some time, and of whose 7 children – all grown up – I was glad to have news. At tea time 2 Miss Sidgwicks (nieces of Prof. Henry and Mrs A. of Cambridge who were keen on Psychical Research), the Ensors and Cecily Becker came to a café at my invitation and we had a pleasant time. Cecily seems very happy in Oxford and was most bright and lively at the tea party, tho' everyone else was so enormously senior to her.

On 29 Oct. I came off to Doncombe very glad to settle down again after my 3 months Odyssey, tho' I greatly enjoyed the 13 visits I paid during my wanderings. I'm delighted with this cottage, and have a charming bed sitting room. My cat Tony is quite glad to have me on the scene again and is grown into a coal black beauty! Buster, the spaniel whom Dick, on departure to Hong Kong, passed to Jack, is flourishing and still hugely enjoys a day's shoot with his master. So far I haven't found much to do here, except helping Jack[43] with his War Savings Group.

However, I hope that 'they also serve who only stand and wait'."

I am not the only one to be in awe of Alice. Cousin Ivy, in the next contribution, says:-

From Ivy Crompton
"I am bound to admit I feel a little diffident of including anything with the editor so adjacent who will report anything there is, so much more worthily than I. However this is the first issue since we have moved into the cottage so I will try to describe a little of what it is like. A good sized room to live in with rather a jolly open fireplace and I was lucky to have a rather lovely old fireback and a pair of dogs. Upstairs we have 3 bedrooms and a Bathroom there are 2 radiators upstairs and we have also 2 fitted basins so we are quite comfortable, the kitchen is pokey and hot, the worst feature which ought perhaps really to be the best, but so it is. We have let our house for 6 months with the option of a further 6 which I fear is almost certain to be expected. Our tenant is truly odd, very charming and quite a Lady but alas in her way of life hardly able to be called a "perfect lady" for she has swarms of dogs and we fear for our poor little house which I think must feel rather unhappy. Mrs Allan (tenant) lives almost entirely in the kitchen also eating there and she turns night into day and often doesn't go to bed at all. The garden is covered all over with kennels and wire netting which is a sore trial to us but we try to turn a blind eye. It does not really matter very much to me as I am out so much on my various but very unarduous war works and the kennels etc can be very easily removed and the place restored when we get it back again. Our chief reason for letting was I fear a very selfish fear of having to take billets so perhaps a rather

---

[43] Ivy's husband, Jack Crompton

unsatisfactory tenant is poetic justice."

The dog-loving Mrs Allan was their first tenant. Later, in 1943, Jack and Ivy let the house to the commander of the RAF station at nearby Colerne: Air Commodore Reginald Pyne, his wife Nancy, and their two children Andrew and Angela. I have beside me now the book that Nancy Pyne wrote in 1974 in which she describes arriving at Doncome Mill.

"Into the tiny village of Ford we came, through an entrance gate and facing us at the end of a short straight drive was our house. We crossed a stone bridge over a stream, passed three ancient cottages on our right and on to the front door where the owner of the property came to meet us. It was a wide, two-storey building named Doncombe Mill which they had rebuilt from an old mill house, and fashioned in the style of a Cotswold house, of grey stone, with many wide windows facing south.
We all went indoors where Mrs Crompton had made it really beautiful with vases of flowers from the garden enhancing the elegant drawing-room. The stream actually flowed under this room and at the back was the kitchen garden and beyond, a wooded hill which protected the house from north and east. She was delighted with our appreciation of everything, and she and her husband returned to their own house close by, two of the cottages we had passed which they had converted into one dwelling.
It was charming little estate with a lovely garden, woods, the stream with a waterfall and beyond, a large pond with an island in the middle. It was a children's paradise. There were two small paddocks, one containing cows and the other a pony."[44]

The Pyne family were still renting Doncome Mill when Air Commodore Pyne was killed in May 1944. The Hurricane plane he was flying on a checking mission over Bolt Head, south Devon, caught in the cable tethering a barrage balloon and crashed. On his death, his widow Nancy and the two children moved out of the house and into the small cottage beside Jack and Ivy's in the drive. When the war ended, Jack and Ivy moved back into the house, and let the bigger cottage to Nancy Pyne. "Yes, it was a children's paradise," Angela said yesterday, agreeing with her mother's words. We'd met for lunch in Wells where she now lives. She and her older brother Andrew each had a rubber dinghy which they rowed to the

---

[44] Extract from memoir written by Nancy Pyne, tenant of Ivy and Jack Crompton, Doncombe Mill. This was kindly lent to me by Angela, Nancy's daughter.

island on the lake. To a child, it was just as good as Swallows and Amazons on Windermere.

Returning to the time of the Chronicle, Ivy continues her contribution written from the cottage on the drive:

> *From Ivy Crompton*
> "Alice seems awfully well and has settled in quite happily I think. I don't think there is anything of interest to report here. We seem so much out of the world and but for the sound of German planes passing over at night can hardly realize that we are at war, the few shortages in the commissariat are so trivial and, even in the country, so little trouble. The rain it raineth every day; Alice was remarking today that she has been here 14 days and only one of them dry. We are a bit anxious when the stream gets too high as it likes coming into this cottage.
> Peggy and George[45] are now at Bordon and have taken a furnished house. They are very glad to have their own domain again but have not got the children with them as Hampshire is not very healthy from the point of view of bombs, as I fear Aunt Cissie knows well.
> George took his tank to Nottingham for War Weapons Week not long ago, it is a very rich town and they did magnificently and the men were most generously entertained and feted by the town, they were all very sorry to return to Warminster where they were then stationed.
> I do hope this is legible but doubt it, I am writing on my knee and nodding a little, the hour is late but so am I with this contribution and Alice protesting."

The German planes passing over Doncombe Mill would have been on their way to bomb Bristol and targets in south Wales. Alice noted that many babies born in Bristol around this time were christened Sireen, after the constant sirens. Imagine going through life with such a name. I can still hear, with a sickening lurch of my stomach, the siren's high-pitched, penetrating wailing.

In this issue, Grace Werner's news was entirely of her sons:

> *From Grace Werner*
> "Paul had a horrid attack of poisoning from the gas which is made at his firm and was away from work and here for ten days. I was glad to be able to have him here. He is alright now and I hope won't get another attack, he went so thin again."

---

[45] George (Errington) was Ivy's son by her first marriage; Peggy, his wife.

Gas?? Being manufactured for use??

"John has been having a rotten time with boils at school and I felt inclined to have him home but not so Henry; he said it was a bad principle. Anyway I expect he was right for he's back in school again now after nearly two weeks in the San – and says he is quite fit again. They seem little troubled with air raids. Although in his last letter he has put '*We have just finished a game of rugger rather abruptly. The guns have been firing and we actually saw the 'Jerry'. Last night we also had the guns about nine o'clock and had to go down into the corridor away from possible flying glass. I do hope you aren't getting many raids.*'"

A letter from Charles is added to her contribution.

Letter from Charles
"9/9/40 Time just flies past now and one only has time to breathe at the weekends before being caught up in the swirl again. I think I can honestly say that I have never had to work harder in my life before. Up at 5 am flying until 8.0, breakfast until 9.0 Lectures from 9 to 1.15 Lunch until 2.15 Lectures until 5 o'clock and compulsory study from 7.30 to 8.30. By the end of this there is nothing one wants more than to slip into bed and to sleep and then, before one knows where one is, it's all on top of one again. Still, only another five weeks of it to endure and then we sit for our Wings Exam and, with any luck, we think that we will pass somehow. So all this toil will be worthwhile. Amazing as it may seem – and it never ceases to amaze me! – I seem to have taken quite naturally to my new machine which - frightening as it appeared at first - is really far easier than a Tiger Moth to fly. In fact I was the second person in the course to go solo after only three hours instruction. I'm now quite accustomed to swishing through the air at 200 mph and the mass of instrument dials no longer bewilders me, instead they reassure me and warn me, as the case may be, and are a very great help. So far too I have not had the slightest recurrence of my air sickness. Strangely enough, the fact the one is in an enclosed glass-roofed cabin seems to help a lot and the steep turns and spins which used to make my head whirl in a Tiger are now almost unnoticeable. I think it must be that my giddiness comes from my eyes and it is looking at things whipping past that upsets me, and now there is so much to watch inside the cockpit that one hardly notices the way the sky and earth tilt so crazily. So there we are. Yet - as I say each time I clamber out of that mass of streamlined metal and see myself a weird figure in parachute, helmet, oxygen mask - I really wonder who on earth I am. So life goes on and it is made now more bearable by the fact that our stripes enable us to eat in the Sergeants mess and we have a great big lounge and a radiogram. So it is quite pleasant really. Also we each now have a native boy to act as

batman and he makes our beds, polishes buttons and sees that we have a nice clean starched set of khaki drills to wear each morning and generally 'does for us'" for which I pay the vast sum of 3/-.

I was glad to hear you were now all safely settled at Wilmslow and that so many people had welcomed you back. Maybe - though I hardly dare let myself think of it - I shall be seeing you all towards the end of John's Xmas holidays. There has not been the slightest hint of where we are going when we have finished our training here – but we all of us are hoping we shall be sent home and perhaps Peter and I will be attached to a Spitfire or a Hurricane Squadron. Its no good pretending that I don't long for the old life and my old friends – but there is no alternative but to see this thing through now to the end and to be thankful that one is capable of doing useful work and perhaps following in the footsteps of those men whose deeds one reads about every day. And really I have a great deal to be thankful for. I don't mention the Air Raids for I'm pretending that I don't worry about them either. I'm very fit and well, so good bye until next week."

Roger had written from India, and his letter was also included in the Chronicle. Unlike Charles, he sounds heartily fed up.

Letter from Roger
"Werner 2/4 P.W.O. Gurkha Rifles, Loralai, Baluchistan, India
Well at last I'm getting settled down in this ruddy army. Its exactly like going back to school only much more boring. Compared with life in tea, it's ridiculous: everybody seems to think they are being worked frightfully hard here, but the hours are half as long as they are on a Tea garden and one does half as much in them. I feel an awful fraud and am pretty fed up with things. I joined the army to fight or at any rate to be of some use, whereas all I'm doing at the moment is swindling the Indian Government out of about Rs 400 per month. I'd feel much happier back in Assam – at any rate I was earning my pay there.
I wish I thought there was a hope of getting home to fight - or at any rate into things - fairly soon. I feel such a swine doing nothing here, while everyone at home must be going through a kind of hell let loose. I hate to think of you all during this damnable time – but please don't have any worries about me. I'm in revoltingly good health and likely to play at soldiers here in India until the end of the war. Its horrid to think I was due leave from Assam in 41, now I don't suppose I'll get home leave from the Army for years as I imagine I shall have to stay on for a bit after the war is over. I find everything more expensive in this childish army. I get less pay here than a newly joined 19 year old infant from Sandhurst which makes me mad. However in spite of all this they seem to have accepted me quite well here, possibly because I'm about the only man in the

battalion who can put a lorry right if it breaks down. Shall be glad of more news of everyone."

Family news was desperately important with so many family members dispersed. Cousin Alice's experience of the First World War, whatever that had been – perhaps a potential husband killed, an experience like that of so many others – no doubt informed her decision to create the Chronicle. Her generation of cousins had lived through it. My father had fought in it. Here they were again, just two decades later.

My mother in Devon reported that my father had a week's leave in early October. As I was aged only two and a quarter, I have no memories of this occasion, yet perhaps my fondness for cream teas on Dartmoor could be traced back to an autumn day in 1940.

From Molly Withington
"Dick got back for a week's leave early in October, which was a great excitement for us all. He looked very well and was very cheery and thoroughly enjoyed his little holiday and the society of his family. He played golf every day except one when it was too wet. Our dear old friend General Curtoys (who has since died after some months of illness, I am sorry to say) lent Dick his beautiful sports Bentley two afternoons and we had a lovely drive one day through Dartmeet and Ashburton, Bovey Tracey to Mortonhampstead and back across the moors by Postbridge where we had tea in an 'otel', much to Susan's joy. "Tea party in 'otel with Daddy" was her theme song for the afternoon! The week went all too quickly of course. The country was looking beautiful with autumn colours which is the loveliest time on Dartmoor, I always think.
We still remain very quiet from an aerial point of view down here, for which we are duly thankful. The local W.V.S. is really beginning to function at long last and I am on the Committee of the Tavistock Branch. We are now busy preparing to start a Club for War....or Evacuees, but we are having difficulty in getting premises as everything suitable seems to have been already commandeered by the Military authorities. However we shall no doubt find something and I am sure it will be a good thing.
I have also taken on a small canteen job in Whitchurch where one company of the Regiment here has its H.Q. I only go once a fortnight on Saturday evening from 4 – 7 as my nannie is out every other Saturday. Anyway, canteen work is always so popular, they have no difficulty in getting helpers.
The children are all well, Jane and Antonia have been inoculated for diphtheria in case there should be an epidemic, it is 98% immunity for

life so well worth doing. Susan has just started dancing lessons, she thoroughly enjoys it, she is the youngest in the class, but follows reasonably well and is not in the least shy, as Jane was when she began at 2 ¼. Jane is now one of the best in the class and she and Antonia "coach" Susan at home!

Dick has been in high society lately as the King spent the night at his H.Q. last week and as President of the Mess Committee Dick had all the arrangements to see to. They seem to have had a very jolly dinner party and the King was in excellent form, and so natural and has a great sense of humour.

My people have just had my brother's first letters from Abbotttabad, which are very cheerful. He lost part of his kit en route, unfortunately. I have heard no other details yet, as the letters are being passed round before being sent on to me."

Abbottabad. That's where Osama bin Laden was finally found and killed. In the days of the Raj, it was the headquarters of the Hazara District in northern India. At the time Uncle Dicky was posted there, it was an important garrison town for a brigade in the Second Division of the Northern Indian Army. Roger Werner was also in India, in the 'ruddy' army; he was stationed in Loralai, Baluchistan, now known as Balochistan, one of the four provinces of Pakistan after partition in 1947. Both Dicky and Roger had been sent to areas in which the Raj had established cantonments in defence against Russia. The region borders Kandahar province in Afghanistan, still frequently in the news.

How the two armies, the British and the Indian, arranged matters to fight alongside each other, I have no idea. I suspect that British army officers were seconded to lead Indian troops. It certainly wouldn't have been the other way around. Independence didn't come until after the war. Despite the ambivalence of individual Indians towards the British war effort - why help your oppressor against its enemy? Why not help that enemy? – the Indian Army made a huge contribution to the Allies' eventual victory. A commander-in-chief of the Indian Army in 1942, Claude Auchinleck, believed that the British couldn't have won without the Indian Army.

My uncle Dicky fought in Burma against the Japanese, but the details of his wartime experiences are unknown – and there's no-one left alive to ask, even if he had talked of them. All I know is that he was not among the many thousands taken prisoner. Unlike Roger – but we'll come to that later on.

The cousins made the best of things in the second Christmas of the war. Ivy reported from Doncombe where Cousin Alice was with them:

> *From Ivy Crompton*
> "I find it very difficult to make the second report from a household of this size, so little happens and Alice is the better raconteur. We were alone for Xmas and Alice and Jack had a very quiet day. I went out with the canteen all day and the men were most appreciative of our effort. Alice and I had previously made hundreds of gay paper bags which were filled with sweets and distributed to the men. I forget if I have revealed to my relations that I am obliged to wear an Air Force blue uniform cap in which I look like a broken down pantomime boy or male impersonator. Miss Maggie Muck's positively last appearance and rightly. I think though I lean towards the P.B. (pantomime boy) as the posterior development of the M.I (male impersonator).is always greatly in excess and that in our narrow War would be a major disaster.
> But to turn to less serious subjects, one other event was the children's party which is usually held in the house. I think it was a great success and the gardener brought down the house as Father Xmas, but the room was squashed and the air bad, so I leave the rest for Alice who was the life and soul of the party. The Aerodrome here is being enormously enlarged but it is very high and catches every wind of Heaven, one feels so sorry for the men, and we are glad to have a large shed allotted to us where the men can stand in, out of the blast. I did not get any news of the grandchildren at Xmas, they were to have gathered together with various parents and cousins but one of them started measles and the plan broke down. ….I suppose when one expresses New Year wishes one feels there is a little more hope and justification for them than there was last year, so here are mine for everybody."

Alice the life and soul of the party! That reminds me of the description of her in the pages of the book about the Manchester University Settlement which I quoted at the start of this. How she managed to sparkle in company when she couldn't hear is astounding. Here is her description of her Christmas at Doncombe Mill:

> *From Alice Crompton*
> "Life goes on very quietly in Ford, and December was no exceptional month. My one and only war activity is helping Jack with the village War Savings Branch. We have 42 regular weekly contributors – not a

bad number for so very small a place. The Savings Xmas cards of which I append a specimen, were very popular. The chief event in Dec. was the party which Ivy gave for the Village children – native and evacuated. We got two little Xmas trees out of our wood, and trimmed them for table decoration, and hung paper chains (red, white and blue) about the Parish room, and Union Jacks – all these being what were used in 1936 for the Coronation. Some of the tiny children were a little bit frightened at first by the huge Father Xmas, all scarlet and white, but were re-assured when he opened his sack and dealt out gifts and crackers lavishly. The children did not seem as ready to sing as I think they would have been in the North Country. And two other differences struck me. (1) no 'waits'[46] here. I remember well how they used to come round to Bowden Hall at night at Xmas time, and Uncle Wilfred used to regale them with mince pies and drinks. (2) On Xmas Day I went to the beautiful old Church at Castle Combe, one of the loveliest villages in England and was disappointed to find it almost without decoration. Amongst others I remember how Colne Church used to have all the pillars wreathed with evergreen garlands. Manchester Cathedral too. But at Colne the effect was marred, to modern taste, by cotton wool texts on Turkey red cotton!"[47]

I can just hear Alice's disapproval in that last sentence. And even the children of the North Country may not have been quite as ready to sing in December 1940. The Manchester area was now being targeted by German bombers, as Kathleen reported from Wilmslow.

From Kathleen Smithells
"Since last writing we have had our Blitz or maybe only some of it. The Sunday before Xmas it started and soon the fires lit up the sky. We had 13 hours of roaring overhead with bombs and guns. We never took our clothes off - just lay on our beds in the cellar. Archie kept a sharp lookout for fire, so was in and out all night.
Our friends in Whalley Range had a simply ghastly time. Dr Neilson and his wife had a land mine in Withington but they were on their way to the cellar when their front door was blown in. They got into the cellar and were lucky to get out with their lives – their house is no further use to live in. A lot of the furniture and carpets are no use. Whalley Range has suffered so badly one can hardly see it ever recovering again. Hulme was another badly bombed area - such

---

[46] Or waifs? Whatever the word, the allusion must be to carol-singers
[47] 'Turkey red"was a natural dye for cotton originating in Turkey. I'm trying to imagine red cloth hangings, on which words formed out of cotton wool have been stuck. Certainly, a curious idea for church decoration, even at Christmastime.

crowds of people rendered homeless.
Archie and I drove over to see how our friends were before we went out to Wilmslow for Xmas – it really did let you see how cruel and dreadful it all is – curtains hanging out in rags where the windows used to be, roofs off, tiles torn up and lying, people trying to stack their furniture to save it.
On New Years night we had one dropped in Withington: Another land mine was dropped in St Paul's Church Rectory Garden in a tree; it had not gone off so everyone was sent out of the houses in Withington; all the shops closed and the traffic sent round by Mosely Road. It was put out of action before the evening rush – the first bomb broke all the windows in Withington ....again, the second time.
It was so nice to get out into the country for Xmas, we had quite a happy busy day. We were a small party and one's thoughts were with Charles and Roger so far away. Charles sent us a cable arriving at the right moment .....
We are now having it very cold and if we are not careful everything will freeze. I have not been into the worst damaged part of Manchester. I don't much enjoy seeing it and there have been such crowds going to see it.
K.M.Smithells"

Cousin Alice's purpose in setting up the Chronicle had been to keep the scattered cousins in touch during the war. How long that war would last and what it would mean in their lives none of them could have guessed. Now, as the war progressed, the value of the shared Chronicle was becoming more and more apparent. The cousins often mention how glad they are to hear each other's news in this way. By December 1940 the circle had spread to Western Canada. Leigh Henderson was now looped into the Chronicle's orbit. He was the son of Joe Henderson, and brother of Kathleen Smithells and Grace Werner.

From Leigh Henderson
"I enjoyed reading your chronicle very much and would surely like to read some more of them.
You know it is thirty three years next February 19th since I left for Western Canada and as I have not been home since, there are several of you people I have not seen, just heard about.
I have travelled all over Western Canada from Brandon in Manitoba to Prince Rupert in north of British Columbia.
I am now in the Okanagon Valley where the best apples in the world come from.
We here do not know there is a war, for everything goes on just as

usual except we are continually being asked for contributions to one thing and another, to which everybody gives willingly and most generously. Well, we should when we hear over the air and read what you people are so bravely enduring for us and the rest of the world.

I have a family of four: the Baby Kathleen is in her first year university and has applied to go into one of the Hospitals for training next fall. If accepted she will be there for three years.

Harold is a first class school teacher and is studying for his B.A.

Evelyn is also a first class school teacher making her specialty the junior grades.

Leigh is travelling in Alberta out of Calgary for the Ash-Temple Dental Supplies."

The name Leigh came from Lydia Kay, nee Leigh, the wife of the 18th century Ernest Becker from Thuringia. A present-day cousin, Susie Becker (now Lothian) tells me that the baby her daughter has just produced will be named Arthur Robert Leigh after Cassandra Leigh, Jane Austen's mother, who they believe is a forbear. Perhaps these threads will be traced back to a common source. The son of Ernest and Lydia, Hannibal, was given Leigh as a second name, as was my father. Joe Henderson gave it to his son as a first name, and he passed it on to his son. Lydia's Christian name was also passed on. Hannibal Leigh and Mary Becker named their first child Lydia [48].

Present-day cousin Nicola Werner christened her daughter Lydia.

There is sadness in losing a surname, as well as excitement in changing it. On marriage, the female half of the couple usually agrees to the loss. Sometimes women choose to double-barrell their single and married names. There have been some wonderfully long, tongue-twisting results of this practice. A famous example was the name of the special envoy to Moscow in 1939. If the occasion allowed, my father made fun of the envoy's full name: Admiral Sir Reginald Aylmer Ranfurley Plunkett-Ernle-Erle-Drax. I grew up with the surname Withington and it felt exclusive: the only Withingtons I'd heard of were members of our family. Now I wonder just how many hundreds of Withingtons are spread across the world, all distantly related. If we go back far enough, whatever our name, we are all cousins, every last one of us.

---

[48] Lydia Becker has already appeared in these pages, see page 22.

SIX

Blitz, Blitz and Blitz again – 1941

"Well, never mind, it might have been worse."

Leigh Henderson was now included in the Chronicle's circuit. In the February 1941 issue – January's is missing – Leigh adds a new perspective to what was happening in Canada at this time.

From Leigh Henderson
"About a week ago an advt appeared in the paper wanting men between the ages of 19 – 21 with Senior Matric. for the Dental Corps to study Dentistry in all its branches. So Harold[49] applied. He got his orders to report at Vernon for his Medical which he did and was accepted but has not got the final call. It is a good opportunity...
3 Feb. Harold has got his call today to report to Vernon for his transportation to Victoria where he will be stationed for the present...Helen had a phone call from one of the School Board out at his School asking her if he had a nice razor (which he has not) so they are going to give him one as a parting gift. She said they were all feeling terrible about him leaving for he had been such a wonderful example and influence to the children in every way.... I have no worries about him for he has no use for liquor and does not smoke, nor does the boy he is going with....
See you had our friend Wendell Willkie in Manchester. He has sure made a name for himself. He was mud here during the Elections but he has surely come back with a bang – everybody is praising him now."

Mud! What had Wendell Wilkie been saying and doing? I've been on a hunt for answers and learnt that he was a Republican who became the Party's nominee for president in 1940, in opposition to Roosevelt. The big issue in this election was over the US's attitude to the war in Europe: should America join in or stay out? Wilkie was an internationalist who advocated the notion of global cooperation rather than nationalistic competition and antagonism. In his campaign, he tried to hedge his bets with the electorate and consequently lost support from both sides. Roosevelt regained the presidency.

---

[49] Harold is the son of Leigh and Helen Henderson

Wilkie spent the next few war years meeting the leaders and people in the allied nations, and wrote an account of his travels, talks and thoughts in a book that became a best-seller, 'One World'.

He visited Manchester and is mentioned by Grace Werner in her February contribution :

From Grace Werner
"Wendell Wilkie was greatly liked here in M/C. I was at a 21st birthday party and met Raymond Street from the Chamber of Commerce and he was full of Wilkie's praises. The people in our Flat lost a lot of valuable property in the M/C Blitz and were actually on one of the sites when Wilkie came along. They had just found a small cash box with a few odd shillings and pennies in and Wilkie asked if he might have them to sell in America for the Red Cross. I sent Leigh a family tree thinking he might get muddled with the cousins he had not seen, but as he put it 'He had figured it all out.'"

Leigh and his family lived in British Columbia in western Canada. There are two more contributions for February from across the Atlantic, this time from Montreal. (Perhaps January's issue was lost as a result of a torpedo?). Louisa Withington, whose pre-war visit to Canada had been forcibly prolonged, was glad of the presence of another Becker descendent in the same country. Like Leigh in Kelowna, British Columbia, she was grateful for the contact that Alice's Chronicle provided. She wrote to Leigh's father, her nephew Joe Henderson. The fondness between her, the youngest of the 15 Beckers, and the son of her elder sister Mary, is obvious. The big age gap between the sisters meant that Louisa was only five years older than her nephew. Cousin Alice copied out sections of her letter to Joe for the Chronicle.

From Louisa Withington
"Extracts from Aunt Loo's letter to Joe dated Feb 9/41
I often think of you all and wonder if I shall ever see you again. No one can tell what the future has in store – but I don't feel at present that I shall ever cross the Atlantic again. I am anxiously waiting to know if I am to get my income this month! Mr Perkins says he is entirely in the hands of the Exchange Control authorities – will do his best to keep me (informed). It is very harassing. I have about 10 dollars in hand, and don't know when I shall get any more!.........I sold my diamond brooch and that big diamond pin – which was

valued at £10 in London as it had a flaw in it – not worth more! I got 150 dollars for the two which was very welcome…..I don't want to sell my ring if I can help it.

Bob is getting 80 dollars a month working in the new C.N.R. terminal and goes 3 evenings a week to classes working for his Senior Matric. It will count as his first year at McGill. He paid 100 dollars fees. He is such a big fellow – went to a dance on New Year's Eve wearing Len's dress clothes! Ted working hard at McGill and Army training 3 days a week. He is going into Camp for the month of May, I believe. He was 21 last month. They are not calling up students who are working for their Degrees. Ted should get his next year. What will happen? I think things certainly point to an invasion, the sooner the better now we are ready for them. The chance they missed was last June when France collapsed. So the poor old Free Trade Hall is smashed up – like Free Trade itself! How many lovely concerts have I listened to in that grimy place! Something much nicer will be built there eventually".

The Free Trade Hall in Grandmother Louisa's day was the home of the Halle Orchestra. After the bombing, it was not replaced by a new building, as Louisa hopefully foresaw. It was rebuilt and later converted into a hotel. It's a typical Victorian building. The solid darkness of its brown-red brick makes me think of the weighty presence of a municipal official with dangerously high blood pressure.

When recently I visited Manchester for the first time, I was struck by the city's oddness and apparent emptiness. It felt like one of those places where, even when you are in its centre, you are sure the centre must be somewhere else. Nor does it seem to know what sort of city it wants to be – dark brick or plate-glass. And where on earth were its citizens? But I did find what I was looking for. In the Institute of Science and Technology I learnt about bleaching cotton in the early years of the industrial revolution, though I was disappointed to find no mention of Ernest Becker who brought his bleaching method from Germany. The man behind the desk was animated and helpful when I told him I was researching the Becker family. I must go at once to the newly refurbished central library, he said. I walked along deserted streets, past darkened and empty shop windows until I came upon the library, a beautiful, circular, ivory-white building.

Once through its revolving entrance doors, I came to an abrupt halt. There, staring sternly at me from twenty yards away, was the familiar image of my great-aunt Lydia Becker, my grandmother Louisa's eldest sister: Her photograph was presiding over a display devoted to her life and the early years of the suffragette movement. In the gift shop I bought a notebook with the same photograph on the cover – a notebook of twenty blank pages. On the back cover is a quotation I like very much:

"Every boy in Manchester should be taught to darn his own socks and cook his own chops."

It is startling that she was my great aunt, as she was to Grace, Kathleen, Leigh and Joey. She was born in 1827; her youngest sister Louisa in 1854; my father, in 1893; and I myself in 1938. Some families pack many more generations into a century. Chasing these dates I discovered that my grandmother Louisa was born on August 24th which by chance is the date today, 161 years later. Happy birthday, grandmother who I never met, yet somehow know. People can live on in their writings.

I did meet my aunt Molly Easton, who came over on a visit in the 1950s. I have a photograph of her sitting among the lobster pots of Port Isaac's harbour, painting the view which included the house we owned briefly forty years later.

Molly posted the news from Montreal on February 12th 1941 and Cousin Alice received it on March 10th.

From Molly Easton
"It is a long time since I sent a contribution to the C.F.C. chiefly because I feel our doings are so very dull and humdrum amid all the excitements of the other Chronicles. But all the family enjoy the C.F.C. so much and read it with tremendous interest and admiration. It is incredible how you can be so cheerful and brave through all the things you have to bear.
I never snuggle into my comfortable bed at night without thinking of all the cellar-dwellers and basement-burrowers and feeling slightly ashamed of my luxury.
All well here – Mother keeps very well in spite of not being able to get out much. The weather is sub zero and the roads very slippery and snowy, so it is really not fit for her, but she puts on her fur coat and sits by her open window in the sunshine, getting the air and goes out in the car when a decent day comes along. She is always happy and busy, does all the family mending – no light task ! – and silver cleaning as well as some beautiful embroidery and lots of reading – and bridge or bezique every evening.

Ted is working very hard and extremely keen on his studies. He works every night and is often in collusion with his father on mysterious engineering problems. There is some talk of keeping the University open all summer and graduating the engineers in the Autumn, for munition work. There is great demand for metallurgists, which is what Ted will be. So there is little chance of his being called up for the Army, thank goodness. He has ditched Elsie, the girl he was so keen on for two years, and has acquired a new girl, also called Elsie! I asked him what she was like and he said she was alright from the neck down! I don't know what he meant, quite!

Bob is very well and growing enormous. He works out of doors most of the time and eats hugely. He is very keen on his job, luckily he finds it most interesting. He is also planning to be an engineer. He went to a dance on New Year's Eve in his father's dress suit, and very smart he looked. He came home at 6.30 am, incidentally the old night hawk Dickie is looking forward to his 8th birthday, he asked me yesterday what time he was born, I said '2.30 in the morning.' He said 'Gee, I must have been up late that night!' It's one point of view! I close with this story of a raw recruit up for medical inspection. The doctor says 'How are your bowels?' "'don't know, Sir, I haven't been issued with them yet!' "Oh, you mean you are constipated?' 'No, Sir, I volunteered'. 'Good heavens, man, don't you know the Kings English?' 'No, sir, is he?'."

I can imagine Molly's eyes crinkling up at this, in the way my father's did. Within the creases, you could just catch a glimpse of a brown-eyed sparkle, which would let you know that whatever mysterious thing had just been said was a joke.

In March Cousin Alice was in Clevelys, near Blackpool, where an old Settlement friend had lent her two rooms.

<u>From Alice Crompton</u>
"Blackpool has enormously changed since my childhood, when my parents used to take a house at South Shore for 4 – 6 weeks and bring cook and nurse. All the rural surroundings have vanished, save at Bispham where I spent a weekend with my hostess's sister. A few little low white-washed cottages are left there, and one sees the long line of fells behind Garstang. When our great grandparents brought their family here I believe they used to go to Church in a bathing machine!"

Alice is referring to Ernest and Lydia Kay Becker. Ernest was the manufacturing chemist who brought his formula for bleaching cotton from Thuringia and set up a factory in Manchester. He clearly had an inventive mind. Fancy thinking of taking your family to church in a horse-drawn bathing machine. Alice, as a small girl, must have heard stories about her great grandfather. She continues:

> "The town is absolutely packed with soldiers and airmen, a good many Poles amongst the latter. Most of the hotels have been commandeered by the Govt for Offices, and there are hordes of typists filling them. Blackpool has just had a War Weapons Week, aiming at a million pounds. Over 2 million came in!
> I have not been in Manchester except driving through in the bus from Wilmslow when coming here. I did not notice any damage in Bolton or Preston en route. Bombs fell in Cleveleys recently, but no harm done. Occasionally, but not often, nights are disturbed by Sirens."

Ivy Crompton also reported an influx of Polish airmen to the local aerodrome at Colerne.

> *From Ivy Crompton*
> "Much excitement has been caused by a Polish flying squadron which has arrived here, they are the most charming people and such a good type. We were surprised to find that hardly any of them speak French and they have very little English so I wonder how they manage to make themselves understood, but there is great fluttering in the village dovecots when there is an Aerodrome dance and it seems that all the pretty girls prefer Polish partners, which rather annoys the village swains and small wonder. I shall succumb to the translation to tell a story which I fear may not be quite new but I hope bears repeating.
> Three Polish officers were dining in an English mess, the following conversation passed.
> (English officer) – Are you married Monsieur?
> (Polish Officer) Yes I am married Monsieur.
> (E.O) Have you any children Monsieur?
> (P.O) Alas no Monsieur.. I have no children, my wife she is unbearable.
> (2nd P.O) Pardon Monsieur. he mean to say, his wife she is inconceivable.
> (3rd P.O.) Excuse me Monsieur, these gentlemen they do not know the English idiom as I do, he wish to say, his wife she impregnable.
>
> I do hope I am not repeating a twice told story but I think perhaps it may not have reached Canada and I think it would appeal to our darling Aunt Loo."

A recurring sentence in Grace Werner's news has been *'We still have no news of Roger.'* At least it would have been a comfort that her eldest son Charles was back in England after completing his flying training in Rhodesia. He was stationed at RAF Catfoss, near Hull. But he was now sharing the dangers of the widespread blitz. Grace forwarded his letters to Alice for inclusion in the Chronicle.

From Grace Werner, Letters from Charles, March 1941
"Dear Mum

Just a short letter before turning in for the night, to let you know that all is well and that none of the many bombs which seem to have been dropping lately have come within striking distance of me!

We had some pretty hectic displays last week but were able to view them all from a nice safe distance and afterwards to sleep quite happily only awakening when the bed was shaken by an exceptionally violent percussion every now and then I only hope that you were all as fortunate and that poor old Manchester didn't suffer any more damage.

Yesterday afternoon, with cloud down to ground level and flying quite impossible I decided to take the bull by the horns or perhaps that's not very flattering – anyway, I decided to visit 'Her Ladyship' at Grimston Garth. As I now own a 1/3 of a fine racing Austin 7 (1931), it seemed too good an opportunity to miss, especially as we wanted to try out the car which Peter, another bloke and myself bought for £5.0.0. As it happened, Peter was attending lectures, so I took a fellow Officer called Clarke along with me to act as chauffeur and also to give me a bit of dual instruction on car driving.

Well, believe it or believe it not, our car - bright red and making a noise like a Bentley - actually did go without a hitch all the way to Grimston, which we traced with the aid of a large Aerial map! The hall itself is a colossal place and standing surrounded by trees on the cliffs half shrouded in mist it looked like some scene from a book, reminding me strongly of Manderley in 'Rebecca'. We left our rather impertinent-looking car out of sight and tramped around the hall looking for the right door and eventually found it; and on mentioning Trevor's name we were warmly welcomed by Her Ladyship!

She is quite young, about 45 I should say, and very good fun and didn't seem to mind my having barged in uninvited as it were. Actually she knew all about me and her letter inviting me over was already in the post and I got it today. We stayed for tea and saw over part of the house which has many Coats of Arms, open fireplaces, bookcases which slide back revealing hidden doors, twisting passages, and round towers, and in fact everything which one could hope for.

We talked of the Beckers (she was at school with Irene) and of Rhodesia which she knows well and altogether it was a grand afternoon and the complete change was very refreshing. And afterwards, when we had left with a cordial invitation to come again for the weekend if possible, our 'red terror' actually brought us home without a hitch – and more amazing still – I was at the wheel the whole way!

Such then was my debut into Yorkshire society! Anyway I don't think I disgraced myself and I have written a 'Bread and Butter letter' today – so all should be well.

I finished off my 'Conversion Course' today which means to say that it is now considered that I can fly a Blenheim safely. The rest of the time here will be spent in flying with our crews and carrying out duties etc. Actually this afternoon I practised every conceivable form of landing, with two engines, with one engine – and even with no engines – and all without a single bump so I feel more or less happy about things now – and I expect my crew feel pretty glad about it too! On Wednesday afternoon I am making my first – and probably my only (!) appearance for the Squadron Rugby Team. It should be good fun – if I can stand the strain!

Well I think that's all the news up to date so I will hie me awa! to bed and see what the morrow will bring forth.

Much love, Charles

Wednesday March 19th.
Dear Mum
Just a very short line in case the news of the Hull raid set you worrying. A slight loss of sleep was all I suffered. It was pretty hectic while it lasted and it lasted most of the night – but the luck of the station held and not a single bomb came within a mile of us. Several came just outside that radius and as I heard their whistle I found myself wondering whether I might not be safer under the bed rather than in it but it was so much warmer in bed so I stayed where I was! The fields round about are quite riddled with craters and I believe one haystack was completely destroyed – what a waste of metal!

Will write again later this week
Much love, Charles."

My mother wrote from her full household in Tavistock. Her newsletter answers my questions about how the extra family of Mellersh cousins fitted in to Markham.

From Molly Withington
"All very well here at present, though Rachel Mellersh[50] was away at the beginning of the month at Godalming and got a mild go of flu at

---

[50] Rachel was the wife of my mother's cousin George Mellersh. My maternal grandmother, known as Mop, was the daughter of Frederick Mellersh of Holloway Hill House, Godalming, the source of. another complex of cousins to rival the Beckers. Rachel and her two children, Antonia and Nicolas, stayed with us at Markham for a number of months.

the end of her visit. She is still sleeping here as we thought it too cold for her to go up the road after supper to her room at Mrs McAlisters. George came down for last weekend for 4 nights instead of an Easter holiday, which meant more re-arrangement of our elastic house, however he and Rachel did very well in my room and Susan and I fitted into the dressing room very comfortably. We are now looking forward to Dick coming for a week at Easter, leave permitting.

George was very glad to find all the children looking so well – spots, pox and coughs being things of the past.

Poor Plymouth had a frightful 'Blitz' about a fortnight ago as you read in the papers. May (our nannie) was in Plymouth on the Thursday afternoon with 2 other nannies for their afternoons out. They saw the King and Queen twice, it was a beautiful afternoon and Plymouth and the Hoe were looking their best. Little they knew what destruction was coming. When the nannies came out of the Cinema about 8.30 to catch their train back to Tavistock they found the raid had just begun and incendiaries were falling all round them. They dashed into the Continental Hotel for shelter and spent the next 4 hours in the underground shelter there and were allowed to spend the rest of the night in the Lounge, and they caught the first bus back in the morning. A good deal of damage was done that night, but nothing to the Friday raid, which was terrible, and the whole of the shopping centre has been wiped out, whole streets in ruins, the Guild Hall and St Andrews mere shells and a great deal of damage to the Hoe and the residential area found there. Rachel and I went in last week with a party of W.V.S. workers to work in a Mobile Canteen, we were on duty from 12 – 5, our Canteen was driven by a Plymouth Corporation bus driver, who was most helpful. The Canteen was very well fitted up with its own water tank in the roof, and its own Calor gas supply for a gas store and 2 water boilers. There was a sink with running water and excellent shelves and racks for china and provisions. Everything except chocolate and cigarettes was provided by the Lord Mayor's Fund. We went round nearly all the devastated areas, except where there were time bombs (we heard no end of these go off at intervals and one got quite used to it!) We were principally intended for troops, sailors, A.T.S and A.R.P people working on demolitions etc but served anyone who came around and in some places civilians made collections and in that way we got about 30/- for the Fund. We served tea, coffee, sandwiches, hard boiled eggs, cakes and biscuits. It was a most interesting experience although rather grim. It was very sad to see so much wanton destruction, it was really much like pictures one has seen of earthquake damage. The troops were marvellously cheery and the ordinary citizens so patient and resigned, some of the older people still had a slightly dazed look, but all were trying to carry on as best they could.

My feelings were first of sadness and then of extreme anger at the scenes of devastation. Of course we were very welcome with our hot tea and coffee and in some places the ruins were still hot from the fires and all the walkers were covered with dust and consequently extremely thirsty. I have heard since on good authority from more than one source that the casualties are very much less than was at first feared.

No news from India lately from my brother – all well at Godalming, Dick was down there for a day off last month and cheered them all up. We have now got a good show of daffodils out in the garden, it is really the only time this 'shrubby' garden looks pretty, and the weather has been nice and warm enough for the three little girls to go out soon after breakfast and play, which they much enjoy."

The three little girls were Antonia Mellersh, Jane and myself. Nicolas was too young to join in. Of the four children living in Markham in 1940, only Nicolas is no longer alive today.

In the next issue Irene wrote from Glossop. *"April has been a month of upheaval and general disturbance to us. Our home in London has been blitzed and all the family has had measles!"* Trevor had telephoned her after the worst bombing and she passed on the news to the Chronicle.

<u>From Irene Becker</u>
"Trevor phoned me with the news that poor old No 70 had been blitzed in the night! And such a night they all had, poor things. It was the night of the last bad Blitz on the West of London, and some buildings 200 yards away were hit by a huge aerial torpedo and demolished; the blast from this blow blew all the windows and shutters in at No 70 – not to say window frames and garage doors etc!!

The furniture in some of the rooms was hurled about in all directions; the dressing table in my bedroom flew over the bed and landed by the doorway into Trevor's room at the other side, the frames of which door also came adrift from the wall. My cupboard doors flew open and the contents which were a legion of small articles, boots and shoes etc, were strewn in all directions; the bed was covered in glass from the large windows – happily Trevor was not in bed at the time – but sitting in his chair in his own room next door until he heard the forerunner whistle of the blow, when he quickly removed himself to the other doorway which just happened to be safe from that blast. Just the one lucky spot apparently since a marble topped table in the bathroom window adjoining was all hurled across the room to the doorway near where he was standing!

The maids and Mrs Pratley were safe in the basement except for being covered in dust and dirt from the falling plaster of the various ceilings there. Ceilings gave way in many parts of the house, a huge wardrobe in Lettice's bedroom was moved right out about two yards into the middle of the room; my heavy cabinet Singer sewing machine turned a complete somersault in Aunt Ciss's dining room on the ground floor. There was soot – an inch of soot completely covered the drawing room floor – fallen plaster, dirt and broken glass everywhere. I have seen Nora, my cook from No 70 since, as she came up at the height of the measles to help me here as Dorothy has not been too well. She said the whole thing resembled an earthquake, or what she had always imagined an earthquake would be like.

She went to the gas stove and tried to make some tea for everyone there and twice when she was there the kettle rocked and came shooting over the stove into her arms! This from other minor bomb shocks in the neighbourhood which came after the worst one, which wrecked all the windows. After that the gas, electric light and water were all cut off and they were thankful when morning came to be able to get a free breakfast from a mobile canteen in the street. They all had to go out in the Mews at the back for the remainder of the night; the great blow fell at about 11.45 pm. There were numbers of the people there with minor injuries, cuts and bruises etc who were glad of help. Nora took out my collection of 1st Aid requisites which I put ready in the basement ages ago now, at the beginning of the War. At last they were in great demand and very useful. I only wish I had been there myself and able to help. However family calls here left me tied and I was unable to leave.

Unfortunately Mr Pratley, our flat tenant, who usually shelters with us in the basement was badly injured. He was out in the Mews on Fire Watch in a house just facing the buildings where the great bomb fell and was thrown over by the blast. Trevor went out to find him but he was unconscious; his assistant warden a woman called Mrs Tangstrom was also injured and bleeding badly so Trevor went out and found an ambulance and sent them both off to Hospital. Mrs Tangstrom luckily soon recovered and in a week was able to go to a convalescent home. Mr Pratley unfortunately was suffering from a cracked skull and remained unconscious for nearly a week and then only had very few lucid intervals. However we have had a postcard from his wife (about a week ago) to say he was definitely better and the hospital authorities were very pleased with his progress, so I do hope all may be well with him ultimately. Trevor has had a horrid shake up altogether and I am afraid he is feeling the effects of it now as his nerves are none too good – but he won't own it and when he wrote to me about 4 a.m. on the morning after it happened to tell me the details, he ended his letter 'well never mind it might have been worse! We still have a house if dilapidated! Tails up!'

Our poor Persian cat Tom had the worst shock, poor thing, or rather I think he showed the effects of it most outwardly by continuing to shiver all the next day. Nora had to carry him about in her arms all the time to pacify him and whenever he heard anyone picking up broken glass, he was nearly frantic, - even in her arms. Then Trevor said he could find no comfortable place to sleep in – everywhere was terribly draughty!! However, happily the following morning was a lovely fine day and Trevor being always on good terms with our builder Dix and Co. went round there at 9 a.m. after the Blitz just as they were opening shop and commandeered them to begin on our repairs at the earliest possible moment. The workmen were round before 11 o'clock and before night the maids had collected what glass they could and cleared the furniture away from the windows so that no serious weather damage could be done the next night. It took some days to complete the First Aid repairs of course but now the house, though very dark with the boarded windows, is more or less watertight I believe and should be I hope until the next time!

The measles are nearly over too now. Wilfred is up at last after a fortnight in bed; Juliet out and about though her eyes are still a nuisance and she has grown a lot. Her head now reaches to my chin which is quite a good height for 9 ½ . The tiresome thing about the complaint is that the wretched patients can't read at all and it seems a moot point when they will be ready to begin! We others have to put up with three different wireless programmes going sometimes one in each room of this flat. One likes only classical music, another all the educational talks and a third any sort of music at all. Mike meanwhile has retired to a lilo at night in his office up at the Vol-crepe works and just comes home for his meals and a bath! He, having had measles in his youth, is happily immune this time!

I was interested to read all Charles Werner had to say about his visit to my friend Armatrude de Grimston at Grimston Garth, near where his billet is (or rather somewhere in the neighbourhood). She has been a great friend of mine for over thirty years now and as Charles says looks young. She has the Irish charm of manner and much to my chagrin at the time married at the age of 22 a widower of 75. Later I grew very fond of him myself. He was a marvellous and most interesting man and had for years before the last war worked for the Federation of Europe. He knew personally at the time many of the crowned heads of Europe and used to visit them in his yacht during the last years before the 1914 – 1918 War. The War came as a great disappointment to him after all his efforts during many years to promulgate peace in Europe. He was a German by birth but naturalised English in his early days and as serious an opponent of the Prussian ambitions then, as the Jews and anti-Nazi Germans are today. One often met many interesting foreigners and diplomats in his house at Richmond and Armatrude used to love the role of acting as his hostess then. She always wore the most lovely clothes which came from the most notable Paris and London houses in those days and she held great court. Lovely to look at with her tall slim figure, fair complexion and large azure blue eyes – all of which she has kept to this day. She is now rather in the danger line in her family castle on the coast but I do hope she will be safe from harm. I hope all this will not bore the family but I ventured to think the description might be as interesting to some others as it was to me: this coming of

Charles from far away Rhodesia straight almost directly to the doorstep of my friend, who by odd coincidence had also spent a good deal of time in that fascinating country. There is no doubt about the old proverb that the older one grows the smaller does the World become!
It makes life interesting though and helps to distract our thoughts for a time from much that may harrow and disturb."

Charles had now been moved to Shetland. Before including extracts of his latest letter, Grace wrote about the evacuees she was expecting.

From Grace Werner
"They have just arrived, the child with a cold and very full of it and coughing very well!!!! Poor things though. One feels sorry for them. They have three small suitcases and that contains all they have in the world. They were under the ruins of their house for six hours before they were found and dug out. Her husband who was on leave at the time was badly hurt and is now just out of hospital, back in the Balloon Barrage. If things get better the mother and child mean to go South again to the husband's mother near London."

My mother also talked of evacuees in the April issue.

From Molly Withington
"Tavistock is still fortunately lucky enough to be on the outskirts of the Blitz, but we get frequent 'alerts' and had very noisy nights when poor Plymouth and Devonport got their bad raids again last month[51], but no bombs dropped in the immediate neighbourhood. Since then Tavistock has been simply inundated with poor evacuees, the Town Hall and the Infants School taken over as Rest Centres and the Old Grammar School as a Feeding Centre, and W.V.S. and other helpers have been hard at work. I have been on duty for one shift every day except Sundays for the last three weeks, and so life has been rather strenuous, especially as the influx has made housekeeping even more difficult. The children all flourish, Jane has now started school in a mild form 2 hours 3 mornings a week at a little Kindergarten, not far off across the Moor, she trots off very importantly with her gas mask slung over her shoulder and her attaché case in her hand. Nicolas has just been 'trousered' and looks very sweet in his 'Buster' suits, he is a very sturdy little chap, and is walking quite well now. The Mellersh

---

[51] April 22nd 2016 was the 75th anniversary of Plymouth's worst night of bombing, referred to here by my mother in 1941. The city centre was completely destroyed. An air raid shelter in Portland Place took a direct hit and 72 people died.

118

family have been here nearly a year.
Another wartime activity I have been drawn into is Land Army work, and I have been out 'potato dropping' rather a nice outdoor occupation, but quite tiring. I found one has to accept payment for this and I was quite proud of my wages.
Dick is still in East Anglia with the same Corps HQ. Trevor wrote for his address, but I couldn't tell him his exact whereabouts, of course, but he is in the neighbourhood of ...(section of paper cut out)......"

Every so often in the Chronicle it is obvious that a censor was at work. Besides the main censorship office in Liverpool, there were 20 other centres around the country. Not every single item of internal mail can have been checked. Instead, there was a certain amount of self-censorship. The cousins occasionally alluded to details they should not write about; information which might have helped the enemy if their letters fell into the wrong hands. This was particularly true of letters to and from anyone in the forces. Yet Grace's April contribution held the uncensored information that Charles was now stationed in the Shetland Isles. She included the letters she'd just received.

From Grace Werner, Letters from Charles
"Here I am safely installed in a quarter section of a Nissan hut but completely partitioned off in cream bricks. We have a stove and a bed, an armchair and a small dressing table and washbasin. All that one needs really and with my photographs and everything I feel quite cosy and at home already, which is as well as this will be my home for the next two months. I arrived at Aberdeen at 10.pm to find good old Peter waiting for me at the barrier. He had arrived only a few minutes earlier himself. So we went off to see the Embarkation Officer who was quite surprised to see us and said since we were here we'd better catch the boat train which went at 1. o'clock. Otherwise we would have to wait a week for the next one!!! So we had a shave and a meal and dashed along to the docks. We didn't have long in the town but did find that our Squadron was very much in favour there. At one place we had to sign a special visitors book, devoted to the members of the Squadron. Everybody in fact was very good to us and we look forward to our return visit. Of the trip over here I can say little I slept most of the way in a tiny cabin which I shared with Peter. It was pretty rough but it did not prevent me from enjoying my meals. In the morning we got our first glimpse of the Shetland Isles under very grey skies and not looking exactly inviting. We got some cocoa at a second rate café at Lerwick and were then all piled into a sort of closed van very like a Black Maria and trundled along the odd 20

miles to this place seeing a lot of sheep and gulls on the way but nothing else. It would be quite impossible to exaggerate the wildness and desolation of this place. The camp itself is just a few huts half buried in the sand dunes with the sea and rocks on all sides. Yet nobody seems to worry – and one never hears a single complaint. They are a grand crowd of fellows. 'What is there to do' I asked in the Mess last night. They just smiled 'to do – nothing at all old boy – abso bally lutely nothing.' 'But I suppose it is not too bad at Lerwick?' I asked. 'We wouldn't know they replied. 'We have never bothered to go there' and that's everybody's attitude. They have just said to themselves, we are all in this together and we shall make the best of it here and if one adopts that attitude one should be quite content. Today the sun is shining in a cloudless blue sky and the sea is sapphire blue and one can smell the salt and seaweed in the air. The headland just beyond is asking to be explored so Peter and I are going to walk there after dinner before bed. As you know I cannot say much about my flying – but we shall get quite a lot of nursing before we are sent out on any big thing. It's a great feeling to know that one is really in a Squadron at last and that one can get to know the fellows and settle down without continually chopping and changing – and its good to know that one is really doing ones bit of something at last and helping to pull ones weight a bit in the war. There is nothing I need except socks so would you send me some – We do our own washing here!!!

28.4.41 Everything has some consolation or other and the fact that every day is exactly alike, one never gets that Monday morning feeling. After a week here I am settling down nicely, my room is cosy and comfortable. I have books to read and the food is reasonable. There is a wireless and papers do arrive eventually and best of all a mail plane comes every day. So letters now have an enormous value and one looks forward to them no end. It was grand to get two letters from Rhodesia which you sent on and your letter stacked full of news.
Our advance into operational flying is being taken in very easy stages thanks to a splendid C.O. who really takes an interest in his Squadron and won't let any of us undertake anything tough unless he's personally satisfied that you and your crew know how to take care of yourselves. I am all for it myself; the death and glory stuff is all very well if need be but when one is not forced one might as well go slowly. Anyway I have had two marvellous flights. The other day I had to go to Aberdeen. We were there in less than an hour and a half. It's a grand station and I thought I was dreaming when I clambered out of my plane and found I was surrounded by about 20 beautiful girls! I soon found out why they were really there. They began to rattle collection boxes under my nose – they were Art students and apparently it was Rag Day in Aberdeen. Anyway they all came along to the mess and we had a wonderful sherry party and before long the

RAF band was playing and we were dancing before lunch. Luckily the lunch was served by some lovely blond WAAF's. After oue week up north- it was a wonderful break. Anyway roll on the day when we go to Aberdeen. Now I must rush off to my dinner((so called) "Brown Stew" or Curry Sir". Still its good plain food so who cares. We get plenty of eggs and bacon for breakfast."

How many times would that letter have been read and re-read. It was Charles' last. Cousin Alice opens the next folder, Volume II, Number 5, May 1941, with this note:

From Alice Crompton
"This number of the C.F.C is very late in appearing. I was waiting for two contributions (which have not yet arrived) when the news came that Charles Werner, R.A.F. had lost his life as the result of air operations. The funeral (military) took place a few days later. Henry and Paul were there (and Graham Henderson). It was all very beautiful and exactly as Charles would have wished it to be.
All we cousins share the sorrow and the pride of Grace and her family. (The lines below came to light in a box of papers of mine a few hours before the Air Ministry's wire arrived).

TO A FALLEN AIRMAN

High o'er the clouds, and aflame with the fire of sunrise,
Poised on the edge of the moment, to die or to live,
Sheer with the peregrine's stoop through the swirl of the skies,
Daring the cost, you struck home; what more could you give?

Dead: - but the flame of your youth cannot fade with the years,
Dead – but more living in spirit than we who draw breath,
Perfect by sacrifice, cleansed of our doubts and our fears,
Fallen, the ransom of many, and Victor o'er Death.

Cyril Norwood.

A.C."

*

SEVEN

The Fallen Airman – 1941

The first of the young cousins to be killed

Charles was the first of the cousins to be killed. Even at this distance the shock wave that passed through the family can be felt in the Chronicle's pages. The death of one of the Becker progeny would have hit all of them hard, particularly Charles' coevals. Yet magical thinking comes into play when you're young: *Death happens to others, not to me.*

The newsletters in the May and June Chronicles of 1941 cover a muddling range of dates. In the issue which began with Alice's announcement in May 1941, the cousins were mostly writing before the news came through. Bombing raids, vegetable growing and Red Cross work were the subjects. Cissie's contribution written on June 14th 1941 gives a picture of domestic normality in wartime Hampshire.

> From A.E.I. Becker, Aunt Cissie
> Extracts from Aunt Ciss' letter of 14th June to A.C
> "I am so thankful the Trevors[52] have left London. Lettice went up for 3 nights to help with sorting out papers and drawers. We have had, I should think, nearly 4000 alerts, but we are not the target area like London, Portsmouth, Coventry etc. We have lots of gun fire and bombs, of course, but we are not really the target Jerry wants to hit. We are very busy, the crops are behind, and birds have eaten all my peas nearly to the quick. I have had to sow each row again. Another year, if still here, I must black cotton all the peas. Of course, the weather has been vile, and things are v. late. I have a magnificent lot of broad beans nearly ready for eating. We took the tops off about 10 days ago, and ate them. Excellent – consistency of spinach with broad bean flavour. The lupins and poppies and white daisies and sweet rocket and violas are a show in my garden here – the veges all across the railway line. I had a job to get tomato plants this year and, with the cold weather, I fear they will only just start to yield when the frost comes. We get a drive very occasionally, short distances as our 6 gall: does not go far, for Lettice's car drinks up petrol alarmingly. We paid a 2 week visit to Loo[53] at Earls Barton, and I must say I enjoyed 2 weeks of complete idleness. I had not been well, and was x

---
[52] Shorthand for Trevor and Irene
[53] Irene's mother, known as Aunt Loo like my grandmother Louisa.

rayed again but they did not find much wrong. It has been a strain working and not feeling well, but I am much better – but was for months all 'anyhow'.

When I come in from outside I have the house to tackle. Tomorrow we have someone coming to lunch, we are glad of the 'offal' sauté of kidney, the joint tomorrow. We have a lot of eggs in pickle, and a lot for Trevor and Irene. It was like asking the farms for a pound for 10 shillings. .But we made weekly collections, a few here and a few there, and we got friendly and we got more then!

We have piles of wood – we never go out in the car without bringing some home, and I got 2 tons coal put in for the winter. But we have no outbuildings here, and the coal is in the garden. There is a Red X fete this next Thurs. Lettice will have to help with a stall, and we are giving food. .I spare ½ hour every day to go and see an old villager opposite – a great invalid and suffers terribly. I go when Lett. starts to cook our bit of dinner – about 7 o'c. We are cutting endless cabbages now and I have the left over for lunch with salad dressing and bread and butter – not bad at all, in fact I like it! We mash potatoes with cabbage water instead of milk, as we are rationed now. We find Eiffel Tower and Creamola milk puddings a blessing, as in 3 minutes you have a milk pudding and no long baking and waste by evaporation. I make potato and other scones for tea most days, as, with jam, you don't miss the butter as much as with bread. Looly is much thinner, and so am I.

I am glad we have some furniture at Earls Barton – a peaceful place, and I undressed and went to bed there, which I never do here. There is no news here – just the daily jog along and hot bottles in bed our one comfort in this cold summer!"

When the cousins received the June issue of the Chronicle, the newsletters, like Cissie's innocently talking of Creamola milk pudding and endless cabbages included at the same time as Charles' letters written in his last weeks, must have made bitterly sad reading.

"I append," wrote Cousin Alice, "the last letter I had from Charles – a characteristic one. The double heel was his mother's suggestion."

From Charles Werner
"Wednesday April 16th (1941) 460468 Officers Mess, Royal Air Force (address crossed out)
Dear Cousin Alice
You have every right to think very hardly of me for my apparent ingratitude in not answering your letter and thanking you for the socks. I can offer you no excuse but try to make amends by this short letter now.

123

The socks came to me at a time of very grave crisis for a search of all my drawers and numerous hopeful explorations under the wardrobe had failed to reveal a single pair which could not have been put on equally well at either end. Hence within five minutes of the arrival of your gift, the socks were on my feet and I could face the world with the confidence which only a good solid 'un-holy' pair of socks can give.

I cannot speak too highly of the "Crompton" or double heel, it really is a marvellous invention which ought to be embodied in all socks for the services and I feel that you would be doing your duty in revealing it to the government in order that harder wear should be obtained from the 'Socks – Airmen for the use of' which fall so sadly short of your standards!

However I will not betray you – on the condition that when my turn comes around again I may receive another pair of the same excellent quality! Blackmail I'm afraid.

I am at home just now on a week's leave and having a grand time before leaving to join my new Squadron in the far distant Shetland Isles. It is a long way to go but I volunteered as it has that touch of adventure which in my life I have always sought and which I shall seek to the end – so that whenever the end does come I shall be able to say without any reproaches – I have lived .

Well, well, before I start writing like Beverly Nicholls, I'd better finish.

Thank you again
Yours affectionately
Charles"

Charles writes with all the verve of a 23-year-old. The mismatch in dates between the writing of the newsletters, the issue of the month's collection by Alice, and the delays in its circuit around the cousins, makes the family's loss even more poignant. Grace herself hadn't known of Charles' death when she'd sent in her news the month before. She happily included a letter she'd received from him dated May 1941.

From Charles :
"The days seem to drift past quite swiftly now, probably because this month I have been kept so busy – my flying hours are mounting up rapidly and I am only one hour behind the Flight Commander who took the biggest total for this month. If things carry on at this rate I will have topped my first 50 operational hours against the enemy by the end of the month. The trips on the whole are quite pleasant though one is apt to get a bit weary towards the end of a five hour trip on which one has seen nothing but an odd ship and mile and mile of grey sea. My navigator seems to cope quite well – we always seem to

land up here on our way back which is a good thing for it's a bit awkward if you miss (censored) and have to go on into the Atlantic!! It's all great fun really and there's a marvellous feeling of satisfaction as your wheels trundle along the runway and you know that you're home again and that the job is done. Then if you're lucky you climb into a steaming hot bath and relax until the next time.

I got a surprise the other day when I came in from afternoon flying and barged into the Mess for tea to find the Duke of Kent!! Apparently he had just shaken hands with all the Pilots. Unfortunately I had missed that privilege, but I now know how the Royal Family eat buttered muffins and I must brush up my table manners. Anyway its nice to know that one member of the Royal Family now knows what I am doing to help the War effort.

We are having some lovely weather. Yesterday the Doctor, my Flight Lieutenant and the Squadron Adjutant and I took advantage of it and got an old sailor to take us over to the Island in his boat. We all had to help with the rowing. The Doctor is a scream and very like a P.G.Wodehouse 'Bertie Wooster' and the Flight Lieutenant not unlike Roger to look at and full of fun. We had only gone about 100 yards when the Adjutant noticed that the boat was leaking and he got terribly concerned. So we took it in turns to bail and row. The doctor always rowing completely out of time with everybody else – until he 'caught a crab' and at the same time caught the poor old sailor who was steering a nasty crack on the head with his oar and nearly swept him out of the boat. Anyway more by good luck than good management we did get to the Island. Roger would have gone mad with delight at the rare sea birds to be found there, their nests were everywhere and we had difficulty not to step on them. We saw numbers of seals who flopped off the rocks and then watched us intently from a few yards off-shore. It was great fun. We brought back a few eggs but unfortunately they were all in rather an advanced stage and not too pleasant for eating.

During this week (censored) have been giving us a taste of what they can do in the way of weather. For two days it was snowing hard – not very spring like! Anyway yesterday was warm and a lovely evening and I went along the cliffs with a rifle and tried to get a few birds – not I may say with a great deal of success, but it relieved my feelings and was really quite good fun. Such little expeditions help to make life bearable here – for on occasions, when one realises that flying is over for the day and there is nothing whatever to do, one does feel a bit cut off. On the other hand it's very beautiful and a fine warm day makes it well worthwhile to be here.

Today we have been issued with our Blue Battle dress. It really looks quite smart. We also have a white jersey with a Polo collar which we can wear instead of a shirt for flying. So now my Rhodesian Wings which my instructor gave me have come into their own and I have them on my Battle dress tunic. We have been given too some lovely woollen underpants and vests all lined with silk."

In her own contribution for June Cousin Alice talks of her month-long stay with Grace and Henry at Sunnyside, Wilmslow. On June 7th they went to see the film of 'Pride and Prejudice'. They enjoyed it very much, says Alice, but 'one deplored the alteration of the story at the end when Lady Catherine urged Elizabeth to marry Darcy!'

I was once miscast (in my opinion) as Lady Catherine in an amateur dramatic society production. The director kept urging me to be more horrid. I felt I was being as horrid as I could possibly be. I would have done better, perhaps, if the director had wanted an aider and abetter type of Lady Catherine as portrayed in the film that Alice saw with the Werners.

Alice continued:

> "This was the last entertainment poor Grace and Henry had, for 3 days later came the news of Charles' death. On the 14th Henry and Paul went to his funeral. On 26th June Grace was told by a policeman who came to the house that Henry had had an accident, and was in Warrington Hospital. With much difficulty she got through to Warrington on the phone and learnt he had been run into on his bicycle by a motor car. Four ribs were broken and collar bone injured. It was too late that night for G. to get to him but Archie drove her over first thing next day, and she found him v. well looked after in the Hospital Nursing Home and tho in pain, not in danger. He stayed there till 6 July, doing well.
>
> For 3 weeks I was very busy helping to write up the new Ration books in Wilmslow – I went to the Council Chamber every morn. and aft. returning to Sunnyside for lunch and a short rest. There were a great many voluntary helpers, each of whom had a cup of coffee and a biscuit at 11 a.m. and a cup of tea and a biscuit at 4 pm. (Sugar with both). I felt we ought not to have it – it was a very soft job and we could choose our own hours. However I didn't refuse it, as it was there! We all had a good deal of amusement out of Little Blitzie, Sal Small's kitten – a very engaging creature with blue eyes and a dear little pink mouth. His uncle has gone to be mascot to a R.A.F. Squadron in Cornwall and is called Spitfire."

Grace herself wrote a contribution for the Chronicle after hearing of Charles' death. She included his last letter, two letters of sympathy, and a cutting from the Glasgow Sunday Post, the newspaper he had worked for.

From Grace Werner

"Alice has been with me through it all and a great help with her kindness. We had a letter from Charles dated June 1st saying he had gone to censored and that was the last letter we had from him. I feel so glad he had the move, for he hated censored and seemed so happy to be in censored. We got the news that he had been killed on the 10th. I had been schooling myself to take it, ever since his Easter leave when he seemed so much more serious about what was before him, and I know he felt that he would not see the war through. He left a message for me by Paul – to say he had no regrets. A happy life – and the two greatest moments were when he got his wings and then when he joined his Squadron. He wrote saying what a splendid lot of fellows they were and what a grand thing it was to be with them all.

Poor Father broke the news of the telegram to me – I had stopped the telegraph boy for weeks on the way to the village – but that morning I went on my way. I arrived back at 1 o'clock to find Father waiting for me. And I knew at once what it was before I saw the message. The next day we got another wire saying he was found and we could either have him home or let him have a full military funeral there in censored with the men he had loved and been with for the last few weeks of his life. I had to decide myself as Henry and Paul were both at their jobs. And I feel still that I decided right in leaving him there where he was happy. Henry and Paul were able to go over for the funeral. I felt I could not face it and I don't feel Charles would really have liked me to have gone. In part of Paul's letter to Roger he put 'It was all very very beautiful and I feel just what he would have wished. A little country churchyard and village church, all so beautifully done. Mum had sent flowers and there were some from his squadron and Graham (Henderson). Many of his companions were already there and one from 1918. The peace and beauty of the countryside made me feel that Mum was quite right to have him buried there among those other little white wooden crosses.' John was sent home by his headmaster – he was very brave and a great help to us all. Henry could not get back from Risley until the day he had to start for the funeral – but Kathleen came and stayed for three days and was a great comfort. Paul was such a help to me too although he too feels it terribly. Paul, Roger and Charles have always been the best of friends and the gap can never be filled.

I think perhaps those who knew and loved Charles would like to hear what he wrote to us in his last letter, written on 1st June and received on 10th."

That was three days after she, Henry and Cousin Alice had enjoyed the film 'Pride and Prejudice'. Could his parents have been in the cinema at the time he went missing? I am not sure what the actual date of Charles' death was. He had been moved from the Shetlands to somewhere further south. From his letter it sounds as though he might have been in Northern

Ireland and shot down over the Irish Sea. There's an airfield called Sandy Bay which could fit his description. Grace adds his letter here:

> Last letter from Charles
> "We have never had much money but we do see life and the world!- I can hardly believe that my exile in the Far North is over and that I am within easy reach of civilisation once more – yet it is definitely so. As always in the R.A.F. when things do begin to move they move rapidly and no sooner had the news come through than we were in the air in mass Squadron formation and here we are still a little breathless but nevertheless with (censored) far behind us and with every prospect of a nice long stay here. We may of course have to return there sometime but is very unlikely as we have had far more time there than any other Squadron. and it has not been by any means a quiet time. Even after a very short five weeks the strain and tiredness were beginning to tell on me and most of the other fellows had had five months. So we have got our break at last and I for one think it is well earned and we should be able to take things more easily here. censored Why they call this (censored) for never in all my life have I seen anything to equal the green of the fields and trees. When our formation crossed the coast (censored) after mile after mile of sea you could almost see each machine stagger as the Pilot had his breath taken away by the sight of the tiny fields below and the green hedges and trees and tiny white cottages. As we followed the broad river into (censored) at about 50 feet up – my observer summed it all up very well by saying that it was all like scenes in a coloured 'Silly Symphony'. It all shows how distorted one's ideas can be, for I always imagined that (censored) was all heather and marshes and I would never have credited that it was so very green and beautiful. My seasons have all been so jumbled this last twelve months that I had lost touch with them – but here with apple blossom all over the place and yellow honeysuckle and masses of flowers I know that it is spring and I have caught up with myself again. You must forgive all this rhapsodising – but it is not my fault it seems that I have seen nothing but sea and the short colourless grass (censored) for ages and ages. We live in a brick built mess now and are waited on for our meals by beautiful blonde W.A.A.F.S instead of hard-faced orderlies! The orderlies may have been more efficient but it does make life a great deal brighter when one can gaze into a pair of beautiful eyes as one munches ones breakfast cornflakes. Actually they're not as beautiful as all that – but you must remember that I've seen nothing but sheep for weeks and weeks! –(censored) too is a 'big city' with 'real cinemas' and 'bright lights' so what more can one ask. Also I am only just across the way now and I could be at Woodford in under an hour in my plane from here."

Woodford is or was an aerodrome near Wilmslow. It does sound as though Charles was in Northern Ireland 'just across the way.' What was the broad river, and the big city? I guess it was the estuary of the river Lagan leading to the city of Belfast.

> "So there we are – all's well that ends well. I've survived (censored) and come away bronzed and fit with my lungs full of sea air and I think I am very lucky too . Will post this now and write more again when I have extra time. Much love Charles
> PS Is Graham still in these parts?"

Extra time was to be something he would never have. Grace adds below the letters of sympathy she and Henry received.

> <u>"From Joan Hayton (now Forsyth) a very old and true friend of Charles</u>.
> Dear Mrs Werner
> I went over to Brooklands today and Mother told me of Charles. I can understand little of the bitterness of your loss because the goodness and unselfishness of Charles has been a very real thing in my life ever since I first knew him. We have always spoken of him amongst ourselves at home as 'dear Charles' because he was so young and charming when he came to us or wrote to me. On his last leave just before my wedding we had lunch together in M/C – he looked so happy and so very much at the beginning of life – afterwards he wrote to me and said he hoped I hadn't found him too "horrid and tough". There is something in his death which would have pleased him because I think he enjoyed being thought tough really and I believe he only made himself brave through his own strength of will which is perhaps the hardest thing of all to do. He was to have come and visited Scott and myself on his next leave. When this is all a little further away I would welcome you with all my heart if you would come over one day instead. I am sorry I express my sympathy so badly. I wish I had some small comfort to offer you but I can only send you my own sorrow and my love. Joan"

> "From The Editor of The Sunday Post.
> In this sad hour I know you will be cheered by the many messages you receive paying tribute to your splendid son. I would like you to know that all his colleagues in the Glasgow Office of D.C.Thomson & Co have heard of his passing with the deepest sorrow. He was not long with us when he joined up, but long enough for us all to win his friendship and to appreciate his qualities of mind and heart. He was very happy among us and he spread his joy in life to others. For that

was his nature – big in body, great in heart. I know from what he told me he entered the Air Force with no illusions, but he had made up his mind to serve where he thought he could be most useful. There was never any thought in his mind to seek the easy way. He was doing his work brilliantly here until the call came; in my time I know of no young man who promised so well. Its hard that war should take our very best.

In your time of mourning, Mrs Werner, remember that the sympathy of all those who knew Charles is with you. By his daily work and conversation he honoured you, and reflected your spirit. He was a great gentleman. Your pride in him was ever justified, never more so than in his death on behalf of others.

My own personal sense of loss is very deep; but our thoughts are with you and all the members of the family, and I trust you will be sustained and comforted and given the strength to bear this great sorrow.

Yours very sincerely, J.M.Borthwick."

Grace ends her contribution with a cutting from the Sunday Post:

"SUNDAY POST MAN KILLED
Pilot Officer Charles Leslie Henderson Werner, who has been killed during flying operations, was a member of the editorial staff of 'The Sunday Post'. He was 23 years of age, and the third son of Mr and Mrs C.H. Werner, of Sunnyside, Brown's Lane, Wilmslow, Cheshire. Educated at Manchester Grammar School, P.O.Werner joined the Manchester editorial staff of D..C.Thomson & Co. on leaving school. A most likeable personality, he made rapid progress and showed a distinct flair for journalism. Before the outbreak of war he was transferred to the staff of 'The Sunday Post', Glasgow. On the declaration of war he volunteered for the R.A.F."

*

EIGHT

The war intensifies – 1941

Rationing, Vegetables and Hens

What highways and byways the cousins have led me into. I've spent the past two hours hunting the internet to discover how and where Charles was killed. In the days of our mutual forbears there was no Google, no Wikipedia. I'm sure the Becker family scoured encyclopedias for facts that cropped up during meals around the dining room table at Foxdenton Hall. 'Why is seven such an important number?' At the start of the Chronicle, that was the question I imagined Alice's mother Victoria asking of seven-year-old Alice who then passed the challenge on to me.

I have some partial answers to my questions about Charles' end. He was with 254 Squadron, Coastal Command. Originally formed in 1918 (at Prawle Point in Devon) to fly anti-submarine patrols, 254 Squadron was re-formed at the start of the second world war and based first on the east coast, then in Scotland, to provide fighter escorts for shipping. In May 1941 the squadron moved to RAF Aldergrove in Northern Ireland where its duties included reconnaissance. The station, operational from 1918 until 2009, shared runways with Belfast airport. The wide estuary Charles described was Belfast Lough. From the base, long range aircraft patrolled the Eastern Atlantic for U-boats. On the internet I found a video giving an all-round view of a model of the plane Charles would have piloted: a Blenheim Mark IV. It showed two seats in the cockpit as well as a gun turret. Charles talked of his crew. It must have numbered three: Charles with the co-pilot – or the navigator? - in the front, and a gunner sealed in a vulnerable-looking bubble on the plane's mid-spine. I also found the squadron's Roll of Honour, 1940 -1941. Charles' death is recorded as occurring on 9th June. On the same date two other names are listed.

Sergeant Robert Shaw and Sergeant Jack Jean Eugene Marie O'Donnell. It is likely that they were Charles' crew, and their Blenheim Mark IV was shot down somewhere in the Atlantic.

The squadron was only at Aldergrove from its arrival there on May 29th until it was moved elsewhere on December 12th. Charles flew missions from the base for just 11 days. He had been relieved to reach his new station, after five weeks of intense action, flying from the Shetland base. "The strain and tiredness were beginning to tell on me. So we have got our break at last and I for one think it is well earned and we should be able to take things more easily here."

His letter rings with optimism and cheer. To read it knowing he was to die within days is affecting enough today; how it was for his parents is beyond imagination.

In the same month my mother wrote her contribution while on holiday in Cornwall.

From Molly Withington
"I write from a lovely spot on the North Cornish coast, where we have taken a bungalow (belonging to our Tavistock friends, Admiral and Mrs Wollaston) for a fortnight. We look over Lundy Bay in the direction of Tintagel and Boscastle. We have had the most marvellous weather the whole time we have been here, except for one day of sea fog. The children are thoroughly enjoying the sands and the deep pools, and even the 'big sea' as Susie calls it, with its rollers, for the first time. Unfortunately both of them are struggling with horrible whooping cough, which was brought us by some children who came to tea at Markham, and started 'whooping' a few days later! Although Rachel and I had our 4 inoculated 3 times, they all caught it, but it has been fairly mild. Poor Sue is the worst and has bad attacks of coughing, especially at night. It is a most distressing complaint, but they seem very well and jolly in between whiles.
We have Mrs Wollaston's sister here as a p.g. and she is a most pleasant companion for me, she is (fortunately!) fond of children, also Sam, the Wollaston's Aberdeen, who is a keen rabbiter, and finds the cliffs round here a perfect Paradise!
The flowers in June are quite lovely, we now have iris, orchid, thrift, honeysuckle, campion, scabious, valerian, wild thyme – heather and ling just beginning, also tamarisk. The most striking feature here being the masses of red poppies in the cornfields, and growing on the grey stone walls, quite a lovely sight, and the sea and sky have been a

brilliant blue. If only Dick were here to enjoy it and his small daughters capering about in their green bathing suits!

Last weekend my friends Brigadier and Mrs Johnson were staying at a nearby hotel and I had 3 games of golf at St Enodoc, which was a great treat, especially as I had not played golf for 7 weeks owing to neuritis and I was very glad to find it had completely gone, thanks to the treatments at the Hospital. The Brigadier and I are very level opponents, he won the final game by a putt on the last green. I wish to inform Archie 'the Himalayas' did not defeat me on any occasion and I got over in 2! But one time the poor old Brigadier was caught on the highest peak and had to toil up in the hot sun!

Another delightful feature of this little bungalow are the masses of roses growing on one wall of the house, and some very nice rose bushes in the garden, too, also in full bloom now. The sea is rather cold still but I have had several excellent bathes, and good surfing. We return to Tavistock next week, and will find the house very quiet now the Mellersh family have departed to Gloucestershire, but we are looking forward to Dick coming on the 16th for a week.

I had a very nice visitor in the early part of June, Vi Sharpe – my old friend General Curtoy's cousin, and I hope she will pay us a longer visit later on. She rides an autocycle and was breaking her journey from Badminton to Minehead. I persuaded her to stay 5 days in the end, as the weather wasn't very favourable for motor cycling and she had had a tiring visit to a cousin, helping with spring cleaning and was glad of a rest.

We are now hard at work in the local W.V.S. organising the Communal Feeding Centre – the Ministry of Food is most insistent this must be got going before the winter, both for Tavistock itself and the rural areas. Tavistock itself is much less crowded, but will always be a 'first line' in a (censored) Blitz and must be prepared to accommodate hundreds at short notice. We had a very successful War Weapons Week and got over £200,000 (aim £75,000).

My sister in law is getting on very well, though very slowly, and is still in bed and still has a nurse. We have had no letters from Dickie lately."

I remember the Lundy Bay holiday in a few sensory snapshots. As an adult revisiting the place, I was on the look-out for fragments of childhood feelings and images. From the car park at the top, the path runs beside the bungalow where we'd stayed and leads down through a steep combe to the cove. In hollows where the air grows warm and slumbrous, buzzing insects took me right back to my three-year-old self. At the cliff edge, I looked over the stone wall and felt dizzy with the thunder of the waves below. This was the *big sea,* so much greater a presence than the small, green, silent pond at

Markham. Looking back up the combe, I tried to make a house high on the far side match my memory. The harder I tried the more elusive the picture.

But my memory of Vi Sharpe is clear, maybe formed later than this 1941 visit. She came to stay every so often, a woman on her own who wore tweed suits and stout, leather, lace-up shoes which she could stride about the moor in. She wound her hair into two long, thin, grey plaits which she then coiled over each ear like headphones. On arrival at Markham she would hoot the horn of her motor bike. The horn was attached to the handlebars, a black rubber balloon which we were allowed to squeeze. She'd give the bike – called James – a heave onto its iron legs before coming up the steps with us – six, then five, then four – to the front door.

So Vi, I learn from my mother's contribution, was General Curtoy's cousin. According to an earlier issue of the Chronicle, he had lent us his Bentley for a trip on the moor. Tavistock was full of retired army and naval officers who'd fought in the first world war and Vi Sharpe was typical of the many single women of the time. She became translated, as it were, into an Aunty Vi in a novel I wrote, in which I wanted to catch a flavour of that generation.[54]

My mother ended her letter with news of my father's mother and sister in Montreal.

> "I was thrilled to see the snapshots of the Easton family and Mother in the last C.F.C.
> I think Ted is very like his father as a young man. Mother looks so well and pretty and smart."

My grandmother Withington (Aunt Loo) had now received her allowance from England and had bought three new frocks. I can imagine her pleasure – frock is a frolicking kind of word. And she bought three, a triple frolic!
Cousin Alice in her Editor's Note at the start of the July 1941 issue reported:

---

[54] Ste*phen and Violet,* Collins 1988

From the Editor
"Several of us have heard from Aunt Loo that the April C.F.C. reached her in a very dilapidated state, mutilated by the Censor.
In future I hope contributors will continue to write in as full and detailed a way as hitherto, and I will copy out a bowdlerized version to send to Aunt Loo. It would be a great pity to cramp our style, since there seems to be no objection to it for home circulation.

Please send August pages to me <u>on Sep 3</u>, to c/o R.C.K.Ensor Esq. Sands, High Wycombe, Bucks which will be the best address for me throughout August."

Whenever we have anyone to stay, it is never for longer than two days. Cousin Alice would have been a delightful guest for that length of time. Benjamin Franklin thought visitors, like fish, should not be kept for longer than three days. The Ensors had Alice with them *throughout August.*

Irene Becker had also learnt from Aunt Loo in Canada that the censor had been at work.

From Irene Becker
"I feel rather guilty as I expect I was too communicative about the Blitz. It evidently behoves us all now to keep to purely family matters which I fear may be much more dull to the readers abroad, though safer and more likely to reach the ultimate destination."

She goes on to describe how busy – *'up to our eyes'* – she and Trevor had been. They'd decided to move the remainder of their belongings, goods and chattels out of No. 70 Eccleston Square.

"We came to the conclusion that it wasn't worth paying all the rates and taxes it involved for just two of us to live in what would probably be a certain amount of discomfort. Smith our Handyman has been called up on National Service, Mary has gone to work at the Army and Navy Stores, all the family still away and likely to be so now until the War ends. We don't feel justified in taking on any more men or women now in the way of staff, when all hands are so much needed for National Work. It would be quite out of the question for us to run a large house during next winter without any staff to do repairs and mend leaks etc. and, as we don't need it either for our own convenience or the family's, we feel quite justified in flitting and relinquishing our large bill of rates.

But the removal and disposal of all the contents of the house meant a great deal of sorting out, packing and repacking not to say dividing out from all the different owners what had to be done with the belongings. The first question was where to go. Where could we live Trevor, myself and Nora our cook, plus one large and devoted cat! – the few who remained from our former establishment of fourteen, all told, in peacetime days, not to mention the cat, 2 parrots and 2 canaries. First of all, we heard of a furnished flat at Epsom which we thought might do and then we should have had to store most of the furniture somewhere else. We had just warned our usual removal people we should need them and provisionally fixed the date, when to our joy the tenant of one of the flats at Epsom belonging to the Porkellis Co[55], which Trevor directs, wrote to say he wished to relinquish his flat immediately as his work took him elsewhere. Trevor thereupon telephoned and took over his lease on the spot, almost before we (or rather I) had even seen the flat! It is a dear little flat, cosy though small, but on the ground floor which is very convenient for Tom our cat. We found we were then left with nearly all large furniture, as I had especially picked out the smaller stuff and wardrobes, chests of drawers, tables etc, which would be more easily placed in any establishment, for Earls Barton whither they had all gone in February. We had kept all the big things in London thinking they would be the ones to stay put at No 70 where the space for them, thinned out of the Earls Barton furnishings, was quite vast. So I had to think and plan a great deal; first of all on squared paper with everything measured to scale, then by doing some rearrangement when they arrived. Of course it was pouring with rain the day everything arrived at Ashley Court (Epsom) and four large wardrobes, Aunt Ciss's beautiful old oak Court cupboard from her bedroom, Lettice's large desk for Trevor's room, my old oak bookcase desk, the beds, chairs, and the piano all turned up, not to mention sundry other chests of drawers, and the kitchen table and stores - all of which had to be carried by the five removal men down the garden path, round the block of flats all the way to the back door to get inside, without the removal of the large air raid shelter which, for safety's sake, blocks the front entrance entirely except for pedestrians. We had no gas stove the first day we arrived and nothing was unpacked so we and the men were all most grateful when Mary Macgowan, Tom's wife who also lives in the same block of flats, made us a cup of tea all round.

We got it all settled in eventually, including the piano into Nora's bedroom. Trevor had absolutely refused to have it in the sitting room

---

[55] Irene frequently alludes to Trevor's business interests: the boot factory, a colour photography printing business, and various board meetings of unspecified companies.

as neither he nor I ever use it and he said (quite rightly) that we would never get in anything else we wanted if we had it there. But it is a good piano and Cecily loves playing on it whenever she comes home so it seemed rather a pity to leave it in the garage where I am sure no piano tuner would ever deign to keep it in order for us! The balance of the furniture we may want again but can at present do without, is all lodged and carefully arranged so as to be get-at-able in two small garages quite reasonably near the flat. So all being well we are really very comfortably fixed up for the time being. The little flat is very cosy and though full there is quite enough room for the two of us and Nora to live in. We just have to go out if it is necessary to walk about. The walls of the sitting-room are panelled with oak wainscoting which, though a little dark, gives it a dignified air and the large oil painting (of the Italian School) which used to be in the drawing room at No 70 looks quite pleasing though it does take up too much wall space for true elegance!

Cecily laughed when she came back from Oxford and saw the flat so full but I told her she must just consider it a home for the furniture (and the cat) which it really is rather than a home for us! And after all we have quite a number of books and other tools and implements for the mild preoccupations of two quite peaceable people, so if left in peace we really ought to be very happy while it lasts at any rate.

Since fixing up the flat at Epsom and arranging the blackout etc, we have been in London at Aunt Loo's flat in Eccleston Square which she has lent us also for the duration of the War, while we tidied up the remnants at No 70 and arranged the dispersal of the books etc."

This Aunt Loo was Irene's mother who had gone to live in the country, first of all not far from Trevor's mother and sister, Cissie and Lettice, in Ringwood, before moving to Earls Barton. I suspect it was a habit among the cousins to refer to their own parents as Aunt and Uncle, as all the nephews and nieces did.

"We had so many of these (books), amongst all the family possessions that we waited until Cecily came home and she was able to do a great deal of the sorting. A large proportion of them are stored now in the basement at No 70 as is also a certain amount of surplus furniture china etc and pictures we couldn't find room for at Epsom. We also sorted out a lot of books for the children's hospital which has moved from Great Ormond St out into the country and a collection also for the troops. We were able to store a certain number of things in the basement at a very great reduction in the main rates which is convenient.

We spend quite a bit of time at Aunt Loo's at Wilton Court and always leave enough things there so that we can stay anytime without making further arrangements. It is convenient for Trevor when he is alone and needs to be in London.

In the middle of our removal I had to send Nora, my cook, up to Glossop. We had an SOS telephone call from Mike in the early hours of one Sunday morning to say Dorothy was ill in bed at their lodgings with a septic throat and could they have someone to send Julie to school in the mornings and cook their dinner for them all. So Cecily and I had to run the flats between us wherever we happened to be and continue our sorting efforts at No 70 at the same time. There is a lot to be said for a flat these days when one is short handed in the house I think! We managed to do all we had to do in time to get up to Glossop for Juliet's birthday at the end of July. Since then I have been busy with the allotment garden here finishing off the planting out of some of the spring vegetables, weeding etc!

Mike has a collection of hens, some cockerels for fattening and two rabbits in a hutch to look after as well as the garden which always needs much attention at this time of the year! They also have taken on some shooting on one of the moors here this season with Russell Tallis (from Chapel en-le-Frith); too many irons in the fire I think to get on with as well as their daily job at the factory! Wilf has just bought himself a secondhand motor bicycle cheap which he has been repairing, doctoring, cleaning etc all in his spare time. He wants to go for a week's holiday with it in what they call "Wakes" week here, and take a friend in the side car. They intend going camping as they know they will not be able to get a room where they want to go and will take their tent, blankets stove and pan and food with them in the side car I suppose. A hard work holiday I imagine it will be but I suppose it is what boys like!

He has been so busy that he has had no time for the garden so Julie and I have been doing our best whenever it is fine. But the Derbyshire climate is not very kind to growing plants I fear and the results of one's efforts are not very great I'm afraid.

However we are having beautiful lettuces and really good cabbages which is something and I think the onions will be good as well as the potatoes when ready, and we are hoping for some runner beans, though they are still but in flower.

I am expecting Trevor up here at Glossop on Wednesday for a week or so and Cecily later on in the week. She has gone to stay with a friend at Hawes on the Yorkshire moors and is enjoying herself very much.

I am sorry this is such a rambling screed this month and I hope everyone will not be bored with our removal details. I for one am very thankful it is over for a time at least and hope we may be left in peace at Epsom. It really would be a terrible undertaking to move out of that flat now!"

Irene's trials were typical of the times. There were so

many comings and goings throughout the land as people moved from one temporary lodging to another, escaping bombs or being billeted on others in the course of service. Archie and Kathleen Smithells had a second BBC girl; the first one had met another billettee and they'd married. The war created wonderful opportunities for meeting people.

From Kathleen Smithells
"I have had a busy week getting Margaret my BBC girl off to London, where she has got another job and can now get to see her husband at the weekend. I never saw such a lot of luggage. We shall miss her very much. She was always so bright and cheery. She has been nearly a year with us."

Cousin Alice reported news from Doncombe where she was staying in June 1941:

From Alice Crompton
"There are 4 charming R.A.F. Officers billeted in the house now. Mrs Allan is quite glad to have them. Her tenancy expires in October, but probably it may be hard to get her to turn out. Bobby Errington has had a fortnight's embarkation leave, and has been coming and going to and from Doncombe. sometimes with a nice Air Force girl friend. Jack is extremely busy digging for victory, and they have been hay making too. Short of rain of course, like other places. Jack keeps well on the whole, Ivy is busy with Mrs Bowes-Lyon's Mobile Canteen; so is Mrs Harcourt-Harding – Ivy's life-long friend, who is at Doncombe 'for the duration'."

Doncombe Mill had become quite a village. There were the four RAF officers billeted with Mrs Allan and all her dogs in the house. Jack and Ivy were in the larger of the cottages, which had three bedrooms. Cousin Alice was a frequent visitor. So was Ivy's son Bobby, sometimes with a girl friend. Now we hear that a lifelong friend of Ivy's was living at Doncombe for as long as the war would last. Perhaps she occupied the smaller cottage.

From Ivy Crompton
"The heat in our Canteens is almost unbearable, and the sight of the Polish Squadrons present has to be seen to be believed. They have scarcely a rag of clothing on and the place is literally teeming with torsos burnt almost black with the sun. The sight of Poles with nothing but bathing trunks on, riding or wheeling bicycles is quite

fantastic. I must say, though, they have the most fascinating smiles and manners, and well do they know it! They sometimes succeed in melting the stony heart of Kitty Bowes-Lyon for an extra sandwich or piece of cake. Our supplies are certainly getting a little more difficult but we still do well. Mabel and I are doing shorter hours but more shifts. There is much more aerial activity overhead than there used to be, and many new and very noisy planes have arrived. Aunt Loo[56] would sigh for the peace of Doncombe. Jack's War Savings Campaign is really doing wonders: he has started a rivalry between Ford and Slaughterford (the neighbouring village) as to who can first buy a Bren gun, and they are all agog."

Molly Easton wrote from Canada. *"I am afraid I have not contributed for a long time but my news is all so tame as compared to the adventures you all go through."* But she included a letter written by Ted.

Letter from Ted Easton, June 1941
"Copper Cliff Ontario. International Nickel Mines.
This is the weirdest country that I have ever seen. There isn't a tree or a blade of grass or even a particle of soil outside of the town, nothing but bare brown rock. This is due to the smelters before their chimney stacks were raised and before the company were forced to reclaim the sulphur and arsenic from the flue gas. Years ago there wasn't a plant within a radius of twenty miles. On bad days people were forced to hang cloths soaked in ammonia over their windows. Now the towns look quite normal, there is even a nice park in Sudbury – but outside the town there is no greenery whatever until about 20 miles away, you reach the farm country.
I start on Monday in the smelter, sampling ore. I am going fishing this weekend with my boss, June 5th. It gets very warm on my job now and I do copious perspiring. There are drinking fountains all over the place and beside them are bottles of pills – you are supposed to take 2 or 3 every shift, to avoid heat exhaustion. I went into the barbers the other day – he was quite amused by my lack of hair on one side of my head where I was splashed with molten slag. The slag was pouring from the converter in a rather large stream and when I shoved my bar into it, it splashed up over me and some of it went inside my gloves. Naturally I wasted no time in getting my gloves off and after I had done so and rid my hands of the slag I went on with my sampling. When I had finished getting my samples I happened to look up and saw the skimmer on the other side of the stream of slag dancing around and pointing to his head. When my ears began to feel warm I got the idea and whipped my hat off. It was in flames so I

---

[56] This Aunt Loo is the one in Canada, Louisa Withington, my grandmother.

> dropped it into a drinking fountain and got busy on my hair. Actually I didn't lose very much, just a small handful on the left side of my head which absolutely ruins my parting but does not otherwise detract from my beauty. One of the most intriguing things I have seen in the smelter is the sign language. The noise is such that the human voice is useless for people more than 2 ft apart so that a language of the hands has evolved which is almost as good. I find it quite amusing and am catching on to most of the signs quite well. I can even tell a man to go to H-----! Most of the old hands can tell dirty jokes or anything else to another man when they can't even hear themselves think. To look at them you wouldn't give most of these birds credit for the intelligence some of their manual conversations show."

Molly ended her newsletter with a mother's concern for her absent son's well-being.

> "….Ted has a very comfortable boarding house and belongs to a club run by the Company where he can play games, swim and anything else he likes. Please excuse horrible paper. (M.E.)"

There was a shortage of paper in Canada, too.

*

NINE

The Battle of Moscow, Pearl Harbour – 1941

"Absolutely okay, don't worry"

Three headlines greeted me on my computer screen this morning, August 27th 2015, courtesy of the US edition of the Guardian newspaper's website:
Virginia shooting: how Vester Flanagan forced the world to be his audience. This was the gunman who shot dead a TV interviewer and a cameraman on live television. He thought he'd been unfairly sacked by the company.
Donald Trump wants to deport 11 million migrants: is that even possible? Trump is campaigning to become a Republican presidential nominee.
At least 20 migrants found dead inside lorry in Austria.

That last item affected my night's sleep. Last night's UK television news showed the lorry drawn onto the hard shoulder of an Austrian motorway. On its rear doors was a large cartoon of a red-combed chicken's head. In my half-sleep the image kept re-appearing, accompanied by the snatches of the story: *seen stationary for a number of days ... driverless ... putrid liquid leaking onto road ... bodies ....migrants... on their way to Germany.*
Later we learnt that the number who had suffocated inside the frozen chicken lorry was 71, three of whom were children under ten and a year-old baby.
Germany is the humanitarian hero today, taking in the greatest number of people fleeing from the devastating conflict in Syria and violence in African countries. We are told that Europe is experiencing the biggest mass migration of people since the chaotic end of the Second World War. Random shooting, suicide bombs, wars, migrants: the news is full of such things. We are horrified. We keep asking why.
The Great War was called the war to end all wars. Twenty years later we were fighting another world war. In 1945 the two atomic bombs dropped on the citizens of Japan altered the pattern of international conflict. The possibility of

mutual annihilation has stopped any nation risking a nuclear war. The deterrent has led to years of peace, we tell ourselves. Yet wars are still being fought. They may be localised and smaller scale than the first and second world wars but that's no comfort to the people affected by them. And the whole world is at risk from the greatest danger of all: the possibility that nuclear weapons will *get into the wrong hands* – the expression is used in the same way as it is when referring to individuals and guns. In 1968 when the treaty for the non-proliferation of nuclear weapons was agreed, five nations possessed such weapons: US, UK, Russia, France and China. Now the number has risen to eight, with the inclusion of Pakistan, Israel and North Korea. The deterrent factor may still hold good on a rational level but when a nation is led by someone who is not rational, a kind of Vester Flanagan, what then? There always are leaders who can whip up followers with an inspirational credo – Churchill for one, Hitler for another. We – whoever the we is – are good: they – whoever they are – are bad. Isis terrorists are as convinced they are right as we are convinced they are wrong. What would Islamic State do if they captured a nuclear arsenal?

As Lawrence LeShan wrote in '*The Psychology of War'*, published in 1992, 'there is no hope for our species but Peace.' His book explores why it is so hard for humanity to live in peace, and what might possibly be done to achieve worldwide harmony. He quotes the question Arthur Koestler asked Freud: "Why war?"

"Why the army?" I might have asked my father if I'd thought of it in time. It was only after his death in 1969 that I began to wonder what had led such a quiet, gentle, even-tempered man into the army in the peaceful years before 1914. If you'd met him in retirement, you would never have believed he'd ended up as a Brigadier.

"*Dick has been up north to Matlock lately on a short course for Brigadiers(!)*" That's my mother's bracketed exclamation mark at the picture brought to mind: a classroom of stout, khaki-clad figures crammed into rows of desks – the sort which had inkwells in the right-hand corner and initials carved deeply into the grainy wood of the sloping lids. Despite the course for brigadiers and years of being in commanding positions, Dick remained someone who liked to stay in the background, an amused, sometimes sardonic observer.

In my bookshelf I have a gilt-edged leatherbound copy of the complete works of Alfred Lord Tennyson. In the fly leaf is the inscription *School Prize R.L.Withington Xmas 1907.* Incised in gold letters on the cover is

ἀνδρίζεσθε
BOXGROVE SCHOOL

Boxgrove was a preparatory school in Guildford, *Be a man* [57] the school's motto. Dick went on to Uppingham and Cambridge. He became was an engineer who liked discovering how things work, designing and making things, and reading poetry. After the war, the semi-underground room below the stairs in which we'd huddled during air raids became his workshop. I still have the broad spoon onto which he'd welded a hook to park it safely on the rim of the marmalade jar. He made us a model yacht which sailed proudly across our murky green pond before its hull became waterlogged. *"Full many a flower is born to blush unseen and waste its sweetness on the desert air."* This was said with a twinkle that glinted somewhere between a tease and an expression of sympathy. I'd left school and was moping at home without a boyfriend. I didn't like the idea of wasting any sweetness on the desert air, and very soon went to live in London, first staying with Aunt Irene and Uncle Trevor at No 70 Eccleston Square.

Not many events in childhood were allowed to pass by without an apt quotation. A picnic on the moor would be accompanied by the lines from the Rubaiyat of Omar Khyam:
> *"Here with a Loaf of Bread beneath the Bough*
> *A Flask of Wine, a Book of Verse – and Thou*
> *Beside me in the Wilderness –*
> *And Wilderness is Paradise enow."*

From his mock-solemn delivery we would know that we were being invited to laugh. *"This mounting wave will roll us shoreward soon"* - pointing at a slight rumple in the sea ahead. We'd be sailing the hired, clinker-built 'Arrow' in Salcombe harbour – *"and in the AAAfternoon, they came unto a land in which it seem-ed AAAlways AAAfternoon."* I once heard a

---

[57] *Andrizesthe* – behave in a manly way, have courage.

scratchy recording of Tennyson reciting his own poetry. Oh, I thought, so *that*'s where my father's extraordinary delivery came from. He must have heard Tennyson.

'Other Men's Flowers' was a favourite source of quotations. This was an anthology of poetry published in 1944, by Archibald Percival Wavell, a distinguished soldier; in fact, a Field Marshall. Wavell, one of a number of literary-minded soldiers, memorized a poem a day.

My poetry-loving father fought in two world wars. I now guess that the army, in the days he chose it as a career, was the best route to a life spent designing complicated things and making them work. Fighting in France was not his aim. Yet there he was, not once but twice. Boxgrove School's message worked its magic: *Be a man, have courage.*

Courage he had. He got a machine gun across the Yser canal under fire and was awarded a Military Cross. This was in the first world war. In the second he was in France from the start. A diary he kept from 1919 to 1969 provides clues to his movements. The entries are brief and factual. He sailed from St Malo on 17th June 1940 and arrived next day in Southampton. He was based in Hertford as the chief engineer of 11 Corps. This meant frequent trips around the country: cousins in the north and west and south reported his swift visits. No mention was ever made of what his job involved. In 1942 he was moved to the anti-aircraft command at Stanmore as Engineer Adviser. In 1944 he reported to the War Office as A.D.F.W. (I'm trying to discover what that stands for). He was billeted with Miss Wotton, Church Road, Watford. I know that his landlady had a cat which used to jump across her kitchen sink while she was washing up, making her exclaim. 'Going whoops like Miss Wotton' became useful family shorthand to describe anyone's surprised reaction.

In the summer of 1941 the cousins were acutely aware that Grace and Henry Werner were waiting anxiously for news of Roger, made even more anxious by Charles' death.

They heard at last in August, with a cable from Baghdad.

<u>From Grace Werner</u>

"I am glad for the moment that fighting has ceased in Iran as we gather he was in there. I expect he would be glad to see something of the war, he was so tired of doing so little in India."

Roger's letter is added to the Chronicle's pages.

Letter from Roger
"Dearest Mum
Well I have changed my address again but it doesn't really mean anything so don't worry about me. It doesn't look as though I'm ever going to see any real action in this War. I've been a bogus soldier for over a year now and have been bored stiff the whole time.
I wish I could get home to share some of your troubles, you must be having a pretty damnable time, but its absolutely impossible. I've been away from home for nearly 5 years now and there's not a hope of my getting home until the end of the war. I've only had a few long weekends' leave since I came out and could do with a few months at home. How is everybody? I haven't heard from you for months, I hope you got my letters from Poona.
By the way, the address at the top of this letter is the one for you to write to, it's not where I'm writing from. I will try and send you my proper address as soon as I am allowed to.
I met quite a number of men from the Assam Co a few weeks ago, most of them quite senior to me in the company but all very junior to me in the Army. Did I tell you about McFarlane (who came out with me) he has just married his Colonel's daughter obviously trying to make a career out of the Army. I only hope he does because the company aren't likely to take him back as he left a lot of big debts behind him in Assam. I sounded quite a number of people as to how I stood with the Company and everybody said I was absolutely certain to be taken back as I had been held up as an example to people joining up, as the only man of the first lot to go who had paid off all his debts and left his job in a decent state. It was a great relief to hear this as I was rather worrying about it all. I'm determined to go back to Assam after the War; having seen the rest of India I now realise how much better a place Assam is and how much more genuine Assam planters are, then either the Army crowd or the box wallahs of the towns.....
Well I have got to hand this into the P.O. so will finish this off now.
Love to John and you all and as this might just catch your birthday many happy returns to you.
Your loving son, Roger.
P.S. Please let me know at once if you are in a hole for cash as I can generally raise a little, especially now as I expect to be able to save quite a lot in the next few months."

In the following month's Chronicle Grace reported that Roger had sent a cable from Iran. *"Absolutely O.K. don"t worry. Hope getting my letters. Love to you all, Roger Werner.*" He'd given his address but Grace thought it wiser not to put it in the C.F.C. She would send it to anyone who would like to write to him.

It was a lottery whether anything sent by mail would escape the censor, even arrive at all. This added to the willingness of the cousins to write individual letters as well as ones for Cousin Alice to include in the Chronicle. Even when they thought that there was nothing worth writing about, they wrote. They would be surprised that the ordinariness of their daily lives could ever seem extraordinary. At the time, the benefit to them lay in the sharing of anxieties and experience. Their younger generation was constantly in mind.

Grace and Henry Werner, having lost Charles, had three surviving sons. Paul was in a reserved occupation and safe. But the factory where he worked was making gas and he'd suffered breathing problems. Roger was in the army, stationed far away from any action, that is, up to that moment. John was still a schoolboy but growing dangerously older. The family prayed the war would be over before he was called up. Trevor and Irene Becker had two sons: Michael whose health was problematic and Wilfred who was just 18. They were sharing the flat above Barclays Bank in Glossop and working at the boot factory. This must have been considered a reserved occupation. Wilfred had joined the Home Guard. Cecily, their elder daughter, was up at Oxford – for the time being. Juliet was only 10 and safe, so far as anyone in Britain was safe from bombing. Her wartime tragedy was being separated from her family for so much of the time. At the beginning of the war, she and her nurse Dorothy lived with Irene's mother in Bournemouth. When the school she attended was closed, she and Dorothy went to live in Glossop, after a brief and unsuccessful time lodging in Hertford and sharing a governess with the hostess's daughter who always had to be top. Irene did her best to see Juliet during the school holidays. But September 1941's Chronicle shows that this was not always possible.

From Irene Becker
"The first two weeks of September I spent at Bournemouth with my Mother; her house had been broken into by some naughty boys who

had a feast of tinned fruit, raisins, camp coffee etc, but luckily did no further damage, so she wanted to go there to see how everything else was getting on after a year's absence.

I enjoyed this time very much; the weather was lovely; Juliet was at Ringwood with Aunt Ciss. She had come down for her holiday with Dorothy as they both needed a change - Juliet after the measles – and Aunt Ciss had invited them to go there. We were all able to meet frequently. Trevor came down for a weekend and, although I was busy as we only had the gardener's wife for two hours in the mornings, it was altogether such a happy time and a holiday while it lasted. We were able to let Juliet bathe two or three times on the beach and she thoroughly enjoyed her swims and play in the sands. We got a lot of blackberries at Ringwood and I was very pleased to be able to make some jam for the store cupboard – a great luxury these days."

Kathleen Smithells, Grace's sister and daughter of Joe Henderson, had heard from Irene. *"She does seem to have had a busy rushing time. She is wonderful the way she tends her family – here and there."* As she and Archie did not have children, the young people she writes about are her Henderson nephews and nieces. *"We are expecting Joey to have leave, also Graham, Roy is going into the Navy soon."*

Grace had been staying with Ivy and Jack Crompton and in her letter she also mentions these names. Joey is her and Kathleen's brother. Graham and Roy are two of Joey and Gladys's four children.

From Grace Werner

"Roy, Joey's second boy has got his School Cert: and has left school. He is going into the Navy about Christmas time. He is at the moment doing Farm work. Graham is still in Ireland, both he and his father hope to get leave together in about three weeks time.

Alice came and spent the day with us here on Thursday 25th. I was glad to see her looking so well and rested, she was not looking very fit last time I saw her – I hope she will be very happy at Rye.

Paul is still working most weekends. He looks terribly tired. I do wonder how long these men will be able to keep it up. He never grumbles. He longs I know to be released for the Army or R.A.F. but as he is now a key man I am afraid he won't get his wish - and I for one am very glad although I know it's selfish."

September's folder ended with my mother's contribution:

From Molly Withington

"September has been a lovely month for weather and we had some picnics and some nice expeditions blackberrying, it has been a very good season for them. Unfortunately I could only make 8 lbs of jam as I had no more sugar left. I have had several half days of agricultural work, weeding turnips and lifting potatoes – but cannot go often as I get no petrol provided and one's allowance soon disappears. I have also been busy in the new 'Feeding Centre', two days a week, where we serve dinners for 90 or so schoolchildren every day. I see Dr J.J. Mallon[58] wrote in the Times strongly advocating midday meals for schoolchildren – Tavistock has two of these centres now going.

We are now looking forward to Dick's next leave which he hopes to get on 22 Oct. He has been very busy on manoeuvres again and quite enjoyed them though he was glad to get back to HQ for a bath and change of clothes after 6 days of it.

I much enjoyed the contribution to the last C.F.C. sent in by Juliet. What about one from Cecilia as I know she writes excellent letters. I also very much liked the snap of Cousin Joe and his daughters and send some of my daughters for this number!"

An earlier folder had included a photograph of Grace and Kathleen and their father Joe Henderson fishing in a small rowing boat on Lake Windermere. Kathleen mentioned that she'd caught 12 fish and been eaten alive by mosquitoes.

I look with great interest at all the photographs, particularly – naturally enough - the ones which include me. I'm searching for some inkling of the person I was at the time of the Chronicle. Aged three and a quarter, I posed on the moor just outside our garden gate. My right arm is raised high and pointing straight ahead while my head is turned to the camera. I guess I was being 'sweet'. I'd overheard myself being described this way. For some time I did 'being sweet' on purpose, until eventually I decided I was too old for it. I'd joined Jane at Miss Atridge-Smith's kindergarten, which entailed an adventurous walk over the moor to Whitchurch, braving on the way any long-horned, wild-haired cattle as well as 'Big Boots', the keeper of the cricket pitch who would shout and wave a stick at us.

Today, September 3rd 2015, a photograph of a three-year-old is being passed around the world's media. Aylan Kurdi was

---

[58] J.J. Mallon was a friend of Alice's from her Settlement days.

washed up on a Greek beach. He lies face down where gentle waves lap the sand. His five-year-old brother also drowned. So did his mother. His father says he now only wants to join them in a grave.

The refugee crisis has grown to apocalyptic proportions. Will the image of the little boy bring leaders in Europe to their senses? Ordinary citizens do their best, bringing blankets, water, soup and sandwiches to the refugees at the bottlenecks of Europe. For others of us, further away, what can we do? There are petitions. I've signed this one organised by Avaaz.

> "To German Chancellor Merkel, all Heads of State and Government of the EU, and the President of the European Commission:
>
> We, citizens from around the world, call on you to lead the world to a humane 21st century global refugee policy that saves lives and protects the people fleeing war and hunger. We urge you to significantly increase the number of refugees to be resettled and relocated across Europe in a way that shares responsibility across the EU and reunites families, give financial and technical support to countries on the frontline of the crisis like Greece and Italy, and oppose any military action that hinders rescue efforts or puts those seeking sanctuary at risk."[59]

*

---

[59] Petitions get us nowhere. This footnote added September 2016.

TEN

Leningrad, Pearl Harbour and the Fall of Singapore - 1941/1942

"A nice warm feeling of stretched-out hands."

When Russia and Germany were in alliance at the beginning of the war, both countries were our enemy. Even if some of us had earlier been in favour of communism's ideals or, at the other extreme, entertained sympathy for fascism, the two dictators had become an evil pair in our eyes. Both were as bad as each other. The Soviet Union was ruthless to citizens who opposed its will. We knew that thousands of Russian peasants' lives had been lost in the course of industrialisation (six million, in fact) while numberless dissidents were continually sent to Siberia. So it was disconcerting to find in the summer of 1941 that Stalin's Russia was now on our side against Germany. Hitler had invaded the lands of his erstwhile ally, who was still supplying him with tanks, fuel, and the use of ports for u-boats. As the Germans advanced into Russia, we breathed a brief and selfish sigh of relief. The two big bullies in the playground were fighting each other.

Not until much later were the details of the brutality and carnage in this War of the Titans known. Both leaders were ruthlessly single-minded. They were equally able to coerce their nations into obedience. They saw this as a righteous war against a subhuman species in which any atrocity was possible. The cause was just. The enemy's lands and resources must be appropriated and its peoples converted to Soviet communism or German fascism, depending who was speaking. Prisoners were starved to death or shot. On the Soviet side, Stalin ordered that there was to be no surrender and deserters were to be 'destroyed by all available means'. The numbers of dead, civilian as well as military, in the German-Russian war is beyond comprehension, with the sieges of the cities, first Leningrad, then Stalingrad, being perhaps the most appalling result of the intransigence of the two leaders.[60]

---

[60] In the autumn of 2016, Aleppo is suffering much the same fate.

The siege of Leningrad started in September 1941. The cousins didn't mention it, however much or little was known and featured on the BBC News at the time. 'Walls have ears' was one of the slogans to stop the population talking about anything that might help the enemy. News for the Chronicle was confined to safe topics, family matters.

While I was in the process of producing a typescript of the original newsletters, Ivy Crompton's handwriting became more familiar, and so did the people she wrote about. Several squiggles which first had to be typed as question marks were later recognised as names for people who could be fitted into the picture with some confidence. George was her son by her first marriage, with the surname Errington. Peggy was his wife. Bobby was another of Ivy's sons. Ivy was a somewhat reluctant mother and grandmother, judging by her contribution for October 1941.

> From Ivy Crompton
> "It has been a strenuous month for us but so dull for other people to read.
> It seems hardly worth recording the evacuation of our odd and oh so dirty and doggy tenant and all the redecorating and lifting of carpets and scrubbing of everything possible and impossible that had to take place. It was a herculean task to get through it in the allotted time, specially as I had an S.O.S from Peggy who was literally all alone, except for her 2 little girls, Caroline and Daphne, 2½ and 5 respectively. George having measles, Peggy was feeling things badly, so I went off to be with her and grapple with the offspring, no foolish grapple either, they are full of spirits and most unruly but very fascinating withal and difficult to suppress, though I find, thank goodness, that I can be a much sterner grandmother than mother in the back ages. I wonder if anyone remembers a wireless debate by G.K.Chesterton, and one other whom I forget, on "whether mothers were the proper people to look after their own children". The talk was flippant and very amusing but I felt relief immeasurable when it was decided that they were not.
> The major disaster of the month for us (and how small a disaster really) was the departure of our nice man Earl leaving us sans a gardener. We have been lucky enough to let our house and garden again with upkeep, but even so the cottage garden with all his other activities keeps Jack working harder than he ought to.
> Bobby and George are now both overseas and we were relieved to have cables of safe arrival from them both. Last month I gave a blood transfusion, a very simple process without any sensation, if nobody

has done it. I am glad to have experienced it as I now have to beat up the Ford people to volunteer. I find most people all agog so I don't suppose it will be difficult. I don't think there is anything else to report, and we are most warm and comfy in this cottage and almost .it is almost difficult to be sufficiently thankful.

I wonder so much if any cousins other than Grace and I keep chickens and if anyone has any rays of light about how to make the poultry ration go round?"

Grace wrote about hens in the same issue, October 1941.

From Grace Werner
"I like what my hens produce but I find they take up a good deal of my time. They get cleaned out each day and then they must have a warm meal in the afternoon. I give them the Government meal in the mornings. We get mostly two eggs and sometimes three a day and they have been a wonderful help with the invalids. The people in the Flat have been here just a year so they wanted to give me a present, because they said they had been, and still are, very happy here. To my great joy they have given me a wheelbarrow. I needed one so badly too. We think it most kind of them. My evacuees have gone, they have got a little house. I miss the little girl - she was a dear little thing, always singing round their part of the house or in the garden. I don't know what I shall be called upon now to do. I am offering to take parents or wives of the R.A.F who come up to visit the hospital. It is quite near here – so I feel the bedroom could be used that way.

It was lovely to have Joey home on leave and Graham too they both look so well. I saw them twice and they all came and spent a Sunday here too. Graham is still in Northern Ireland and Joey on the East coast and both seem likely to stay there for the present. Gladys has been looking at new schools for Josephine. She is getting too big for her present one. I think they have found one at Seascale – and she is to go at Easter. We still have Sam Small but her kitten has gone with the Barnes (evacuees) the little girl loved it so – and she always called it Little un so Little Un it will be to the end of its days."

As the Chronicle progresses, children grow and cats proliferate. Cousin Alice started the cat line with Tony who turned out to be female. At the start of the Chronicle, Tony was taken by Alice to Doncombe where he/she had kittens, one of which was christened Sam Small. That, too, turned out to be a kitten producer.

In September 1941, my mother follows Grace's contribution with news from Tavistock.

From Molly Withington
"We have a new member of the family, Scottie by name (after the Downderry cat) a very attractive black kitten, a son of Tony! He came by train from Doncombe in a basket and seemed an excellent traveller – the children were delighted with him and it is nice for them to have a pet as Dick has taken our black Labrador back to Headquarters with him. Although Cousin Jack wrote that the kitten was rather hideous we think he is decidedly handsome and he is full of character, moreover, he gets on very well with the cook, which is very sensible of him!"

At much the same time as Scottie, the Markham cat, was getting titbits from the cook, Russian cats were being eaten by the starving citizens of Leningrad. As the siege progressed, it wasn't just cats that aided survival; there were those who resorted to eating human flesh. Thousands of people were dying *each day*. Stalin would brook no surrender, although the privileged could escape.

Cousin Alice in November 1941 wrote that she and a friend called Agnes Guest had gone to see a film, 'A Day in Soviet Russia'. They were so enthralled by it that they saw it again two days later. I expect it was a propaganda film showing happy workers bringing in the harvest. We were to forget any of Stalin's atrocities against his own citizens that we may have heard about. We were urged to admire rather than fear Soviet Russia.

In this autumn of 2015, President Putin of Russia is presenting us with much the same puzzling proposition. As in 1941, we have to decide whether Russia is a valuable ally or a threatening enemy. Yesterday, September 30th, a Russian general knocked on the door of the American Embassy in Damascus with a message. The Russian air force was about to bomb Isis positions in north eastern Syria. US planes should keep out of the way. Short notice, but better than no warning at all. For a moment, the possibility hovered: was Russia going to lend its weight to the common cause, the defeat of the fundamentalists fighting to establish an Islamic State? It seemed so. Putin, in a speech the same day, evoked the alliance of Russia and the West in the war against Hitler. We are allies again, he said, this time fighting against the spread of Isis terrorists. Later in the day, it was clear that the Russian bombs had fallen, not on our common enemy but in the west of the country, on positions held by the rebels of the Syrian president Assad. The West supports the rebels, Russia bolsters Assad. We are allies, only in speech.

Meanwhile, Jeremy Corbyn, the newly elected leader of the Labour Party, was being pressed at the Labour Party conference on a crucial question: would he put his finger on the nuclear button if Britain was attacked? The motive lying at the heart of such a simplistic question is plain to see. Corbyn wants the UK to give up its nuclear deterrent. A large part of the parliamentary Labour party are against him on this and many other questions. They don't want him as leader taking them too far to the left for their comfort. So they throw doubt on his ability to win an election and become prime minister. A prime minister, they say, must protect his country's citizens against nuclear attack. Therefore, he must say publicly that he is willing to press the button of the deterrent for otherwise it does not act as a deterrent.

To such crude tick-the-box questions are politicians subject, in order to provide fodder for headlines. The more honest and straight-forward the politician, the more difficult it is to give a brief and simple answer that won't open the trapdoor to oblivion. How much easier it is to be a ruthless dictator, with a whole host of quick and lying sound bites.

I'm sitting in the sun with the original Chronicle's typescript open at page 197. The cousins are writing about the run-up to Christmas 1941 – the third Christmas of the war that at the start of the Chronicle they thought would be over before it had barely begun. The landscape spread before me lies silent and serene, the epitome of peace. The placid Red Devon bullocks in a distant field are as though fixed to the spot, brown-headed drawing pins stuck in a map. The depth of silence is broken, and accentuated, by a sudden, muffled clatter – something being unloaded or perhaps built – in the village out of sight behind the shoulder of our hill. I am at the garden table in the centre of the terrace, the prime seat in a rural dress circle. Between the two framing outposts of hills either side of the view, horizontal lines recede in fading colours into the distance. First, in the foreground, is a long bed of flowers where tortoiseshell butterflies flicker and rest on the wine-red heads of sedum among sea-blue anemones and the imperial-purple sprays of buddleia. Beyond lies a swathe of lawn and a border of shrubs, roses and dahlias in front of the rusty-green sycamore hedge that hides the lane below. From here the land drops steeply away to a receding expanse of fields that fit together like a satisfactorily completed jigsaw. Billows of hedgerow trees throw shadows across the varying greens, merging gradually into indistinct, grey-blue shapes of the far horizon. The tors of Dartmoor - sometimes seen clearly on the furthest horizon where my childhood home lay - do not exist today. Apart from the occasional stirrings in the invisible village, nothing can be heard but the breeze turning over the drying leaves and the occasional clatter of a pigeon's wings in the cypress tree which rises to my right, a mountain of sombre green against the clear blue sky. Then along the lane below comes a white van, its top half appearing above our boundary hedge. It's a supermarket delivery for the holidaymakers staying along the way. Food delivered to the door! – a re-emergence of a luxury that was sorely missed by Irene Becker among others.

> From Irene Becker, December 1941
> "Shopping these days is quite a problem. One has to collect all stores now as the shops cannot deliver very well; if you want fish it is only available at Glossop once a week and then it means a long wait in a queue. Everything has to be collected as required except greengroceries and there is all the cooking for the hungry family, the mending and much enlarging and making where Juliet is concerned! Not to mention the hens and the garden."

It is hard to imagine the wartime housewife's life, keeping a household clothed and fed on limited coupons, without electrical equipment like vacuum cleaners, refrigerators and washing machines, and without antibiotics to protect against measles, mumps, chickenpox and whooping cough. The children of the cousins were always down with one thing or another. Coughs and colds were much more severe and lasted longer. Clothes were passed on, patched, mended, let down, taken up, let in and let out. The first dress I had which was entirely new and not a cast-off came in a parcel from Canada. A friend of our parents sent two identical dresses, one for Jane, one for me. They were made of crisp cotton which had a sheen to it. Lavender-coloured flowers clustered on a dusky pink background. The dresses had puffed sleeves and a sash. We put them on at once and went out onto the moor to be photographed. It was only in retrospect that the idea dawned on us that we might have missed out by growing up in wartime.

<u>From Ivy Crompton, November 1941</u>
"I had such a fellow feeling for Kathleen when she said 'There is nothing to report which is always such a good way to begin.' Our little affairs are bound to sound so trivial in these fateful days – but the C.F.C gives a nice warm feeling of stretched out hands (which I am sure Alice meant it to have) to all our nice cousins and the beloved Aunt Loo.
<u>My</u> chief excitement this month is the very unexpected engagement of Bobby's ex governess, of whom I am immoderately fond. We had ten years together and I have since seen her through 2 bad operations. She is some 50 summers and I had given up all hope of anything of that kind for her and thought she must grow old alone – now a most wonderfully suitable partner has appeared in one of her boarders, a suitable age, a teetotaller, a pillar of the church, who looks as though he scrubs 3 times a day. The one crab is both are a little deaf so one feels they may have to spend days presenting each to the other their ears. But perhaps they will enjoy it. It is regrettable also that the wedding garment must be sternly let out down the side seams. I am terribly delighted about it all, and am to be her matron of honour (or whatever it is) and am frenziedly searching through my garments which grow less and less glad, so as not to let down the old firm. The only thing I feel any confidence in so far is a voile veil which I find is always the refuge of the destitute and gives an unfairly gala appearance to the head and face, but the rest remains and is difficult.
Our disappointment this month is a sailor-cum-gardener which we thought we had but had not caught. He was a curious old article who had spent most of his life in the navy and the police force, not good preparations for the post of gardener, but he seemed keen and called me everything he could think of from Mrs. and Mum to Milady and insisted on shaking hands warmly on departure. Jack and I decided that he might do to keep the place tidy and was at least a pair of hands but now even he has failed.
The cottage gets very damp if it is not lived in and is not an alluring habitation I fear though we spent such happy days in it. I have no fresh news of the boys, but it seems almost certain that George has not yet arrived on the Libyan front which is a blessed relief for the moment. Peggy seems to have succeeded in capturing a maiden of 19 to look after the children. I suppose it will give her a rest for the moment but I did hope she would manage to find somebody of a more

suitable age and a lady to help with them, they are (illegible) and want somebody properly trained to look after them but I am afraid Peggy is getting rather over done and has anxious days ahead. I sometimes feel like throwing up my canteen work and going to help her. I have a nasty but growing conviction that the care of the young is a task of 1st importance but I am not sure that I should shine in that particular sphere. I still go on with the canteen and there still seems to be plenty of food including really good plum cake to give the men which seems amazing.

We like our new tenants very much – she is going to have a baby (I now observe that I need not have underlined she - he could not of course) at the end of February. They wanted to take the house for a year and it may be rather difficult to dislodge them in April, if we want to which I fear we may. They are quite ignorant of horticultural matters and so far do almost nothing in the garden. Jack is the sole pillar and prop at present and it is far too much for him. I think I am rather sorry for gardens and ultimately perhaps for their owners, it is so sad to see them neglected but I expect they will have to go largely with so much that is beautiful and comforting. Jack is out shooting today and gets back very tired so I must cease and feed the fowls (or is it fouls) and prepare the dog's food before he gets back. Old Buster enjoys his days out enormously still, but is very tired and stiff by the end of the day. That happens to them both now and they are so devoted that I almost expect to see Jack developing brown and white spots and Buster check knickerbockers. Even the game seems to know there is a war on and bags are not up to standard this season.

Now, who has toiled through this tiresome tosh?"

I hesitate before excluding any of Cousin Ivy's 'tiresome tosh'. It is the detail in all the cousins' contributions that give the Chronicle its essential quality, in the way that the brush strokes of a painting create the picture.

In the present issue of the London Review of Books, T.J. Clark writes about the way Frank Auerbach's paintings communicate with the viewer.

"What Auerbach takes from the French tradition is easily stated. The qualities in a painting that command our attention, and strike us as making our existence in the world more comprehensible, do not essentially change as Delacroix gives way to Courbet and Monet and Pisarro and Van Gogh. What we demand is totality – unity in the concrete, unity containing complex difference within itself, unity made out of the detail and recalcitrance of the real... Painting has to give itself over entirely to unity and difference in the thing seen. ...The unity of

a picture is only compelling – only non-trivial – insofar as it persuades us that it is an instance of an order in the material of experience."

The Chronicle presents a picture of a family in a particular time and place - 'an instance of an order in the material of experience'. The context in which this picture was created was a global event with all its horrors against which the minutiae of English family life is seen. I take T.J. Clark's thoughts as permission to include 'the detail and recalcitrance of the real', even when – or perhaps particularly when – the content is as quaint as Lettice's instructions on how to make a hat from rug wool.

<u>From Lettice Williams, December 21 1941</u>
"In case you can make use of the tip for yourself or others, I have discovered that Rug Wool is to be had without coupons. The range of colouring is v. good – many of the same soft shades as tapestry wool. It is as thick as clothes line & 1/3 buys a hank sufficient for a hat & enough over with which to trim a jumper to match. I got a wooden meat skewer & bent out a hook with a red hot nail. I use the rope thickness for the brim &, as it is 6 ply, I unravel enough to do the crown. You get either 2 persons to hold 3 strands each or 3 persons to untwist it, holding 2 strands each. You can make a hat in an evening, & it is quite an amusing enterprise. I do the brim quite separate & make the finer wool crown & a sort of snood at the back all in one. Then you fiddle with the brim & set it on to the crown & snood at the desired angle. I sew it firmly. I consider it is a more becoming mode of head gear then the present 'street accident' bandaging of female heads so very prevalent just now.
 Mother & I will be here for X'mas & make no fuss at all of the occasion. I have made a large fruit cake as we decided our currants & raisins would go further this way rather than in an X'mas pudding bolted at one meal or only lasting 2 at most.
 Have you read 'Moment in Pekin' by LIN YUTANG. If not, do try to beg, borrow, or steal. It is completely fascinating & gives the reader a real insight into the tremendous changes from the old China of pre-Boxer days until the present horrors of Japanese invasion. LIN YUTANG is a genius of course. I read the 600 page novel twice over immediately & felt quite sad & lonely when I had parted with all the characters."

By Christmas 1941, the war had gathered momentum across the world. Japan had been unofficially fighting the

Chinese since 1937, with the vainglorious aim of conquering the vast country. Now the Japanese were engaged in freeing Asia from the clutches of western empires, an aim expressed in a field manual distributed to all Hirohito's soldiers as 'a noble cause to establish peace'. Their invasion of the Philippines and Malaya was preceded by a pre-emptive strike against America. On December 7th Japanese planes bombed the ships at anchor in Hawai's Pearl Harbour. The next day America declared war on Japan, and so did we. For us, Pearl Harbour was a boon. At last America with her vast industrial capacity and manpower was in the war with us. Throughout the world nations were taking sides: the Axis powers were Germany, Italy and Japan. The Allies were Britain, the Commonwealth nations and the United States. Allegiances, and the fortunes of war, wavered. In Iraq there had been a pro-Axis regime in April. By June there was a pro-Allied one. Greece which had rebuffed the Italian invasion in 1940 was now under the Nazis, as was Yugoslavia. In the desert sands of North Africa the scenes of combat moved from east to west and back again, as the fortunes of each army flourished and faded in turn.

From the pages of the Chronicle we understand, despite censorship whether official or self-inflicted, the ways in which members of the family were caught up in the war. Ted and Bob Easton in Canada were on the brink of enlisting; George Errington was serving in Libya; my uncle Dicky, my mother's younger brother, was on a gunnery course in Poona, India. Wilfred Becker was registered for military service and was awaiting his call-up. Irene wrote that Cecily's prospects of remaining a student at Somerville College *"for another two years or at any rate long enough to finish her course & get her honours degrees seem all to have faded out with the new call-up of women in their early twenties."*

<u>From Cecily Becker, December 24th 1941</u>
"I am hoping the war will end some day before I am too old to get my degree at Somerville, or at least to continue at whatever kind of post-war university there may be. I shall have to register on 10th. Jan. & want to get fixed up in some job before then if possible. At present I am rather more smitten with the idea of the Land Army than of any Forces job."

Grace Werner thought there was little of interest to write about. After her son Charles' death, it must have been hard to contribute to the Chronicle, especially at Christmastime. Yet she continued:

From Grace Werner
"One's life is shopping and working in the home and garden, also looking after my hens, which are a great joy. I have managed to get my ex-woman help to come back two mornings a week for a couple of hours each time. It's not much but better than no help at all. I was so glad to get a letter from Lettice telling me how to make a hat out of rug wool. If anyone wants to get the instructions I could pass them on. I am trying to do one myself at this moment.
In spite of everyone saying they were sending no cards, we have had quite a number. We spent a Christmas that was quite different from any other we have ever had. Kathleen and Archie came over on Christmas Eve, we all went to early church on Christmas morning and then off to the Queens Hotel at Alderney Edge for our Christmas Day dinner. It was better to do something quite different this year – we all felt that our usual party at home would be a hard trial, apart from our own heartache inside. I don't think any of us feel much real joy this Christmas, there is so much sorrow and suffering everywhere. I for one am glad it is past and gone.
Paul had another bad attack of gassing at the works which laid him out for a couple of days. Father has kept very well this last month. Now we are having a bad spell of fog and cold we feel he should take care – but it's difficult to make him see this.
We have found some lovely Czechs at the camp near here. Archie and Kathleen gave one of them a lift and brought him here as he knew nobody – all they want to do is to sit by the fire and look at books and listen to the wireless, very easy, we just go on with our plans and they do what they like.
John came home on the 19th. He, bless him, spent nearly all his Christmas money on buying me a lovely pair of bedroom slippers. He told Paul he wanted me to have something extra nice this year. Roger's letter on Christmas Eve was a splendid present – and helped me a lot. Henry seems very well if a little tired. I think he finds living so far from the works a bit of a drag – he seems to have been lucky in his rooms but living in the Club near the works was much easier for him.
Joey has been home on leave. He came to see me one Saturday. Gladys, Josephine, Gordon and Roy all came too. So we were eight for lunch and 12 for tea. Kathleen and Archie came and brought back Father who had been with them a week. Father's legs seem to be bothering him this cold weather. Joey looked very well. He was recalled from his leave – so expects there are some moves on the cards before long.

Sunday last, Charles' great friend Derek Hodgkinson and his young wife came to see us – it was lovely to be able to talk to them of those happy days here when the children were all young and happy. Derek, who only lived across the fields, used to be here every day and all day. I always feel as if he were my fifth son I know him so well. He comes to see us on his leaves without fail.

We feel very sad today. Dear little Blitz the kitten which Sam Small presented us with died today. He was ill only two days. The Vet said it was cats' distemper. We all miss him for he had grown into a charming cat and had such great personality and very beautiful to look at too. John has buried him in the garden and put a wooden cross on the grave. We now have no cat at all as his mother, Sam Small, has been missing since the beginning of December. We shall have to have one or we shall be overrun with mice. Having had such bad luck we feel afraid to get another for a bit.

We had a party for John on New Years Eve – it was great fun. We had six friends including one girl. The party broke at 12.30 and we drank the old year out and the new one in in very weak claret cup, mostly lemonade with some fruit salad dropped in. I quite liked it but Roy, Joey's boy, said it tasted like ink! All of the very best to everyone who reads this for 1942.

Roger's letter, 9.12.41 arrived Christmas Eve
Dearest Mum

With any luck you ought to get this letter for Christmas. Anyway here's all of the very best and here's hoping it won't be very long before I'm home for one. I <u>do hope</u> you have been getting my letters. I've had a birthday cable & one letter from you since you cabled about dear Charles. My letters were written from some pretty queer places so they may have taken some time to reach you. How is everybody? Give all & everyone my love & tell Paul I hope he got my reply to his letter. I have written to my bank in India telling them to arrange for some bonus money to be paid into your account but I don't know how long it will take to reach you. I hope things aren't too bad with you all now. <u>Please don't worry about me here</u> - we've had our spots of fun at various places but I'm not in any shadow of danger & only a little discomfort. I've had some very good shooting since I left India – gazelle, sand grouse, black partridge, duck, hare, snipe, blue cock pigeon & good chances at these & orial. There was such good shooting in various places that we've been to – that I always carried my shotgun (Pop's) ready in my truck even when we were supposedly driving into battle. I am sorry about this bad writing but I'm writing it in my <u>very small</u> tent & my torch is on the point of going out. I wish I could get home if only for a week or two. There is so much I should like to know but it looks as if it will be a hell of a long time before I can even hope for home leave. How's the garden at Wilmslow? Are the pigeons still there and has John managed to put some fish in the pond? Are the Williams still at Styche & do you see anything of them? Tell Mrs. W that I've caught some pretty queer kinds of fish since that day he gave me on his river. If John has any chance of using a fishing rod or a gun & wants one please ask him to write & tell me. I will send him the cash. No more room and my torch has nearly gone. I shall keep on writing & you do the same. Some of our letters should get through. I am always thinking of you. Love to you all & my New Year's resolution is <u>more letters home</u>. Roger."

Roger Werner had been in Assam for five years before the war broke out, making his career as a tea planter. I suspect he had not been a regular writer of letters home. All had now changed. His brother Charles had been killed and now he too was fighting in the war. Letters to and from his family had become vitally important, as had the Chronicle to its readers.

At the start of the issue for November 1941 Alice urged the men of the family to contribute:

From Alice Crompton
"We shall all heartily welcome the contribution in this issue from Joe. Will not some of the other men in the family follow his good example – Jack, Trevor, Dick*, Henry, Archie, Michael, Paul, Wilfred, John? We should all be glad to read their words. (Editor)
* Dick is quite ingenious enough to obscure his identity and his whereabouts, and yet tell his Cousins much of deep interest."

It wasn't until the end of the war that a contribution came from my father. He typed up notes he'd made on his journey out to Kenya for his final posting. Brief and to the point is the male style. Joe Henderson's contribution, from Sunnyside, Wilmslow, was about hens.

From Joe Henderson
"In the last C.F.C. Ivy asks about the care of hens. Grace has been very successful with hers and we put it down to having a good breed, Light Sussex and Rhode Island Reds, a dry house and regular feeding, a warm feed at night and not to give them more than they can consume in about 15 minutes. She has 6 hens, 3 of each breed and gets 15 to 20 eggs a week. She also gives them a lot of green leaves, hung up so that they have to jump up to get them and plenty of ash to scratch in, the outside run is only about 6ft by 6ft, very small, but wire netting is hard to get.
I was at Kathleen's for 3 days last week and tried to get some backgammon but my old Scotch friend was unable to come for a game. K and A are at Newby Bridge for tonight and tomorrow.

Archie has business to do in North Lancashire. We are undecided what to do at Xmas, a Turkey or Goose up to now seem very difficult to get, the few that farmers have to spare here are all spoken for and a family gathering with Joey and Graham unable to get leave would be very incomplete."

Irene responded to this in the next month's issue.

From Irene Becker, December 1941
"During Michael's illness I have been attending to his hens at Glossop (during December) and so was most interested to hear what Cousin Joe had to say about Grace's most successful venture. At Glossop we have seventeen hens between us – four White Wyandottes, 12 Light-Sussex & Rhode Island breed, all pullets and one brown hen from last year. They have all been laying fairly well since the middle of October but began to diminish slightly in the number of their eggs daily the week after X'mas. Of course the weather turned much colder then so that may have accounted for it. We always give them a meal of hot scraps & potato peelings boiled up and old carrots, which we get from the greengrocers, every afternoon at tea time and they have their balanced meal in the daytime and a quantity of cabbage stumps and outside leaves to scramble for during the day. It is very cold at Glossop and the water inside the hen house is nearly always frozen in the mornings and the poor creatures are very glad of a drink when anyone goes up. We have to keep the hen house locked as the run is a little way off from our flat up a hill into a frozen (just now) streamlet running down it. I am always very glad of a pair of Lancashire clogs I bought at Glossop last August before the leather supplies ran out. They are a god-send to keep up in the shed and slip on for tramping about in the wet and muddy (or frozen) hen run."

Trevor, despite Cousin Alice's prompting, only contributed once to the Chronicle. This was when he added a note explaining that the delay in forwarding the Chronicle had been caused by its becoming confused with an envelope containing the fees for Wilfred's schooling. Irene sometimes alludes to Trevor, excusing his lack of contributions by emphasising how hard he has to work.

From Irene Becker (continued)
"Trevor is very busy all the time and works all day in the City and at night after his dinner and the News on the wireless until very often 1 or 2 A.M. What with rubber crises, labour shortages and other difficulties it is as difficult to carry on at business as if one was directing a war on the Home Front! There seems to be always some new obstacle turning up and it is lucky he has an elastic mind for it

certainly seems stretched to breaking point sometimes these days! I hope Michael may be better before long and be able to help him a bit."

My mother's contribution ended the year. There are nuggets in it for me.

> From Molly Withington, December 1941
> "Not much news from Tavistock for the C.F.C. It has been a quiet month, no visitors or excitements at all, unless one expedition to Exeter for a day's shopping can be called exciting!
> Dick is well and very busy, and has a new General. He has been getting some shooting about once a week and Sam (the dog) is doing very well, although he wasn't trained in his youth, but he has good gun dogs as his parents."

I remember Sam, the first of our Labradors. When Jane and I were away at school, our mother wrote to tell us he'd drowned in a neighbour's ice-covered pond. The image of Sam struggling to get out has stayed with me. Only today do I realise why this name was bestowed on Sam, often known as Sambo, and on so many other black pets in the bad old days before we learnt better. In the news today is someone calling for Britain to apologise for our part in the slave trade and pay reparations. I might disapprove of the attitudes of previous generations but I can't blame them for being products of their time. What are we doing nowadays that in the future will horrify generations to come?[61]

My mother was typical of her time and class – a memsahib used to having native servants. "Little Black Sambo" was one of our favourite children's books. Her pre-war life of privilege did not stop her from volunteering for war work, some of it on the land. She continues:

> "I have been doing a good deal of war work of various kinds – thank goodness the potato lifting season has now finished. I did a good many days (or rather half days, as I find a morning at it quite enough) last month. I am now on a job for the billeting office, sorting our

---

[61] Today's taboos are yesterday's accepted behaviours. Today's accepted customs become tomorrow's taboos. We can evolve into something better than we are at any one time. I remember notices on buses "No hawking and spitting." The notices were necessary: men did hawk and spit !

forms into different parishes. It is rather like playing Happy Families. This district, rural and urban, is now a restricted area. The census has been taken for billeting purposes. It is quite amusing to read the reasons people produce for not having people billeted on them. One old man wrote 'I have 2 bedrooms, I sleeps in the front, and keeps potatoes in the back.' !"

She ends with the news that she still has her '*very nice young F.A.N.Y.*' billeted at Markham.

There was one FANY[62] Jane and I disliked extremely. In fact, we were frightened of her. She'd take us through the garden gate onto the moor to play. This involved making us lie the ground so that she could tickle us. We co-operated, knowing we musn't hurt an adult's feelings. We also knew that she didn't do the sort of tickling that would induce giggles, if it were done by someone other than her. This memory – where nothing happened that could be described as *wrong* though it felt entirely so - has helped me understand the slippery slope down which paedophile victims may slide. Our generation was particularly vulnerable, perhaps. Be polite! Don't hurt people's feelings! Co-operate!

My uncle, like Roger Werner, was in India and writing home regularly. My mother would often talk of him. I think it was at bathtime that we had her company, so I connect Uncle Dicky with the view from the bathroom. The window behind the basin faced west and was warmed by the setting sun. A bumpy line of trees on the hills the far side of the town, which lay unseen in the valley, became the land where I imagined my uncle lived among elephants. It was suitably 'far, far away'. On my windowsill today are two black elephants which I brought home from the flat where Dicky's widow died last spring.

My mother ended her contribution for December 1941 with the news that Dicky had been in Poona on a course before being moved to an anti-tank brigade at somewhere she called Trimuleguerry.

---

[62] Acronym for the First Aid Nursing Yeomanry, a charity founded in 1907. Members were originally mounted on horseback to tend the wounded in the front line of battle.

I've tracked this place down: Tirumalagiri is north of Hyderabad. Towards the end of 1941, the Japanese were spreading with little hindrance through Asia. After Burma and Malaya, India would be in their sights. There were many Indians who would welcome them, as a means of overthrowing the British Raj. Even highly educated Indians, often far more cultured than their masters, were treated as second-class citizens, excluded from clubs and forbidden to travel in the same railway carriages as the British. To quote Max Hastings, '*There was a mutiny in the Hyderabad Regiment when an Indian officer was ordered home for having sexual relations with a white woman.*'

Wherever they were in Asia, Westerners lived a life of such privilege that they felt invincible. The Japanese could not possibly take them over. Yet on December 8th, the day after the bombing of Pearl Harbour, the first Japanese bombs fell on Singapore. On December 10th two British ships, the *Repulse* and the *Prince of Wales*, were sunk off the coast of Malaya by Japanese aircraft. In the jungles of Malaya, British units disintegrated before relentless waves of Japanese soldiers. The army retreated further and further south. Max Hastings quotes from an officer's report. There were '*small leaderless parties of Indian and Gurkha troops firing in every direction.*' Singapore was surrendered on February 15th, a week after the colony was invaded. The terrible fate of prisoners in the hands of the Japanese is notorious.

*

ELEVEN

The Baedeker Raids – 1942

Snow, Burst pipes, Bombs, Epidemics

Alice starts January 1942's Chronicle with her Editorial Notes:
"*Two volumes of C.F.C. have now been completed, & this present number begins the third. I only hope the Cousins get as much pleasure & interest from it as I do! It seems to me rather unusual, & very delightful that our four groups know each other so well & are so friendly. In many families, as Trevor once remarked to me, cousins barely know one another.*"

It was not only the close relationships between the four groups of cousins that was remarkable. I'm even more impressed by their stamina in keeping up with their contributions to the Chronicle, despite the fullness of their daily lives and the haphazard nature of the mail in wartime. By the time January's folder had been circulated and returned to Alice it was May 19th. It's clear from the dates of receipt and despatch, although not always filled in by everyone, most of the cousins still managed to read and pass on each month's folder promptly – as well as writing their contributions for the next month. Up to January 1942, only January 1941's folder is missing. For 1942, Volume III, only December is missing. Looking ahead, from 1943 onwards, the number of issues falls sharply.

Irene's contribution is the first for 1942:

From Irene Becker
"There seems to be very little fresh news about our family for January. We are four of us collected in London now as Michael has just joined us. He, I am delighted to say, is very much better and has definitely profited by his ten weeks sojourn at Ruthin[63] Castle. He is to go on with his dope prescribed by the doctor here in collaboration

---

[63] Ruthin was a medieval castle which became a private hospital in 1923, specialising in the treatment of obscure digestive complaints.

with the Ruthin doctor and is going to help Trevor with some of his work in the meantime. Cecily is here, still awaiting the call to her war job and filling in the time with a course of first aid and Home Nursing lectures – an intensive course of a week for each with an exam at the end.

It has been a wretched month here, all January: snow, frost, thaw with streams of water everywhere as soon as it was all melted away, with the streets refusing to dry up before the same thing occurred again: another heavy fall of snow, frost followed by a very rapid thaw during which many pipes burst everywhere - in all the empty houses particularly! We had three which burst in different places in our old home, No. 70, and such a flood as the house had never seen! A man from the fire-watch came along to our flat early one morning to tell us our house was flooded and he could not turn off the stop-cock so Trevor and I hastily dressed and went along. Trevor collected a tool from his workshop and managed to stop the worst of the flow whilst I collected baths for the drips and swept gallons of filth out of the hall into the street, down the front door steps. It first had to pass over the well of the front door mat (about 4ft x 3ft in size & fairly deep for the thick mat), so I tried to collect the water into a bucket with a garden syringe Trevor found on the "late" roof garden, but this was a lengthy process and very stiffening for the back so I gave up and continued with the old yard broom! It gradually got swished out of the door and after some days dried up for a time until the next pipe burst and it did it all over again! We had some furniture in the basement in two rooms but luckily this was alright for, although a small stream had penetrated across one course of one stacked-up room, the furniture was mostly on legs, so didn't suffer any ill effects. The water froze after this and there was ice all down the stairs and on all the landings. It was quite a feat getting up and down!! And another flood when it thawed again. How thankful I was there was no furniture above the basement level! After this we got the plumbers and, after a good many hours' work and a visit from Metropolitan Water Board plumbers, the damage was repaired and now all is well and drying up. I am afraid a good many other houses about here have suffered the same way this winter.

Juliet has chicken-pox and was still getting more spots when I last heard, so sad to relate she has missed all school this term since it began on Jan. 19th. And it is now Feb. 6th. It is an odd thing that all the years we lived in London and all four children went to school – three of them to day schools, we never had any epidemics. Now, living in the Country - in the bracing North at that - within ten months three of them have had measles and Juliet chicken-pox as well!"

Measles, mumps, whooping cough, chicken pox – epidemics of these childhood diseases were commonplace. Each became a kind of rite of passage. Heavy colds and bouts of 'flu were routinely expected. Where today children might be dosed with antibiotics, in those years we were tucked up in bed. The gas fire was lit, a towel hung over our heads. We breathed in steaming balsam from the enamel basin held in our laps. When we were better but not yet allowed up, a tray was brought, laid with a napkin in a ring and perhaps a boiled egg in a special eggcup covered by an egg cosy in the shape of a hen, which we might have made ourselves from felt. Or the tray might carry the beginnings of a picture to be created from the numberless pieces of a vast jigsaw. Bits of a bright red train and some patches of sky would beg to be completed. Being ill would be heaven if only we weren't ill. We had to swallow spoonfuls of sticky brown medicine and whole glasses of concentrated orange juice with bits floating in it. Our heads were gummed up and aching. Nothing helped, except the passage of time.

I write these memories in a way that excludes the bearer of the trays. Was she my mother or Nanny Guerini, our Irish nurse? I only remember my mother being there for bathtime. A comment I saw somewhere in the Chronicle has stuck in my mind. "Susie is very good at amusing herself." In becoming a writer, I found a never-ending way of amusing myself.

In January 1942 the Werner household was also suffering from illness.

From Grace Werner
"A dull month, with beastly weather. Father went to stay with Kathleen for two weeks – he had been seedy with a cold – & we felt the change would do him good. He got back a week ago – but finds this snow bad for getting out & about.

Henry had a touch of gastric flu & was at home for a couple of days. Then Paul had it but they both got better surprisingly quickly.

John went back to school on the 23rd & has settled down quite happily again. He has to work hard this term for he takes his school cert. in the early summer. If he doesn't get it, we are wondering if it would be better to take him away from school & give him a few months with a tutor. I feel this might be a good idea – but Henry is against it – so we shall have to wait & see if he gets it, before we make any plans.

No more news of Roger. I expect it will be more difficult than ever now to get letters through. I had a nice long letter from Bobby – Ivy's son – from W. Africa, he seems to find it not too bad. I did tell him my impressions of it before he left. So he had some idea of what to expect. It was nice of him to write & I very much appreciate him doing it.

Paul's Czech friend spends a good deal of his time here – he is at the Camp here – a nice fellow - & no trouble. He expects to be on the move before long. I have a god-child of mine staying with me. I haven't seen her since she was 1 ½ years old. The day she arrived we were overjoyed to get a telegram from Dick to say he was up in these parts & could we have him for the night. In the end we had him here four days. He looks very well & cheerful – Father loved having him here. I did not get as much time as I would have liked to talk to him, as with a house full & no maid, one just never stops, I find. Dick & Paul swept all the snow off the paths on Sunday, we had such a heavy fall on Sat. night – but tonight they are all covered again & the sky looks grey with snow. How one hopes for the summer & some nice warm days.

A nice long letter from Aunt Loo last week – she sounds so full of life – it was a great joy to get her letter & to hear she is well & cheerful. Father had a nice long letter from Leigh. He has had his boy Harold home on leave. He is in the Dental Corps. The older boy is married & had been to stay with them with his wife, whom they all like very much. Evelyn, the older girl, is to be married in the "fall". They like her husband-to-be very much too.

We miss our two cats, Sam & Blitz. Paul has his eye on a nice one at the Works so I expect he will be bringing it home. He's so fond of a cat & we need one badly for with hens one always gets mice. Poor hens, how they hate the snow & the damp when it goes."

This contribution was followed by my mother's.

From Molly Withington
"News from Markham, Tavistock, Devon for January 1942.
I feel sure all the Cousins' letters this month will be about the snow as the weather seems to have been very severe everywhere except in West Devon & Cornwall; we have actually had our first sprinkling today (7th) - previously we've only had hailstorms. The children have been quite looking forward to snow & disappointed there is not more of it!
Dick got his orders on 12th Jan. left on the 14th. for *(piece cut away)* where he has joined the A.A. Command Headquarters as Engineer Adviser to the General Sir Frederick Pile."

In the original handwritten letters of the Chronicle there are pieces cut away, which I noted in the typescript as in the excerpt above. It's a surprise that the censor did not cut away more details of my father's new appointment. As I have no previous knowledge of his wartime career, I seize on snippets of information. The pages of the Chronicle give me rare glimpses of him as he visits this cousin or that, helps clear snow, plays backgammon with Joe, and - now in 1942 - becomes an engineer adviser in the A.A. Command Headquarters, under General Sir Frederick Pile who was the head of the Anti-aircraft Command throughout the Second World War. Batteries of heavy guns defended key targets such as airfields, the cities, and industrial sites. Perhaps an engineer adviser would advise on where to place the guns, and oversee the building of the emplacements. It seems he travelled around the country a good deal, as my mother goes on to relate.

> "It was lovely having him home nearly a fortnight and he had reasonably good weather, & was able to play golf most days. He also did some gardening and various useful jobs. He will have to do a lot of touring in the new job, as his area covers the British Isles, so he will be popping in on friends & relatives all over the place. He has just been away about 10 days in the Midlands, Lancs. & York, & spent several nights at Wilmslow, which was very nice for him. I expect they enjoyed having him. He was pretty well snowed up at York when he last wrote & I haven't heard if he was able to travel back to London on Wednesday.
> We have managed to stay clear of infection so far, touch wood, both mumps and gastric flu have been rampant here. My very nice young F.A.N.Y. *(piece cut away)* …billeted here since July – left this week on transfer to Salisbury & I miss her very much.
> My dear old Aunt Fanny[64] is in a poor way I'm afraid, the intense cold makes her so breathless, she has been in bed a fortnight and has a night nurse & we are naturally being very anxious about her."

By the time my mother wrote her contribution for the next month, Aunt Fanny was near the end of her long life, as my mother put it. I remember seeing this very old lady lying in bed, her head making a small dent on mountains of pillows. We were staying at Downderry, a short walk from Holloway Hill House where Aunt Fanny lay dying. She was, however, 'quite alert in her mind' as my mother reported.

---

[64] Fanny Mellersh was the sister of my grandmother 'Mop' and the unmarried daughter of Frederick Mellersh, whose bank in Godalming was taken over by Lloyds in the 19th century. Out of loyalty to the family tradition, we still bank with Lloyds.

> "She has been up to having visitors for a short time every day, and seeing the children has been a great pleasure to her.
> We came to Downderry, Godalming on 18 Feb. for a fortnight, really a belated X'mas visit wh. had to be postponed. It has been bitterly cold weather. Everyone has felt it except my Father, who is always clothed in layers of flannel & wool & tweed, & says we, none of us, wear enough underclothes."

I must interrupt my mother with a memory of Pop who had decided views on many subjects. At breakfast, he would bark at us in his retired Colonel way. "What? You're not having porridge? You ought to have porridge. There's nothing like porridge for starting the day."

To hand back to my mother:

> "Dick has been here both week-ends wh. has been v. pleasant, & we managed to get our family foursome yesterday at West Surrey wh. is always a popular event. The Club House has been taken over by the military, & there is a gun on the first tee!"

The family foursome would have been Mop, Pop, and my parents. This was before Mop's accident in the blackout, which occurred in November 1942. Mop was one the earliest women golfers. I have a photograph of her taken in the late 1890s playing in a long dress that covered her ankles. By the 1940s, she would have been wearing a tweed skirt that just covered her knees.

> "It has been rather too cold for the children to play in the garden, under the indulgent eye of 'Marshie' (the gardener) who is their willing slave, tho' the last few days have been better.
> There have been a lot of letters of various dates from my brother Dickie lately. He is now instructing in gunnery at Deccan College, Poona, which he quite likes.
> Jane has been having lessons every morning from her Aunt Mary (Mrs. Dickie Phillips) wh. she thoroughly enjoys. Mary is such a good teacher & makes her lessons so interesting & amusing, & I am sure Jane has learnt a lot from her."

I sat at the dining room table too, with a mug of pencils and a sheet of paper to share with Jane. I remember delighting in the satisfactory arrangements of dots which Aunt Mary pencilled within the squares she'd drawn on the page. I particularly liked the shape made by five dots. While Aunt

Mary's gentle presence hovered at our elbow, all you had to do was count up the dots in each square; say, five linked with a large, firm, plus sign to a square holding only two. Then you carefully entered, in the blank square after the equal sign, the figure which represented the total number of dots. The result earned a red crayoned tick. It was mesmerisingly neat in all kinds of ways. My love affair with numbers went sharply downhill after Aunt Mary died soon after the end of the war. She was in her 30s.

In the early months of 1942, the cousins in England, Montreal and British Columbia expressed relief that the news was getting better. America had formally declared war on Germany on January 3rd 1942. At the first session of the 77th Congress, a joint resolution was signed by Roosevelt:

"That the state of war between the United States and the Government of Germany which has thus been thrust upon the United States is hereby formally declared; and the President is hereby authorized and directed to employ the entire naval and military forces of the United States and the resources of the Government to carry on war against the Government of Germany; and, to bring the conflict to a successful termination, all of the resources of the country are hereby pledged by the Congress of the United States."

The wording - *thrust upon the United States* - acknowledged the reluctance of America to become involved in the conflict in Europe. After all, many of them had not long emigrated from European countries which were now allied with Germany. They'd have preferred to concentrate on fighting in the Pacific. Not only was Japan a closer threat on their western seaboard, it had also committed an unprovoked atrocity when it bombed Pearl Harbour in Hawaii. Churchill's eloquence came into play. On January 14th he persuaded the Americans to establish a Combined Chiefs of Staff and make the war in Europe the priority over the war in the Pacific.

Even so, and as the year progressed, increased anxiety is evident in the pages of the Chronicle. More of the younger generation had reached an age to be serving or were being trained to serve. Roy Henderson was in the Navy; Ted and Bob

Easton were on the brink of training in Canada. Cecily Becker was in the army, at an ATS training camp. The Errington boys were serving in Africa, George in Libya and Bobby in West Africa. My uncle Dickie was teaching gunnery in Poona. Paul Werner was training as a pilot. Graham Henderson had set sail for 'somewhere' in February. No word, Grace reported, had been heard of him since. Neither had there been news from her son Roger for a long while.

There was also renewed bombing. Ivy Crompton described the scene in Bath.

From Ivy Crompton
"I think Cousins may like to have an eye witness report of the damage done in poor lovely Bath. We are thankful, first of all, that not any of our friends & only one acquaintance was killed. But the place is pitiful – it seems to have been quite undefended &, as all know, was heavily raided on Saturday & Sunday night. I did not see it for a week as the public were not encouraged to crowd in to the city. I found the place strangely tidy & orderly & the people here taking the raids with marvellous control & fortitude. Everyone who knows and loves Bath will be glad to know that the Abbey, the Pump Room & the historic Circus, also Pulteney St., have suffered nothing more than broken windows. The Assembly Rooms, which have only lately been most beautifully restored, are completely & utterly gutted & were still smouldering when I was there. Mrs Bardsby's house (who some may know, beside Alice) was completely ruined. I went & found her scratching among her possessions, brave as a lion & entirely undaunted. I went up the stairs with her & surveyed the landscape, as the whole of the back of her house had been shattered & thrown down. One of the very beautiful houses exactly in the centre of the Royal Crescent was completely defaced & hollow & a house at the Victoria Park end, but nothing much besides. The poorer quarters had it the worst of all & the famous Lansdown Crescent has been almost completely wiped away.
It all seemed strangely orderly & I missed the tragic note, which I feel certain must have been too pitiful, as I was a week late on the scene. What I noticed was a certain stir of expectancy as the King & Queen & Winston Churchill were due to arrive. I was lucky to see them but was disappointed at the quiet & lack of enthusiasm of the crowd but I think they were still tired & tragic & dazed from suffering, poor dears. I was away both Saturday & Sunday night & so heard nothing but Jack & Mrs Harding said it was noisy & rather scaring here, but I found them both very well and none the worse for rough nights, on my return. I can hardly yet take in that the lovely city where I lived for more than 5 years has been so tragically battered. I have been told by several people that it was far the heaviest & most calculated raid

that has taken place outside of London. Mercifully the shelters must have been very good & well used, the loss of life is so far put at 335 which is unbelievably small when one sees the devastation wrought. Jack was there of course many more years than I, but I think we are a little glad that none of our 'haunts' have suffered."

This was in April's folder which Alice began with one of her admonishing notes.

"The MARGIN still seems a difficulty! Will people please <u>turn down each sheet</u> (like this one & like Grace's), & then the margin thus formed is right for both sides of the sheet. (There is no need to waste paper by leaving a margin on <u>both edges</u> of each page)."

Irene contributed what was, for her, a shorter piece, which included two contrasting paragraphs. The first described her recent stay with her mother in Bournemouth.

From Irene Becker
"We went over to Ringwood several times and Aunt Ciss & Lettice spent two odd days with us. We thoroughly enjoyed the continual meetings. They both seemed very well and cheery and we all went down to the cliffs at Branksome together to have a lovely drink-in of the sea-air, view of the bay and distant cliffs. The weather was lovely, clear and breezy with the sea as blue as the Mediterranean and the gentle white waves rolling away a hundred or so feet below us made one forget all about the war and the sordid things one reads about. What a beautiful world it seemed and we all felt so refreshed at the loveliness. The blackbirds & thrushes were full of song, the pine trees swishing and waving to & fro against the background of blue and there were masses of lilac of all shades and many wild cherries ablaze with colour and almost exotic perfume!"

The next paragraph passed on news of more bombing.

"I had a letter from a great friend of mine yesterday telling me a marvellous story of how she, her husband, son of thirteen and a land-girl billettee all escaped from the ruins of their home the other day after a direct hit by a high explosive bomb. Three of them were in the basement, the boy and the land-girl threw themselves forward on to the floor towards the door of the basement room in which they were sitting and the drawing room floor came down into their room and left a nice little hole just where they were! They all got out unscathed and walked down to a neighbour's – looking like mixtures of millers and chimney sweeps with bombs raining all round them! Such a lucky escape, though unfortunately their house and possessions are a hopeless ruin. I wired to her straight away to tell her to come up and get some clothes as soon as she can get some coupons, but I have a postcard today to say since writing to me she has been having a grand salvage party in the dank dark basement and has unearthed quite a lot of gear – all filthy, but she must now wait until it is all sorted before taking a trip to town! What a life! But I was thankful to receive her letter & know they were all safe at any rate."

My mother follows on with news of Aunt Fanny's death.

From Molly Withington
"Those of the Cousins who knew Aunt Fanny (Miss Mellersh) will be sorry to hear of her death on 19th March. When we left Downderry on the 4th, I knew she couldn't last very long, as the dropsy was gradually increasing, but her mind was unclouded to the last. Her passing leaves a great gap, as she has been the head of the Mellersh clan for so long – she would have been 93 on the 23rd of this month. It also means, alas, the end of Holloway Hill House which my grandfather built in 1850 – it was left to my mother, but it is quite impossible for her to keep up, especially in war time; the house requires 3 maids, and at one time there were always 3 gardeners, though they have been reduced to 2 for the last 3 years. Both the Military and the Surrey Education authorities are after the house. We would really prefer a school there, the lesser evil!"

In fact, the house was pulled down after the war and the land sold to a developer. A number of houses were built on the site, leaving no trace of the Mellersh home. This morning, on Google Earth, I took a virtual walk down a residential road lined with Scots pines in a cul de sac named Braemar Close. Cars were drawn up in front of garages, gardens extended around each of the many houses. I wondered if any signs lingered under lawns of the bombs which had fallen in the garden in 1941, as reported by my mother earlier in the Chronicle.

"Aunt Fanny (91½) has been in the frontline lately, 3 small H.E. bombs dropped in her garden, the nearest being a yard from the dining room window. She was writing letters in the dining room at the time – no damage done at all, not even a pane of glass broken! She was marvellous & insisted on walking all round the house & garden to see if there was any damage done. A greenhouse had some glass broken & two trees were damaged, but that's all."

After Holloway Hill House was demolished and before the developer got to work, my mother led me past the lodge and down the curving drive lined with overgrown rhododendrons. It was very quiet, just the sound of our feet crunching on the gravel. On we walked. The drive led to a clearing. Then my mother said "This place is full of ghosts." I pictured phantom figures flitting about behind the bushes, grey, gauzy shapes with eyeless sockets watching our progress. I dragged my mother back to the lodge and normality as fast as I could. She of course was simply mourning her Mellersh family. She had spent years of her childhood with her relations in Holloway Hill House while her parents were abroad, her father serving with the Royal Artillery in India and Bermuda.

> " I went up to Godalming for the funeral on the 23rd, and stayed on a few days helping my cousins, Beryl Lucas and George Mellersh, clear out drawers, cupboards, attics, etc. sorting out silver and various other jobs, a sad business. Dick was on tour in Scotland & couldn't get down for the funeral. He is going to Downderry for the Easter weekend, & will be due for his week's leave about 20th. April."

Downderry still exists but the only part of it which is still in the family is one quarter of its original garden. This was the vegetable garden where Jane and I used to take turns in a clattering, red pedal car to career along networks of sandy-soiled paths watched by Marshall the gardener. Jane and her husband Peter built a house in this part of the garden when the rest of Downderry was sold in the early 60s. They live there still.

My mother ended her days in the converted stables in the third quarter of the garden. She called it Markham, after the house in Tavistock which she had so loved. Even though rented, it had provided her with the first settled home of her life - thanks to the war breaking out after my father's appointment as commander of the Royal Engineers in Devonport. He'd gone off to France. She stayed put and became a steady hub for visiting friends and relations. I remember a constant stream of visitors all through my childhood.

From Molly Withington

"We had Roy Henderson, Joey's second boy, over for a weekend from (censored) and he is coming for Easter. He got on very well with Jane and Susan, who thought him a great acquisition in his 'sailor boy's' uniform. He much enjoyed his good meal and a comfortable bed."

I can almost feel the rough serge of his uniform and see his strangely shaped, bleached white, navy blue-trimmed collar. He – or was it his uniform? - was my first love.

The Mellersh cousins, who had lived with us for months to escape bombing in the south-east, had left to live in Gloucestershire, so there was more room for visitors. Cousin Alice always included Tavistock on her peregrinations (an Alice kind of word) around the country.

From Alice Crompton
"For the whole of May, I have been enjoying Molly's very kind hospitality at Tavistock....Jane is an earnest interesting little person. Susan is full of pranks and not in the least shy."

The whole of May! Alice was not a here-today, gone-tomorrow kind of visitor.

From Molly Withington
"Alice left us on the 1st June. I miss her companionship very much, she fitted into the family scheme most happily & took the greatest interest in the children. It was very amusing one day. I heard Susan (down the tube) inviting Alice to play "Hunt the Thimble" directly after breakfast. Alice couldn't quite make out what she wanted, so Sue marched off & fetched a thimble, so there should be no misunderstanding. However, Alice firmly said it was too early in the day for such goings on - very wisely! Susie is really very good at amusing herself while May & I are busy with our household duties. Jane is at school 9 – 12.30 five mornings a week."

In the following month's folder Alice returns to the thimble incident and comments:-

From Alice Crompton
"Some weeks ago Molly described little Susan's efforts to get across to me her wish to play 'Hunt the Thimble'. Soon after, I saw quoted from a book by the deaf son of my and Uncle Wilfred's old friend Sir Alfred Hopkinson, *"It seems to me that the difference between blindness & deafness is that a blind man loses things & a deaf man loses people... He is more handicapped in friendship, the world's*

greatest joy ...Worst of all it makes an impenetrable barrier between children & me ... To get into touch with children again will be one of the foremost attractions of life after death." (Pastor's Progress by A.W. Hopkinson."

Well, Cousin Alice, I feel in touch with you now while I work on your Cousins' Family Chronicle, even though I'm no longer the child called by my mother Susan, Sue and Susie, all in the same newsletter. My name is still as fluid, vacillating between these three names. I sometimes wonder if my personality is as indefinite.

From Alice Crompton
"I intended to keep a sort of Diary in Sep. for the C.F.C. jotting down happenings & considerations as they occurred, but it never came off, tho' I'm sure it wd be a good plan, & I hope to do it in Oct. – The chief events in Sep. have been our 2 raids. On 16 Sep. I went down at 5.55 a.m. to make my early cup of tea, & was drinking it in bed when Tony (cat) rushed in to the room & out again as if she were mad. She's never done this before, but, as she's still mother kittenish, (altho' a grandmother) I paid no heed. However, when she did the same again in even a more frenzied style, I realized that something must be happening, & at that moment, about 6.15 a.m. I heard & felt a terrific crash, & the air thickened. Fortunately I'd undone the black-out at 5.55 so from my window I saw the street covered with tiles cement & broken glass. I pulled on a garment, but could not open my bedroom door. A big bit of the latch side had been torn off, & wedged across. However I managed to wrench it away, & went out to see people gathering in the street, but no house actually fallen. Dressing as quickly as possible – quite forgetting to wash – I made a big teapot of tea, & went out with cups in a basket. Various people were glad of a hot drink, tho' it was a fine warm morning. I noticed my neighbour was sweeping in front of her cottage, (tho' it was rather like Mrs Partington & the Atlantic) I got my yard broom & cleared a fair way from my house up to Watchell St. – there I saw that a warehouse near the river had fallen & 2 dwelling houses (or more) were absolutely uninhabitable. Within an hour or two, men were at work mending. The next bombing was on 22 Sep. abt 2 p.m. Happily it was early closing day & no one was injured by the shattering of many big shop windows. Also the Cinema was empty, save for the Manager. It was totally wrecked by a direct hit, & he was killed. On

---

[65] Alice often referred to her home as her 'cot'. The dictionary describes this as an archaic and poetic form of the word 'cottage'. I think Alice used the word with these overtones in mind. I agree, having now seen Number 26 Mermaid Street. It is definitely an archaic and poetic cot.

the 2 raids there were 7 deaths & 40 injured (the majority slightly). The Church has lost some of the glass in the not v. beautiful or ancient E. window. The other old buildings are almost unscathed. My own cot[65] suffered <u>very</u> little tho' some of the houses close to have no windows, & big holes in the walls ...

At the time of the first raid, I had all the beautiful old Leigh & Becker dresses etc hanging up in my bedroom, as I was having 2 or 3 tea parties for people to see them. Happily they were none the worse when the dust was shaken out of them. But I was v. glad when I got them packed away again!

My chief interest in Sep. has been trying to organize help from Rye for China. Since the raids I feel all the more zeal for the Cause, for China has been suffering for 5 years what we have had for less than 3. So far I have 4 strings to my bow:-

1) a Bring & Buy or White Elephant Sale which the Women's' Voluntary Service will run.

2) a Whist Drive wh. a lady experienced in these things will run.

3) a Dance wh. I hope some of the local Military will run.

4) a Play (about China) plus a short Address (about China) plus a Show of Photos wh. I've asked the Min. of Information to lead. A show of Chinese dresses, curios, pictures, etc.

If any Cousins or friends will send objects (new or old) for the Sale, or lend things for the Show, I shall be deeply grateful.

I went up to town by an early train on 16 Oct. & saw 4 Exhibitions that day –

(1)   Modern British paintings bought by C.E.M.A. at National Gallery.

(2)   Chinese Exhib'n at Lady Cripps' H.Q.

(3)   Greek Art at Burlington House.

(4)   Architectural designs for rebuilding London.

All very interesting, & none of them so big as to be wearisome! I got bed & breakfast in Camden Town as p.g. with the daughter of one of my Settlement working man friends & was v. comfortable. Next day, early to Toynbee Hall to see Dr. Mallon, who expected to fly to U.S.A. in Nov. sent by the Ministry of Information to see American social work & tell them about ours. The route of the flight was to be via S. Africa & S. America, because of November weather conditions. J.V.M. had been looking up our taxation statistics & said that practically no one in this country has now more than £6000 a year. I then proceeded to Euston to see off to Oldham Marjory Lees, who had been staying with Lady Emmett for the Nat'l Council of Women Annual. Conference. She wanted me to go to Oldham for Xmas but I hope to carry on the China Campaign here in Jan. so am not going North till Feb. when I can stay 2 months or more on my usual round in Lancs, Cheshire & Westmorland.

In the afternoon I went to see the Merchant of Venice at the Westminster Theatre – very well done, (by Robert Atkins) except for

Portia who in the Trial Scene looked very much like the Principal Boy in a pantomime. But, of course, I remember Ellen Terry, I'm not sure that the M. of V. should be played just now. It is rather an encouragement to anti-Semitism. The stalls & pit were full of young school boys & girls. I lunched at Lyons' T Shop, & was pleased that it had adopted (like the ABC) the Cafeteria system of helping oneself. In the evening I dined at the Lyons' Corner House, 3 courses + Coffee & bread for 1/6, & v.g.! On Sun to Westminster Abbey at 10.30. There was on the grave of the Unknown Warrior the biggest & most beautiful wreath I've ever seen – entirely yellow flowers tied with an enormously wide dark green ribbon. The card on it said "Homage from the Delegation of Brazilian journalists." It was just after Brazil had joined the United Nations & was our latest Ally. I wondered if yellow & green are the Brazilian colours. I went out before the sermon, & called on Violet Dale & Lady Watts in Eccleston Sq. lunching with V.M. Dale. In the afternoon to an old Manchester friend Sir Philip Hartog, who retired from the Principalship of Dacca University some years ago. Again I dined at Lyons' Corner House, waiting in a queue a little time for my seat, but well worth it.

Back to Rye by the last train getting to Mermaid St. abt. 10.30 p.m.

On 21 Oct. Trevor had business in Eastbourne, & got here about 5 p.m. We had a stroll round the mutilated little town & then he insisted on dining me at "The George" our big & good hotel. I had meant to take him but had to give way! It was delightful to have him, & he looked well. We talked till midnight, & he left by the 9 o'c train next morning."

I pick up Alice's concern over the 'Merchant of Venice'. How much did she and the cousins know about the progress of the Nazis' campaign to exterminate the Jews? Some news must have filtered through of the mass slaughter not only of Jews, but also gypsies, Poles, Soviet prisoners of war, the inmates of mental asylums. Max Hastings writes that, at a press conference in November 1941, Rosenberg had publicly announced: *"Some six million Jews still live in the east, and this question can only be solved by a biological extermination of the whole of Jewry in Europe."* Hastings goes on to quote a letter which appeared in the Spectator in December 1942, written by a Mrs Blanche Dugdale:

"In March 1942, Himmler visited Poland and decreed that by the end of the year 50 per cent of the Jewish population should be exterminated ... and the pace seems to have been hastened since. Now the German programme demands the disappearance of all Jews ....Mass-murders on a scale

182

unheard-of since the dawn of civilization began immediately after the order was issued."[66]

Cousin Alice may have seen this letter in the Spectator. Her custom, when at home in Rye, was to go to the Club to read the papers, as she described in August 1942:

> From Alice Crompton
> "I've begun taking in the Times Literary Supplement, & find it very much worthwhile. I don't take any Daily papers as I see a great many at the Club, wh. I visit every morning & night. I do, however, very much miss the Manchester Guardian."

Whatever wartime events the cousins heard or didn't hear about, the subjects that were safe to write about were mainly familial and domestic: hens and their diet, the latest progeny in the line headed by Alice's cat Tony, rationing and recipes, vegetables and the vagaries of their growing, voluntary work and news of family members. In 1942 they would have shared in Grace's anxiety that lay behind the repetition over several months

Then in July the Werners heard that Roger had been taken prisoner. They greeted the news with joy and relief. Having lost one son, they'd been fearing the worst.

> From Grace Werner
> "It was a great joy & relief to get a P.C. from Roger on July 9th. ...The best way to write to him is on those Prisoner of War letter cards sold at most Post Offices now – price 3d. His transit camp address is Captain R.L.H. WERNER E.C. 889, Campo Guerra N. 66, PM. 3400, Italia.... All letters will be forwarded to him from there.
>
> We are now busy getting off his "next of kin" parcel – through the Red Cross. We may send 10 lbs in weight, no more – so it's going to be a squash to get all that we feel he may need into it. We cannot send another for three months & this will take from two to three months to get to him – so warmer things are what we feel he will need by the time it arrives. Kathleen has given him a lovely rug, which I was lucky enough to be able to buy here in Wilmslow: real Shetland – and only weighing 2lb 2 ozs. Shirts & Pyjamas are what we are sending as well - & that will be about all we can fit in this time – beyond a bar of washing soap & 1 lb of chocolate – both the latter will be put in by the Red Cross if we send the £.s.d. – they really do wonderful work & it is all so wonderfully well organised.

---

[66] page 513 and 514, *All Hell Let Loose*, Max Hastings.

I had the enclosed letter on July 29th.

"Dear Mrs Werner, This message was broadcast this morning for you – it came from the Vatican, Italy:-

'I am in the best of health, love & good wishes to family & friends. Capt. Roger L.H. Werner.'

For your interest, the boys say they are being well treated & that they look forward to their parcels which can be sent through the Red Cross. You will be able to send him a 25 word reply through the Apostolic Delegation, 54 Parkside London S.W. May I say how glad I am he is safe.

Yours very sincerely,
(Mrs) Gladys Gough.

P.S. I should be most grateful for a stamp when you write so that another Mother may receive news of her boy. Thank you. G.G."

I also had two P.C.s, one from the Catholic Times & one from someone in Scotland, giving me the same message. All of this helps to bring one a little nearer to Roger - & it must help him & others to feel they are not forgotten.

I went away on July 10th with Paul to Caernarvon for the weekend. I had not been sleeping too well - & the brief change did me a lot of good. Father was with Kathleen for over two weeks – so it made it easier for me to get away – one of the R.A.F. was on leave & Mrs Holthum in the Flat very kindly helped with the hens & the animals. One of my 6 young hens has turned out to be a cock. Which is rather a blow – I think he must be fattened for the pot for Christmas. I still have one of the old ones, which lays 6 eggs in seven days – the young ones won't start to lay before the end of August – I expect. Paul has received his papers & goes off on August 17th. He is overjoyed & for his sake I am pleased too for I know how he must feel now – with Charles gone & Roger a Prisoner of War. I should want to do my bit in a more exciting way than working where he is just now.

John came home on the 24th looking tired – I don't know what the result of his exam will be – we don't hear until the second week in September. He starts farm work this week for part of the holidays - & then I hope he will get a short holiday at the sea with the Wedds – before school starts again.

Letter from Roger, 20.6.42
Dearest Mum

I have already written two P.C.s which I hope you have received all right. I can write one letter card & one P.C. per week but I can give you no final address yet. It was all pretty ghastly at the time but I'm darned lucky to live. So I can't grumble I suppose. I never thought I should return to Europe this way. The food is fair … Ewen Kerr was captured in the same show and is unwounded. He was fit and cheerful when I last saw him a few days ago so please let Mrs. Kerr know. We got some Red Cross parcels yesterday they were damn good, please thank everybody you know that is connected with them. Could you find out from the Red Cross what the regulations are about sending parcels to me as they are rather vague at this end. At the moment I am short of clothes but I understand we will get some clothing issued to us by the Red Cross. I will use some of my letters in writing to my Bank (Lloyd's Bank, 137 Ch?, Calcutta) and get them to send you some money as I did not get much chance to spend my pay in the desert and have quite a decent balance, also I want to write to the Assam Co. so don't worry if you don't get a letter every week. It might be worth getting in touch with those distant relations Charles used to stay with as parcels & letters might be quickest through them. Tell anyone who might be interested what has happened to me as there is no limit to the letters I can receive but I can only send one letter & PC per week. Don't worry about me please at any rate I am safe until the end of the war which won't be long. Love Roger.

Letter from Roger, 25.6.42
Dearest Mum
I hope you received my last letter alright, I still can't give you any permanent address and rather doubt if I shall be able to next week. We aren't doing badly for food these days, as we get a Red Cross parcel between 5 of us every two days and can buy fresh fruit in addition to the two meals a day which are provided by the camp. We get 5 English cigarettes a day and can buy Italian Cigarettes which are pretty foul. Being a prisoner is something I never contemplated, I was dead certain that I should be killed and had quite made up my mind to it. I still can't quite understand why I wasn't. I was amazingly lucky. It was pretty unpleasant having to surrender but I didn't feel capable of taking on German Tanks single handed with a pistol. Ewen Kerr is in another transit Camp but I shall probably see him again when we get to our permanent Camp. I am sending a P.C. to my bank to try and get them to send you some money so that you can send me parcels. I don't know what you are allowed to send or how frequently you can send parcels but expect the Red Cross can tell you. Unfortunately, I have lost all my kit - practically everything I possessed including my gun which is about the worst blow of all. I will write and tell you what I need most when I get to my permanent camp. The Countryside here is very lovely or would be if it wasn't for the barbed wire in front of it. At the moment we can get practically no exercise but suspect there will be some arrangement for this in the next camp. Please try and encourage anybody and everybody to write to me. Love to you all. Roger."

*

TWELVE

The Fluctuating Fortunes of War – 1942

"It's a hard time now with so much fighting getting fiercer ...things must be worse before they are better."

It's not clear where Roger was fighting when he was taken prisoner. He had been in Baghdad, then India. Now, in the summer of 1942, he was in a camp in Italy. He was fortunate – for the moment. Prisoners of war in Italy were far more fortunate than those in German concentration camps or those taken prisoner in Russia. By 1 February 1942, almost 60 per cent of 3.35 million Soviet prisoners in German hands perished; by 1945, 3.3 million were dead out of 5.7 million taken captive.[67]

1942 was the year of the Wannsee Conference when Nazi leaders clarified their aims. Up to now, the liquidation of undesirables had not followed a consistent pattern. The Conference decided on the steps to be taken towards accomplishing the 'Final Solution', the extermination of all Jews in Germany's empire-to-be. Towards this aim and alongside the need for an expanded labour force, there would be a division between work camps and death camps. Those in the work camps might well die from starvation but until they did they could be used as slave labour. On the other hand, death came fast for the others. Nearly all who were transported to the death camps were dead within 24 hours.[68] Auschwitz, the most notorious of the concentration camps, combined both functions.

Anyone taken prisoner by the Japanese fared no better. In April 1942 three months after the Philippines capital, Manila, had fallen to the Japanese, 75,000 American troops surrendered from an impossible position, funnelled into the Bataan peninsula of Luzon island. Those too weak to walk the 65

---

[67] Max Hastings, ibid, p.505
[68] *Devoted to Terror*, Thomas Laquer, London Review of Books, 24.09.15 review of *KL: A History of the Nazi Concentration Camps* by Nikolaus Wachsmann

miles to the designated prison camp were bayoneted. The rest were starved and beaten, many to death. The prevailing attitude of the Japanese towards their prisoners was similar to that of the Nazis towards Jews and non-Aryans. The rules of the civilised world did not apply.

News from around the world would be anxiously followed by the cousins with serving members of the family in mind. Ivy wrote for the June folder that "*in spite of the wonderful air news, one feels very overshadowed by the portentous events in Libya & Russia.*"

Ivy may have been referring to the start of what was known as the Thousand Bomber raids, made possible by America's entry into the war. Wikipedia tells me that, on May 30th 1942, 1,047 aircraft were sent to bomb the city of Cologne. Nearly 900 planes reached the target and all had released their bombs within an hour and a half.

What about the '*portentous events in Libya and Russia*'? In May in the eastern Ukraine, the Soviet forces of Marshal Timoshenko's Southwest theatre of operations had begun a major offensive to capture Kharkov from the Germans. The Russian name so beguiled Cousin Alice that she christened one of Tony's kittens Timoshenko. Not such a good choice of name, as it turned out: the Marshal's offensive failed. "*Yet again,*" writes Max Hastings, "*a German counter-attack encircled the Russians and yet again Stalin refused to permit a retreat.*" More than a quarter of a million men were lost.

In the deserts of North Africa that summer, German and Italian troops under Rommel were pushing the Allies back from Libya towards Egypt. Tobruk fell on 21st June. By the end of June the Allied line of defence was at El Alamein, within Egypt. This was a humiliating retreat.

Gurkha troops were part of the Eighth Army fighting in North Africa, so it's likely that this is where Roger was taken prisoner. Two years before, he'd joined a Gurkha regiment from the Officers' Training School in Bombay.

Of other members of the family dispersed around the world, Roy Henderson was on his way from Northern Ireland to somewhere undisclosed. Grace reported that Graham Henderson was 'writing cheerfully' from Bombay, enjoying the life if not the heat. She wrote that he had been at (the name of the battle was censored) in Madagascar[69] and said it was 'a fine show.' No one would admit to not being cheerful. Alice said that the last time there'd been news of George Errington, he had written 'v. cheerfully' from Libya. Bobby was still, as far as she knew, in West Africa.

Grace wrote for the August folder:

From Grace Werner
"We have had three more P.C.s from Roger after a lapse of three weeks. He says he is well enough but lacks exercise (still at his transit camp). With the welcome aid of the Red Cross Parcels, they all get enough to eat ..
Paul went off cheerfully on the 16th, - he had to report near London on the 17th. You will all know how I hated him going. He writes happily & says "scrubbing out the lavatories & doing cook-house duty" has not humiliated him half so much as the fact that they have shaved his hair nearly to his head! He expects to be off any day now to do 6 weeks P.T. - where, he does not know. The house has been full ever since Paul left.
Dick[70] was here again for a welcome visit of two days. I had a friend's daughter here for two weeks & she overlapped with one of my God-children's Mother,.who was (fortunately) a flying visitor – having loads of photographs which we all in turn had to see & hear about!!! Mostly people we had neither seen nor heard of – very trying when one's days are so full.
Father has had a letter from Aunt Loo who says Bobbie is now in the R.A.F. My heart is with Molly for I know only too well how she is feeling – I shall hope & pray he may be kept in Canada."[71]

Aunt Loo – my grandmother Louisa – had lost her initial diffidence about contributing to the Chronicle. A newsletter she wrote appeared in the August issue:

From Louisa Withington
"Bob is still at Ladine – it is a sort of clearing house. They drill the cadets, find their uniforms - & decide what branch of the Air Force they are most fitted for. I expect he will be moved on to a training

---

[69] Madagascar was in the hands of Vichy France, collaborators with Germany. The 1,000-mile long island in the Indian Ocean was one of the places in North Africa where French and British troops were on opposing sides.
[70] Dick Withington, my father, Grace's first cousin once removed.
[71] Father = Joe Henderson; Aunt Loo = Louisa Withington; Bobbie = Bob Easton; Molly = Molly Easton

camp in a week or two now. We shall miss his visits – as he gets weekends off and also Wednesday evenings."

Aunt Loo and Grace's sister Kathleen Smithells seem to have been particularly fond of each other. Somehow I'm glad about that, as Kathleen comes over in her contributions as rather despairing. Her sentences finish abruptly and the subject matter changes equally sharply.

In August, she'd been painting her cellar shelter and her bedroom.

From Kathleen Smithells
"It is an awful thing to begin doing, as one simply goes on finding a bit more to do – I have been lucky to have the paint as it is most difficult to get – otherwise it would not have been done.
Archie has been having one of his do's & looks rather seedy. It takes him a week or so to get over it – we may go up north next week.
Our tomatoes are many but so green I fear they will never be ripe, I can see myself making green tomato chutney – I am trying to save some sugar for that. I have bottled plums & made jam. Lots of people are making apple rings.
We went over to Chapel en le Frith when Father was with us. It was the wettest afternoon we have had, so one got no fresh air, which we would have liked – Archie was kept until after 6 o'clock at his job, he called at Disley on his way out. I always enjoy that & so did Father as it was not raining then. We enjoyed the fresh air on the tops.
I have had a letter & a sweet little case,[72] which Aunt Loo has worked, I am so glad it did not go to the bottom – she also got my cap I made for her birthday. It is a comfort there is news of Roger again. I wish he could get our letters but I hope each week we shall hear he has.
We seem to have had no summer at all up north here. I wish we could get a fine spell.
I will now dash to the post with this, as I never grasped it was due, with all this painting."

Of all the Chronicle's contributors, she's the only one who often sounds despondent. Perhaps that's because she is the least busy. She looks after Archie Smithells, her husband, and – every so often - Joe Henderson, her and Grace's father.

Generally, the mood in the country had improved now that the Americans had at last joined in. *"We have lots of*

---

[72] I imagine this was an embroidered or tapestry sewing case. I keep sewing materials in a tapestry case made by Mop, my other grandmother.

Americans here, & motor cars. They seem very nice, though I have not seen much of them." This was in a letter to Alice in which Lettice enclosed a cash gift for her Aid to China Fund. Alice copied out the letter to include in the Chronicle. This was something she did whenever cousins wrote to her on paper the wrong size or without margins. It must have cost her much time and patience. Here is her copy of Lettice's September letter:

> From Lettice Williams
> "Owing to pressure of affairs in general, I am unable to help further in making or sending objects for the Sale. I can however contribute an idea or two if that will help! I find an empty square Gin or Whisky bottle can be made to look most attractive when decorated with gold & coloured paint applied with a match stick! I did some very pretty ones with a spot design. The gold paint is runny but a little practice makes one handy with it. After the gold is applied you dry it for 2 days, & then do more spots in the green & then dry again before applying the next colour. An empty Chianti carafe is a good shape too. If you have any very hideous well-shaped basins, or even old brown stew pots, you can paint them with white paint & do a nice winter dried flower arrangement in it, Honesty etc, & I saw in the paper that twigs etc painted with a <u>very strong</u> solution of Epsom Salts appear frosted when dry, but I have not tried it. Also toys are almost unobtainable: they can be made from the rag bag & cut out from a good pattern (one can trace one from a child's animal book). Smallish ones are best, but they must be <u>well stuffed</u>.
> I am now running our local C.H.S.S[73]. depot (since last May when my predecessor was called up). My Sec. has just left us to do mobile Canteen work for Miss Wavell so I have her job to do as well as my own. Here as elsewhere, personnel is dwindling with no hope of replacement. I have to keep my car running to get round my district with wool etc & have 5 villages where I go to see the heads of my sub-depots. So we take our tea with us & have it in the local ditch & this combines business with pleasure.
> Of course I cannot stir out by car except on Red X work. Yesterday I had to go to Winchester for the quarterly C.H.S.S. meeting, & I took Mother & our Chairwoman, so we had a nice day out & a <u>real</u> drive of 60 miles. Mother did some shopping while we were at our meeting, & we all had lunch in the car near the Cathedral. It was a lovely day too – so lucky.
> Re: oatcake, it is <u>very</u> tricky to make, & needs lbs of butter or marg spread on it to make it palatable. Here is my receipt – ½ lb medium

---

[73] The Central Hospital Supply Service was a branch of the Red Cross which supplied hospitals with pyjamas, towels, bandages and bed linen

oatmeal, 1 gill hot water, a knob of cooking fat (NOT marg) dissolved therein, ¼ T.spoon C of Soda, cut well together with a knife. Turn out on board. Divide mixture in half & roll out each half very thin. Bake on hot griddle or thick frying pan, scattered with meal until quite crisp & curled at the edges. Place in oven to dry out.

The following is an <u>excellent</u> receipt that deserves a place in C.F.C. for the benefit of the family, & humanity in general. Get a basin & a table fork & squash a medium sized cold cooked potato. Add 2 heaped tablespoonsful of S.R. floor, ditto grated cheese, good ¼ teaspoon salt, generous shake of pepper. Mix with the fork. Add under 1 table sp. milk & mix into a <u>very</u> stiff paste. Flour a board. Halve the mixture & roll each half out very thin. Cut each round into 4. Fry in a little smoking fat on both sides. It takes about 1½ mins. To fry each side a nice golden brown. Eat at once for either b'kfast, lunch, tea or dinner. Sage & onion <u>can</u> be added if liked, a small raw fine chopped onion & 1 tea sp. fresh chopped sage. I prefer it without."

Irene was as usual trekking from one home to another, looking after different members of her family. In March 1942 Irene's main preoccupation was not Juliet, the youngest of the family, but her elder daughter, who had recently joined up. My memories of Cecily (which the cousins spelt variously and usually pronounced Cicely) date from the time when, as a young adult, I used to visit the Beckers at 70 Eccleston Square. She was an attractive woman, probably in her mid-thirties at the time, with enviable hair: thick and copper-coloured, with a natural wave and bounce. I had absorbed the knowledge that she was 'fragile' which is why she lived at home, unlike Juliet who had moved away and trained as a solicitor. Now, with the Chronicle beside me, I guess that Cecily may have had what was later called a nervous breakdown. Joining up may have been a welcome alternative to continuing her degree, though she had trouble at first with army discipline.

<u>From Irene Becker, March 1942</u>
"Cecily says she had no idea before signing on how very much in the Army and under Military Law women can be! It is quite an effort for her so very independent spirit. She went off one icy morning when all the train windows were frozen and covered up in sheets of ice, in company with about 200 or so girls from Bermondsey and elsewhere in the East End of London. She didn't know a soul, so had to take pot luck about where she was to sleep on arrival at the camp. Nearly all the others paired off or went to-gether in parties of friends. They

were lodged in a huge building with many separate bedrooms along the corridors. She found herself lodged with two girls of 22, who looked about 16, from Bermondsey. One was Nellie and the other either Etty or Hetty. Cecily says she hasn't yet discovered which is the correct spelling! They were all very busy for a fortnight or more doing all the work at the Camp. Taking their turns at washing up, 6 girls at a time doing the job for 600! It sounds a good deal to us at home but needless to say the wash-up is done in quite a different manner to home doings and all the grease from the tops of the sinks is saved for salvage! They had their rooms to keep clean (and many of the former factory girls even had to learn to make their beds), the brass buttons & shoes to clean and all the other jobs of servicing the camp, as well as much marching, exercising and P.T. of various kinds, guard room duties etc. A fairly intensive training, as it was all completed within three weeks when they were all given 48 hours leave, and were ready after that to be posted to their new jobs.

Cecily came here for her leave, as it was more convenient to get here (Glossop) from where she was than to London, and although the work had been hard and she had worn through her first pair of shoes in less than 3 weeks, she looked very well – and that in spite of the fact that she had been labouring the whole time under the effects of a very heavy cold, inoculations for typhoid, vaccination etc. She said herself, "At the end of all this I am sure I shall be very tough."

I arrived here the same evening she did, and we all enjoyed her leave and hearing all the stories of events, and amusing incidents she had to tell. As usual she was full of spirits and had much to say about all that went on, a bit of grumbling at non-essentials and a certain amount of longing for Oxford but otherwise she was so fit and will ultimately settle down probably to get quite interested in the new job. She had found a piano of sorts (I think at the Y.W.C.A. hut) and asked me to bring up her Bach arias and a few things which were borne away back from her leave to-gether with one or two other treasures to be hidden under her mattress on arrival! They are not allowed suitcases and have only one small box, like a tuck-box beside their beds, in which to keep all their belongings. I said I hoped the cake and the biscuits would get eaten before they had to retire beneath the mattress!! But she said she was sure Nellie & Hetty would be very hungry on their return from leave. It was too far for them to go back to Bermondsey and besides they being rather homesick felt they might have too much difficulty in getting back to camp in time if they went so far; so they sallied forth to spend their leave at the nearest large town which was a short railway journey away only…"

By the September issue of the Chronicle, Cecily had finished her initial training, and Wilfred was expecting to join the army.

From Irene Becker, September 1942

"This last month I have been at Epsom, where I came on the 11th as I had to attend a committee meeting about then and afterwards wait for Cecily's leave which was due at the end of the month. Trevor unfortunately had to be away part of the time, at Portsmouth & Southampton, where he had to go on business but he managed to put in a weekend with his Mother and Lettice en route; and afterwards he went up to Glossop for a week. Wilfred is expecting to join the Army as a new recruit any day now as he has passed his medical test and is only waiting to receive his orders as to destination etc. At the moment he is very occupied winding up his affairs & finishing off the threads of his work before he goes from Glossop, but he rather hopes to be able to get down here to see Cecily if possible & there is time before he goes.

Cecily left her last depot and arrived here on Monday evening with all her army worldly goods as she now goes on to the O.C.T.U. (Officer Cadet Training Unit) which is in a most convenient spot and she will be able to come home for short outings we hope. Now only long journeys can be undertaken by troops on leave, and even these much less frequently than before, so it is indeed good fortune to be within a reasonable travelling distance of home. I wish Wilfred could be as lucky!

Cecily arrived at dusk at Kings' Cross so Mike and I both went up to meet her on Monday, as porters are getting very scarce these days & can usually only attend to first class passengers - and taxis scarcer still.

We met her finally on the outside-the-train-station-end of an enormously long train, which end had to be un-coupled and brought in on another platform. When we at last found Cecily, we had to return to the other part of the train on the first platform to find her luggage – kit bag, a crate and a bicycle. The bicycle we disposed of in the left-luggage office for the time being and then we made our way by underground, each carrying a part of the luggage, to Waterloo & Epsom. I must say I much prefer the underground as a means of travel to buses in black-out! It is a joy getting down below to the bright lights once more, like going from England in the Winter to Riviera sunshine, in former balmy days!

Cecily has finally said good-bye to what she has termed her first "attery" and friends there, and is quite looking forward to the adventures at the new place. We have been told about two officers there who are known to mutual friends, who have promised to look out for her when she arrives.

I shall be going up to Glossop, in about a week, I expect - probably sooner -after Cecily has departed, to see Wilfred before he goes. I am afraid Juliet will miss him very much as she is always so devoted to him and has spent so much of her life living under the same roof.

Nora, my cook and housekeeper here, has taken a part-time job in a factory now as a war time measure. She was due to register yesterday and, as it would be very difficult for me to carry on with this flat without her living in it & putting in some time when I am away, she thought the best thing would be for her to get a part time job. So she has got one at a place in the neighbourhood to which she can get by 'bus conveniently in the early morning. Unfortunately there was nothing available locally. She gets back each day in the early afternoon so will be able to carry on for me when I go up to Glossop for my sojourns there. I shall be able to do all the morning doings & shopping when I am here so that she can have all her energies for the war-work. But it will be a great relief to have her living here to look after Trevor & Mike; after all, all they really need is their dinner cooked in the evenings & lunch on Sundays. So this arrangement suits very well and I feel now none of us are idle anyway! But I shall be busy I expect and shall not have time to waste or let the grass grow under my feet. At Glossop I always find plenty of occupation with the animals & garden as well.

I hope Cecily will be able to write a small contribution but she is busy now – acknowledging birthday greetings and has no time to-day so I will post this and forward Cecily's if and when it appears! It is a great relief to have her so much better in health than she was a year ago."

Jack Crompton sent in a contribution for September 1942 in which he mentioned another member of the family in the ATS. This was Josephine, the daughter of Joey and Gladys Henderson. Joey was the son of Joe and brother of Grace, Kathleen and Leigh. At the time of the Chronicle, Joey was in his late middle-age. At the start of the war he had managed to re-join the Army as a sergeant in the Artillery but by 1942 he was out, being over 50. Joey and Gladys's children were Graham, also in the Royal Artillery, Josephine, Roy (of the sailor suit I liked so much) and Gordon.

From Jack Crompton, September 1942
"Ivy & Gladys[74] are away at the moment. They have gone to Sutton to see Gladys's daughter in the A.T.S. who has apparently been sent to a rest cure there. She has been in ever since the start and is possibly overstrained. Foot & Mouth still raging round here, tho' no more cases actually in the village.

---

[74] The Gladys Jack refers to may be Grace's sister-in-law, the wife of Joey Henderson, the mother of Josephine. Alternatively, she may be Ivy's sister, referred to by Ivy in her November newsletter as living in one of the Doncombe Mill cottages.

After a fine week during which I began to dig our potatoes, it has become entirely unsettled. Some days entirely wet, but mostly very heavy showers with sunny intervals. We have a bumper crop & I have got some in very well, but the greater part I am storing in a clamp, & I have a lot dug piled in a heap on the ground. I keep them covered in the wet as far as possible but I'm afraid they may not like the conditions. When too wet to work outside I have *inter alia* been getting our car ready for the road again. It has been laid up here since Dec 1939 &, as the garage is none too dry, it has meant a good deal of work as all terminals & connections have to be drained, pump & carburettor taken down & replaced & so on. However I am nearly through now. The car will be used to take Home Guards to lectures, and so on & also she is to haul a gun. It may be rather amusing & she will be all the better for a run. Ivy is very anxious to drive her again & I don't see why she shouldn't. It will of course be solely on HG duty.

There is a lot to do in the garden apart from the potatoes, weeds are growing galore & I can't keep them down. My late sown peas look like doing well, if we can keep the birds from them. Last year we had them up to Nov."

Ivy wrote a short contribution for the November issue, in which she talked of Buster, the springer spaniel that she and Jack had inherited from my parents, when my father was posted to Hong Kong where Jane was born in 1936.

From Ivy Crompton
"I find it hard to write anything at present except a bitter chat about our dear old Buster who was killed in the road earlier this month. Poor old dog, we did not see it happen but Jack found him on the roadside before he died & quite thinks he did not suffer. One misses him at every turn & it will be hard for Jack to get over it, as Buster has been so companionable always, & specially since Jack has been unable to talk or do much socially. However we must not forget the happy years of dear old Buster's reign, or how grateful we are to Dick & Molly who made them possible. There will never be such a beautiful spaniel in every sense & Jack says he will never try to replace him.

It is a hard time now with so much fighting getting fiercer everywhere - & specially in Egypt, where one feels things must be worse before they are better.

I have both cottages full now. Jack & Mabel Harding & I in one & my sister Gladys & her daughter in the other; we have communal feeding & it works very well, we are also fortunate enough to cook & heat by the same weapon & so are fairly cosy, we also cut up a lot of wood for open fires. The gardens look very sad but downpours of rain almost all October have made it impossible to get on the land to any extent. We have lent our car for the Home Guard & she goes out about twice a week to take them to lectures etc. It felt very bitter at first to see her driven off by their people but now perhaps it will be to the good as we shall not get her tyres commandeered if it comes. We have marvellous crops of potatoes but the problem is to store them: this part of the world seems to be suffering from a plague of rats & mice. Everyone is complaining very bitterly & I have heard the theory put forth that it is because all barns and outbuildings have been so disinfected on account of the Foot & Mouth disease that has literally raged all round here. Fortunately it seems to be dying down a little now - there has certainly been enough rain to wash it away but I don't know if it's done good. We have been busy today getting the indoor chrysanthemums under cover as we have had 2 hard frosts already; we look like having a good lot, which is a boon as winter flowers will certainly be scarce & ruinous when obtainable. I am sorry for the gardeners from that angle, though gardens are such a strain in these labourless days & so heart-breaking when they fall into neglect, though of course not comparable with other heartbreaks now, so perhaps we should turn a kind & complacent eye – now that I have written it I think "complacent eye" sounds like a nasty disease. The rainfall here has been quite phenomenal for the last month so that we cannot do even the jobs we could find time for & we are at least a month late with operations.

I don't think there is anything else to report. Peggy hears regularly from George by cable he seems well & cheerful up to date, thank God."

So Ivy had a sister called Gladys living in one of the Doncombe Mill cottages with her daughter. Is this, I wonder, a coincidence of names or was there a doubling up of relationships – Gladys, the wife of Joey Henderson, being also the sister of Ivy Crompton? At the end of a morning's chronicling, I shall leave these questions. Instead I shall try to follow a Lettice recipe for our lunch. [75]

In October 1942 Grace Werner gave news of five of the cousins' young men: her sons -Paul in Scotland in the RAF, Roger in Italy in prisoner of war camp, and John still a schoolboy; and her Henderson nephews - Roy in the Navy and Graham, serving with the Royal Artillery, in an Indian hospital with malaria.

---

[75] Not something I will repeat. See my comment on the result at the end of the chapter.

From Grace Werner, October 1942
"One special thing that has happened this month is that Paul got home for 48 hours – a big surprise & a very nice one. He looks wonderfully well & happy, & seems not to have a care in the world. He loves the life and the fatigues leave him cold - & there seem to be plenty of the latter in the R.A.F.

Four letters from Roger this month too – he seems to be well enough and to be making the best of it, poor lad. I am sure he hates it.

We had Roy here, too, for four days. His little ship had been run into & he had had twelve hours up to his waist in water, but seemed to make very light of it. It does make one's heart swell - these young men are so brave. He looks charming too in his uniform.

John is home at the moment having his eyes tested, also an overhaul from our doctor. So far nothing can be found to cause his sickness & headaches. It may only be that he is growing rather fast. So he is to have a tonic & emulsion. I think the whole thing is caused by him being bitterly disappointed that he failed to get his School Certificate. It really has worried him a lot. He is now to go back to Trent until next July when he will take it again. After that he wants badly to go on to an Agricultural College for a year before joining up, which he should just about be able to manage.

Joey[76] has gone and got a job of sorts - just what I have not really heard, but am thankful something has turned up at last for him. I miss him here very much. He still may stay odd weeks here, as I believe he may have to do night work alternate weeks. Graham, Joey's eldest boy, is still in Hospital - he's been there for four or five weeks, suffering from the after-effects of a bad attack of malaria.

We have all but five trees stripped of apples so should have enough to last us well through the winter. Henry has just had a week's leave here - & has had a good rest. He spent a good deal of time trying to find a Works to take him in nearer here – but so far with no luck. But something may come of some of his interviews in time. Anyway, he went back feeling better & able to carry on again – but he has very long hours & a long trek to get to the works from his rooms each day."

Grace copied out Paul's and Roger's latest letters for the Chronicle. The holes which Alice skewered through the paper in order to thread sheets together sometimes left gaps in words here and there:

Letters from Roger, Sept 27 & Oct 4th.
"Received your two letters dated Sept 4th & 16 (*hole*) this week. I was worried to hear about your ear trouble, but hope it's much better now.

---

[76] Joey was Grace's brother

You must take care of yourself. Sorry to hear two of your letters have gone astray. Glad cigarettes are on the way. I need them very badly. The contents of the parcel sound perfect. Don't worry if you cannot get the corduroy trousers, but send some trousers of some sort, also please a decent shaving brush. Have received a letter from Aunt Juliette and another from Babette Woodward since I last wrote. I wish I could send some more replies, it's very good of people to write so regularly when I can only send an occasional P.C. in reply. I am studying Italian & trying to improve my Gurkhati to pass the time & keep the old brain working. I'm also playing quite a lot of bridge, so am managing to pass the *(punched hole)* days fairly cheerfully.

It's still perfect weather here, wish you could have some of the lovely air. I understand it gets pretty cold in the winter. Glad Paul is enjoying his training. How long will it take - & what is he going to try to be? ... I do hope John is staying on another year at Trent, even if he has got his School Cert., which I fear you seem to think unlikely. Let me know as soon as Pop[77] finds out anything about my pay. Hope it will be possible to send me some books - they will be essential in the winter here. Love to you all Roger.

Dearest Mum, I have had no letter from you since I wrote to you last two weeks ago, but received the following – Cousin Dick, Cousin Molly, one each from Cousin Jack & Ivy, one from Mrs Baker & a very welcome letter too from Babs Williams. It's really incredibly decent of them all to write, & I'm very, very grateful. I shall try & send a P.C. every week in reply to someone, but please will you thank them too – as I have said before, letters mean absolutely everything to me here.

There is a Captain Peter O'Bree here from the same regiment as myself, who is & has been for some time a great friend of mine. His Mother's address is Mrs H.M. O'Bree, Rotherslade, Mumbles, S. Wales – I have given you her address so that if any letters cease or anything should happen for any unknown reason – you could probably get news of me through her, & Peter has sent home your address for the same reason.

We expect to be moving into new buildings in a few weeks, which are a great improvement, four officers only in a room. I expect to be sharing a room with Peter, a British army Captain & a naval bloke. Have you managed to do anything about paper or books? This address can be regarded as permanent as I have said before – so please dear Mum, don't delay in sending the books - & specially cigarettes. Please could you send the odd ordinary letter enclosing snaps of you all? I do hope you aren't worrying too much about me – I'm quite alright a bit flabby perhaps & rather too fat – due to too much liquid food but really very fit. Anyway look after yourself. Yours with love Roger."

---

[77] This 'Pop' was his father, Henry Werner

Between copying out these two letters from Roger and another from Paul, Grace adds an underlined note to Alice. *'Sorry Forgot the Margin.'* Throughout the course of the war and the life of the Chronicle, the margin caused the cousins headaches. Even Alice herself forgot it on one occasion, to her chagrin.

> Letter from Paul Werner, October 1942
> "From Paul. 30/10/42, N. Scotland
> Dearest Mother, thank you for the sugar, & please thank Auntie for the syrup. I do hope it doesn't mean either of you will have to go short. We had Bags of Bull on Thursday. The Duchess of Gloucester was here & she took the march past. She looked very cold. I went to a dance at one of the Wings last night. I almost need an interpreter when talking to the girls. Shall not get a leave out pass for three weeks, as I must pass my progress exam first. I have to do an extra Parade today, been a naughty boy & not made my bed in time this morning!! Please send my Ping Pong bats. Much love - take care of yourself. Paul."

The next month's folder, the last for 1942, had only three newsletters, from Ivy, from Grace and from my mother. Each sounded cheerful despite circumstances. This is the cousins' style: a balancing act between the bad and good aspects of an event.

"*George is not so slightly wounded as we had hoped but he is not in pain which is a blessing*," wrote Ivy. This is the first we've heard of her son's wounding.

My mother's newsletter included news of her mother's accident. "*November was clouded for us by my poor mother's accident. She has been so brave and good about it, but has had a great deal of pain and shock to contend with.*" Mop had been knocked down in the black-out by another pedestrian, an event which I included in the Introduction.

To end this chapter and 1942, I'll finish with a report of my test of Lettice's recipe for potato cakes. I followed her instructions exactly, sternly disregarding my impulse to mash the potato with margarine and break in an egg. Her single tablespoon of milk and the grated cheese bind the dry mixture well enough to roll out on a floured board. Using self-raising flour is important as it responds better than plain flour to the process of mixing and cooking. The result: edible potato cakes, enough for a light lunch for two. I send Lettice a smile and thanks for a wartime recipe that would work well enough today, should times get *really hard*.

*

THIRTEEN

Death camps and Prisoners of War - 1943

"I do feel you ought to have the one letter I'm allowed to send each week."

On Sunday 18th October 2015, an Observer article quoted the view of a citizen of Aleppo where the Free Syrian Army has its main headquarters: *"If Iran bombs us, it is world war three. The Arab world would join us because it would be Persia against Syria. This is why the regime has played it smartly, by bringing in the Russians."* The headline above a photograph of vegetable stalls in a street of shattered buildings read: 'Russia and Iran line up with Assad as brutal final battle for Aleppo begins.'[78]

"We are confused about the Americans," said Malafji of the rebel FSA who'd hoped for more support.

For anyone who remembers October 1962 when the US and Russia faced each other over a chasm of potential nuclear disaster during the Cuban missile crisis, any line-up of a Russian side against an American one is a reminder of that particular precipice.

In World War Two, just a couple of decades before the Cuban crisis, Russia and America were on the same side. Both nations were Britain's saviours: Russia, through becoming Hitler's chief target; and the US, by joining the war as our indispensable ally. Were it not for these two countries, our island history would have been unimaginably different. In 1943 the war was on the cusp of turning in the Allies' favour. In February the Russians won the Battle of Stalingrad. German troops under Rommel were on the retreat in North Africa. The Allies were gaining a foothold in Italy and in Burma.

Despite the better news, this is the point in the war when the Chronicle shrinks. Until now, the cousins had been

---

[78] ***Final*** battle? It continues today, October 2016, as I proof-read this book. About 275,000 people are besieged in eastern Aleppo. *"Tensions between the US and Russia are raised to their highest levels in years but the Cold War rivals do not wield clear control over their nominal proxies."* Anna Barnard, New York Times, Oct. 6 2016.

fortunate in losing only two months' worth of the Chronicle in the three years of its existence. But for 1943 only the folders for three months, January, June and July, exist. Cousins often mention letters which have gone astray, perhaps in mid-Atlantic. *"Maybe the fishes got them,"* as Helen Henderson wrote, referring to the moccasins her husband Leigh had sent to his father Joe Henderson from British Columbia. Ships were constantly lost in the Atlantic to U-boats. In May of that year, for instance, 34 Allied ships were sunk by U-boats. However, improved anti-submarine tactics resulted in the sinking of 43 U-boats.

In January's folder Grace includes letters from Roger written the previous November and December. He'd been moved.

Letters from Roger, November, December 1942
"November 30th 1942. from Captain R.L.H. Werner, P.M. 17 – P.G. 3200, Italy.
As you will see I have moved quite suddenly & at night – but it's all for the better. I am in a kind of bogus Castle – but we have heating of a kind & some fires too - & I haven't slept in a good bed since I left India. Also the food is better & we are not quite so hungry. I only hope my letter & parcel of cigarettes & books will be forwarded on – so far I haven't heard from anyone for four weeks. Peter O'Bree (*I met his mother in London.* G.W.) had to be left behind with jaundice. I saw him once in hospital – I only hope they won't send him to another Camp when he is fit to travel – Derek's crowd have been very noisy round here the last few nights – but I have felt only joy to hear them & have stayed in my bed.
*(*Derek is a friend of Roger's &- before he, too, was taken a prisoner - was in the R.A.F. G.W.)
21.12.42 Have received five letters since I last wrote – they were forwarded on from my last Camp. Two from you, one from Auntie K, one from Auntie Punch, & one from Auntie Gladys. Please thank them all so much for their Christmas wishes – I only hope the books snaps & cigarettes will arrive soon. Sorry to hear about George Errington's wound; I hope it isn't too bad – he must be very annoyed to be out of things just now that they are really interesting. There is a Captain here from a North Country regiment who lives near Lyndhurst, & knows Peggy & George quite well. His name is Robert Ferguson & he's a most amusing bloke. When you next write to Ivy ask her to pass on my salaams to Peggy. No personal parcels have arrived at this Camp yet – I keep hoping mine will arrive. I more than need a change of clothes!!

28.12 42 Received seven letters this week – Auntie Kathleen, Auntie Juliette, You, Babette, Grandfather & the "Count". We had an extremely good Christmas …considering our position: a special Christmas Red Cross parcel & an excellent dinner. I had more on my plate than I could cope with - the first time I've been in that sort of position for many months. We had snow on Christmas Eve – so I had my first white Christmas for a long time. I am glad you are to meet Mrs O'Bree – her son Peter is a great fellow – I hope it won't be long before he comes on here .

All Red Cross parcels are reduced now to one every two weeks, owing – so I hear – to transport difficulties. I only hope it won't mean our clothing parcels will be held up. I do need the change badly – I hate looking so untidy – also I long for some good English cigarettes. Please thank everyone for their kindness in writing to me – I only wish I could write to everyone, but I do feel you ought to have the one letter I am allowed to send each week. I will try & send the odd P.C. in turn. I hope you & everyone had a good Christmas - & let's hope & pray this will be the last one I spend behind barbed wire or at any rate as a P.O.W."

The Becker news in January includes a long contribution from Cecily.

From Cecily Becker

"I was posted from my training centre at Durham to O.C.T.U. in October, and from there came straight on to the A.A. TRG. Regt. which houses the T.C.O. Officers Trg. School for A.T.S., which has only recently come into existence[79]. I did not volunteer for the work but am not really sorry I am about to become a Royal Artillery officer now that the course in gunnery is nearly over. I think that we shall feel we are doing a real war job by taking over some of the male officers' work on gun sites. Very often, there is little operational activity for us to cope with, which may be all very well for most women but the wrong life for men who are wanted in the front line offensive. By learning the job of plotting officers, we shall directly replace the men.

I think one of our chief problems on a gun site is that of keeping the girls interested in their work and play. There is a good deal of time on our hands which has to be used up in educational lectures, discussions etc. No doubt the battery will get sick of the sound of our voices after a few weekly A.B.C.A[80]. sessions! I suppose

---

[79] Military abbreviations: OCTU=Officer Cadet Training Unit; AA TRG Regt=Anti-Aircraft Training Regiment; TCO=Tactical Combat Operations; ATS=Women's Auxiliary Territorial Service. From 1941 all unmarried women between 20 and 30 years old were called up to join one of the auxiliary services: ATS, the Army; WRNS, the Navy, WAAF, the Air Force.

responsibilities will shower upon us when we leave this school, though up till now we have tasted more of the privileges than the worries of a commission.

For a change the other day, I took over Regimental Orderly Officer's duties for the Trg. Regt. to which we are attached. Unfortunately we know nothing about the workings of the regiment other than the people who teach us and feed us in the school, so I was rather at a loss when it came to dealing with an awkward situation in the middle of my night of duty. I was just getting into bed at 12.30 a.m. after an inspection of quarters to see that all inmates and a batch of new arrivals were settled in for the night, when the telephone rang and I was put through to a somewhat perturbed male duty officer who, in my absence, had taken a call from the Wolverhampton police station about an A.T.S. absentee, who had been landed on them at a late hour. My problem was to find some method of removing the girl (of whom incidentally I'd never heard) to army quarters immediately. It is against military law to shut any A.T.S. in cells for the night and the police evidently seemed disinclined to send her straight to the nearest Attery, which is the normal method of dealing with such a situation. The duty officer had promised that I would do the dirty work for them by finding the A.T.S. Adjutant who would be able to put them in touch with the appropriate authorities. There was I in my nightdress with not the remotest idea where to find the said Adjutant; by the time I had dressed, found the officers' quarters for permanent staff (she slept in a spider hut, one amongst a network of some twelve allocated to two regiments) it was getting on for 2 a.m. and the poor woman thought I was at least a burglar, barging in at that hour of the morning. She suggested the girl should be put in a cell for the night if nothing else could be done with her, and confirmed my own opinion that it was quite impossible to send an escort to collect her until the morning, besides being unable herself to get at a location statement which would enlighten the police, without considerable palaver. Eventually, I rang up the police myself and was about to have a spot of bother with them on the subject of cells, when a call came through from A.T.S. nearby who volunteered, as of course they were obliged to, to fetch the girl for the night. I should be interested to have a word with the girl who must now be back in the regiment, but I believe she was ill and not entirely to blame for her behaviour, so I should feel forced to sing softly to her. Had I but known my powers as a Regimental Orderly officer, I should have opposed the duty officer's plan to wake the Adjutant and taken upon myself powers of colonel of the regiment, telling the police to deal with the matter themselves. Such is the price of ignorance! It is rather a strange idea, though, that a temporary population such as ours should take on a job of this kind. I gather it was an emergency expedient for the benefit of members of

---

[80] An abbreviation beyond my decoding ability.

the permanent staff, who were previously taking orderly duties too frequently, and so we were called upon to help out.

I am falling asleep at a fairly early hour as usual in the army – due, I think, to a surfeit of starchy food which satisfies one's hunger but hardly livens one's wits. I will break off for now."

And this from Alice ….

From Alice Crompton

"My other jaunt was to the Pantomime with Marjory Lees & Mrs. Sutherland who is with her "for the duration". It was an excellent show, acting, dresses, music, lighting, all good, & many jokes. They tried without outstanding success to get the audience to do a bit of community singing, & let down on a small screen: the words as follows (as well as we can remember them)

> Rommel's done a double at Agheila,
> Von Bock has got a knock at Stalingrad,
> The R.A.F. has made a mess of Genoa,
> And Malta's driven Mussolini mad.
> McArthur has thrown out Japs in New Guinea,
> The Aussies & the Yanks are doing grand,
> But Montgomery's the one to turn the Desert Song
> Into Alexander's Ragtime Band.

I continue to get in money for China, & have abt. £36 for Part II of my campaign."

This is followed by Jack's contribution.

From Jack Crompton, January 17 1943

"Continuing my account of my efforts to get a war job: after some 2 months of messing about, I finally heard from the firm I had been in touch with that they had nothing for me. Feeling rather desperate, I decided to cut out Labour Exchanges & went direct to the only large works in Chippenham. They met me more than half way & I have taken a job in the factory as Inspector. I explained that transport would be difficult but I am putting the car on the road again & they will back my application for petrol. Meanwhile I get there as & when I can. The hours are 7.30 a.m. to 7 p.m. & alternate ½ days on Sat. & Sun. I started on Tues at 9 a.m. till 5 & continued these hours till Friday night when my transport ceased. However, tomorrow I can get taken in & out at the proper times till such time as I get the car & then I hope to arrange some pooling system & so avoid 2 cars being on the road together.

I am thankful to be at last on direct war work & hope I shall be able to hold it down. I find the atmosphere of a large machine shop exhilarating – I have always felt it like that & am interested & amused at the changes since my early days. There are many old men, even up to 80, with masses of flappers & a good many youths. I suppose about 50% are middle aged men - mainly on the heavier and more skilled work. A permanent black-out but the lighting is extraordinarily good & one hardly notices the difference when coming out into daylight. The canteen is excellent – meat course, potatoes & veg. 9d. Tea 1p per cup, sweetened alas but not aggressively, loud speakers blaring forth music at intervals & always a feminine voice beseeching "Mr. X – Please, Mr. X - Please," then "Mr. B. Foreman Millwright. Mr. B. PLEASE." This goes on all the time & makes me jump if I happen to be under the loud speaker at the time."

This gives a good picture not just of the factory but of the writer, too. Elaine Davis, a present-day assistant at the Chippenham Museum and Heritage, thinks it most likely that the factory where Jack became an Inspector was the Westinghouse Brake and Signal Company. The factory produced, on a huge and intensive scale, metal rectifiers and other components vital for the war effort, such as searchlight control gear, gyro compass gear, junction boxes, cable glands, contact stacks for anti-submarine apparatus, sector lights for aircraft carriers, solenoids for fire control equipment ... the detailed list of essential war products made by just this one factory makes clear the mammoth demands of warfare on manufacturing.[81].

By January 1943, Jack had become a fairly regular Chronicle contributor. Perhaps his sister made sure of that. I look for a family resemblance in their manner of expressing themselves. Here is Alice's contribution which starts the next folder, after a gap of several months.

From Alice Crompton, June 1943
"With a considerable effort, I finished my single-handed spring cleaning of my cottage just before I left it on 22 June. One week I had various little diversions, going out to tea 3 times & having a friend to tea one day. Now that the Cinema is destroyed, there is no public place of entertainment nearer than Hastings.
I put away all my good china very carefully, with the help of my friend Miss Manning, &, by dint of toiling till midnight on 21st & rising next day at 5 a.m,. got off all right by 9 a.m. train on 22nd.

---

[81] *'A Hundred Years of Speed with Safety'* by O.S. Nock

A great complication arose when Tony had 2 kittens on 14th. I kept one, & called it Limosa, as it was born at the time the 3 Italian islands (Pantelleria etc) surrendered. The difficulty was to arrange for cat & kit in my absence. I spent ages trying to find someone to board them out with. Friends & the vet all declined, & I cannot even get neighbours to come in with food. Late in the aft. of 21st, to my joy, 2 kind sisters with whom I have a slight acquaintance, promised to feed Tony daily. So I got off with an easy mind, & went to Guildford on 22nd to see Dr. Jobson. I had some time to wait at his house, & his (2nd) wife, a very pleasant woman, kindly gave me tea.

Then I tried to get to Epsom by bus wh. I've done before & enjoyed the pretty run. But there was such a huge queue that I gave it up, & went by train instead. At the Beckers' flat I found Tre, Irene, Mike & Norah[82] – the two men not too well. We had a delicious dinner including asparagus, peas & raspberries, & a good talk.

Next day Tre & Ir. both went into town with me & Tre saw me into the thro' carriage for Tavistock. Marvellous to relate I was <u>alone</u> till Exeter, & easily got a cup of tea there. Soon after Exeter the train passes thro' a fine country, & there were glorious masses of foxgloves & honeysuckle. On reaching Markham I was grieved to learn that both children were in bed with temperatures & so on, & Susie's birthday party next day was put off. However they were on the mend, & the improvement steadily continued, so that they were soon able to be out & about again. They have grown a good deal since I was here a year ago, & Jane writes v. nicely, spells very well, & is a great reader. They are an attentive little couple, & Molly dresses them very prettily, daintily, & sensibly. The household runs very smoothly, with resident cook & half daily housemaid. Molly gets to the British Restaurant for abt. 4 hrs. once a week, & I go too to wash up for 2 hrs. They provide a v.g. meal for 9d: meat & veg. 6d pudding 2d, tea 1d. It's the best Brit. Rest. I've so far struck, I think. Perhaps not better than Wilmslow, but a trifle cheaper.

I hope to stay at Tavistock till abt. 28 July, & then go to Mrs Watts at Bournemouth, perhaps. Things seem to be quiet in my "home town" so far, but the little place has been much battered. At the end of the month I heard to my sorrow that Limosa, the little black kitten, had died, & that, afterwards, Tony had disappeared. However I heard later that she had come back & recovered all right. I feel I was right to refuse for 6 years to keep any animal. It was mice wh. drove me to Tony, & she rid me of them completely. Of course she has also given me much pleasure & amusement.   I see Irene asks suggestions for stopping a plague of ants. <u>Powdered borax</u> does the trick. A thick layer on the floor of the store cupboard & on the shelves, if necessary, should be a complete cure, as it was with me in Rye a few years ago.

---

[82] Norah was the Beckers' cook.

Before I came away I had been unable for months to buy Salad dressing. It can still be got in Tavistock. In case it may be useful to anyone, here's a recipe.

Salad dressing without oil.

Mix together 1 teasp. each salt, mustard, flour. 1 tablesp. sugar, a few grains cayenne. Then add 1 tablesp. melted butter, yolk of one egg (egg is not really necessary), slightly beaten, ½ cup milk. Then add slowly 3 tablesp. vinegar. Cook in a double saucepan till thick like custard.

I got this recipe in Cornwall at a very comfortable sort of boarding house where they did one well for 25/- a week! (Early in the Kaiser's war).

When I get back from Leigh Henderson the back no's of C.F.C., I don't quite like to destroy them. What does the family think about it? I am quite willing to house them as long as I have a roof. But perhaps it is sentimental to keep them. Any expression of opinion below will be welcomed by A.C."

When Alice asked for the cousins' views on keeping the back numbers of the Chronicle in June 1943, two years' worth of monthly folders had completed the circuit and returned to her for safe keeping. None of the cousins could foresee that the war, and their stamina for writing monthly newsletters, would continue for another three long years. Alice added the responses to her question from Grace and Jack. Grace, naturally enough, wanted to be given all the contributions in which there was mention of Charles, or letters from or about him. Jack Crompton thought that, if some public-spirited person would look after the folders, the Cousins' Family Chronicle would be of increasing interest in the future.

The other cousins must have agreed with Jack that the Chronicle should be kept, and Alice would continue as their curator until her death. Whether she bequeathed them to John Werner or to another cousin, John was the 'public-spirited person' who was looking after the folders when I first set eyes on them. The Chronicle was in his safe keeping until his death in 2013. The original is now in the hands of his middle daughter, Nicola.

In 1943 John was still a schoolboy, hoping to join the Fleet Air Arm on leaving school. He wrote a contribution for the June folder.

From John Werner, June 1943

"A few days ago I arrived home after about the most interesting week of my life, at an R.A.F. Fighter Station "somewhere" in the Eastern Counties, I obviously cannot give many details of aircraft etc., as apart from being a fighter 'drome they experiment with new planes and types of armament.

To give the cousins some idea of the daily routine I will give an enlarged page of my diary for a week last Tuesday. Reveille at 6.30, got up had a (voluntary!!) cold bath, made my bed, folded my blankets & did Barrack Room Orderly. Then marched down to breakfast - the airmen's messing room is worked on the Cafeteria system & we lined up for porridge, sausages, tea & bread, margarine, and marmalade.

After breakfast there is a break from about 7.45 to 8.45. At 8.45 comes the daily Square Bashing (or marching) on the Barrack Square, in the course of which the Warrant Officer tells you, in no uncertain language, where to go. After this come two different Parades. First we went to the Parachute Room & saw the chutes being packed, then we paid a visit to a satellite drome & saw the captured German aircraft, in flying condition, two bombers & two fighters. We had their kites explained to us by pilots who had flown them and the corresponding British type, which was very interesting.

After lunch about a dozen of us paraded at Dispersal point & two of us at a time got about 30-minute flights in Airspeed Oxfords. However, by far my most interesting flight was the one which two of us cadged a few days later. We flew right over and all around the Wash for an hour and a quarter, and got beaten up by a Spitfire on the way home.

I have been told by Mum[83] that this reads too abruptly, so I think a word of explanation might not be out of place. The idea of these camps all over England is to give the poor, misguided (!) A.T.C. Cadet an idea of what service life in the R.A.F. is like. I found this particularly interesting as a part of the station & flying field was given over to the Naval Air Fighting Development Unit, and as I hope to be joining the Fleet Air Arm during the next few months, I may have seen my future aircraft, if I ever get that far, which I, frankly, doubt."

The doubt must have stemmed from his failure to pass School Certificate the previous year. He was now about to re-take the exam.

Ivy Crompton's news in the same month described a visit to Buckingham Palace. Her son by her first marriage, George Errington, had been awarded a Military Cross.

---

[83] We can imagine Grace making sure she'd checked John's contribution before it was sent.

From Ivy Crompton, June 1943

"The principal event for me this month was the diversion of going to see George decorated at the Investiture which was held on June 22nd. As you will know the King was in Africa & the ceremony performed by the Queen. Peggy & I were glad we went, but spectacularly it was a flop: we did not see one inch of the Queen. There was a large crowd ushered in before she appeared and very badly arranged seats. She is so tiny that we could not see even the top of her head or say what colour she was dressed in, but she did it beautifully & said a word to everybody, standing all the time. She must have been tired. George said she looked charming & asked him how they all were in the desert. He had to stand for hours & found it very trying for his lame foot. I expect Molly & Dick know all about going to the Palace.[84] I had never been before. It took place in a lovely long narrow apartment with concealed lighting near the ceiling, stone-coloured walls with gilt-headed pillars & gilded festoons & portraits on the walls. We were interested to notice plain little lamps about with rather a Woolworthian air - to save light consumption on ordinary days, I imagine. The Yeomen of the Guard were beautiful & very magnificent to see. The little orchestra made me laugh, it was just too Victorian for any words, I now know what it means to "dispense sweet music", the opening selection was the Geisha & everything else thereafter to date. Kitty Bowes-Lyon tells an amusing story of how a [illegible] got into the Palace one day, because everyone supposed it was some kind of new drum! [85] A trick of K.B.L, I fancy, & a propos of that she showed me today a letter that she had received in answer to an advertisement for a gardener. It seems a dull subject but the letter is so wondrous that I think I must give you extracts here.

'I have had some experience in private service, & my employer in that case was entirely unsatisfactory, so I used my skill & experience on my own account, but if you require my services you can have my experience & capabilities.– I will now speak for myself, I am hard work & brought forward, honest & intelligent & I know my job. My wife for your information is an ex domestic – we are in fact a capable couple in my opinion without a fault. Why don't you book us & have done with it! The sooner you make up your mind the sooner you will have a capable couple. You have nothing to worry about, let me know the moving day & we will be there go to it! Yours respectfully'."

Ivy while writing all this out had got in a muddle with the margin. She admitted her misdemeanour in brackets - ("It's that margin again") - before continuing:

---

[84] Ivy makes it sound as though my parents were frequent visitors to the Palace. They weren't!
[85] What can the object have been, to be mistaken for a drum?

"I wonder if I have ever related another delightful epistle I had? This from the wife of an erstwhile manservant we had, by the name of Mansfield. He was separated from his wife & I was trying to bring them together again. A letter, full of bitter complaint, which I received from the wife ended up "Mr Mansfield does not understand that he cannot eat his cake & retain it". It is sometimes almost worth being in domestic difficulties & sometimes better still to be without altogether & I fear the genus will grow odder & odder. George has 3 or 4 jobs offered him in the Staff College. He would rather take an attachment here in Yorkshire but thinks the S.C would be wiser as he very much hopes to stay on after the war but fears he is a bit old (35).
We went & lunched & wined (which it seems one may still do), after the Investiture & it seemed quite like old times.
It seems a bit hard to get back to the garden, but my home is my only love really & oh how lucky we are to still have one when so many people are homeless & tragedy on every hand. I heard 2 sad things today that made me feel that if one is allowed to keep one's children intact there should never be any more to ask."

'Keeping one's children intact' ... a difficulty at the best of times, but in wartime even less likely to be 'allowed'; by fate, by God? I don't know what permission-giver Ivy had in mind. Grace's contribution for June gives away the undercurrent of anxiety that all parents felt. She and Henry had attended a commemoration service at Trent, the school where John, their youngest son, boarded - as well as Gordon, the youngest son of Joey Henderson.

From Grace Werner, June 1943
"We, Henry & I, went to Trent for the commemoration service. It was a beautiful day on the Saturday for the Cricket Match. John made a good catch & Gordon, Joey's youngest boy, batted well making the top score for the boys. Tthe Match was against the Old boys.
The service in the chapel on the Sunday was very touching. Over 130 Trent boys have been killed or are missing in this war already & their names were all read out by the Headmaster. After the service we – Gladys & Josephine & Gordon along with Henry, John & I - went to the Black Boy at Nottingham for our Sunday lunch, & very good it was. We then took the bus & managed to get front seats upstairs & rode to Derby - a very pretty town & the countryside was looking lovely. We caught the 5.30 back here from Derby – a very happy weekend – and as it will be our last chance to go as parents we were glad to be able to do it. ...

… Roger has only got one P.C. through since I sent my last account to the C.F.C. He seems well but complains of getting fat through lack of exercise – particularly walking - & they have no room to play a game out of doors. I fancy the German Camps are all better organised than the Italian.

Just received a letter from Roger dated 8.2.43. "I received a really nice bunch of letters on Sat. - 3 from Cousin Ivy, 1 from Auntie Juliette, 1 from John, 1 from Miss Birch & 1 from Cousin Molly & 1 from Cousin Dick written on Christmas Day. Also at last your letter with the photograph. I am so glad to get some of Charles & you all – a great comfort & a joy to look at. Please give my love & thanks to everyone who has written to me."

The letter home that Roger had written on February 8th was received by his parents in June. Waiting for news must have been far more trying than Grace reveals.

There are only five contributions in the folder for the month of July and three of these have been copied out by Alice from letters the cousins had written to her personally. Had the margin problem become too much? Perhaps the cousins needed to take a break from writing for the Chronicle.

The first contribution is from Alice herself.

From Alice Crompton, July 1943
"Almost all July (till 27th) I spent with Molly at Tavistock, so I haven't much to add to the current notes from her. My 5 weeks were most enjoyable. M. was kindness itself, the children very sweet & amusing, & Tavistock one of the three most attractive little towns in England to my mind, (Rye & Kirkby Lonsdale being the others). I liked doing the cooking for the fortnight of Bessie's absence, and I appreciated the Refrigerator as I hadn't used one before. The children came to the kitchen one day to "make pastry". They each had a little paste board & a tiny rolling pin. I gave them dough, & sausage & other meat, & they each made a small Cornish pasty & 3 little sausage rolls. Great excitement when the finished goods emerged from the oven! Jane was very neat-fingered in handling her paste, & Susan not bad for her tender age.

I travelled very comfortably to Bournemouth on 27 July where I came to take Irene's place with Mrs Watts, I am staying till she returns at end of Aug. probably. On 30 July we went to lunch at Ringwood with Cissie & Lettice, both of whom were well, but thinner than they were. The "Homestead" garden is a blaze of colour, & was even brighter when the rambler roses were out. Lettice said they had better whitewash something. Vera Spafford was staying with Lett. She is now working in Dr. Macgowan's former parish, Holy Trinity, Kingsway.

> I don't expect to go back to Rye much before Oct. as I have invitations to Ringwood, Doncombe, H. Wycombe & Sutton (W. Sussex), & also want a few days in London."

What drove Alice to travel around so? At the start of the Chronicle it seemed wise to be away from Rye, with bombing and invasion in mind. By this stage of the war, was this still the reason for absence? Letting the house for income could have been her motive, but she only let the cottage on one occasion, as far as I can make out. Perhaps she simply wanted to help the cousins in their various households, and share their anxieties. My mother's contribution, next in the folder, seems to support this.

> From Molly Withington, July 1943
> "Cousin Alice was with us till the 27th & was most helpful & "obliging" while Bessie was away on her fortnight's holiday! Alice took charge most ably in the kitchen & produced the goods with most commendable punctuality! She also came each Tuesday to the British Restaurant, (which is the day I go to every week) for a couple of hours during the rush period, to help with the washing up. We didn't have particularly nice weather, very few picnics, but it was luckily a beautiful day for Susan's birthday party, which was on the 1st July, postponed from 24th June.
> We had a small tea party the day before Alice left & a little meeting afterwards to hear her give a most interesting talk on China. It seemed very appropriate to drink tea out of my Chinese "Dragon" tea set, among our various Chinese possessions & then listen to Alice's plea for Aid to China. My friends were most sympathetic & most enthusiastic & "China" benefitted accordingly. Jane & Susie came to the meeting & sat on their own little chairs as good as gold listening intently to the discourse! They simply love anything in the nature of a party, a trait inherited from both Mellershes & Beckers, I think!"

I want to tell my mother immediately that yesterday, October 25th 2015, we had a lunch party here. I made Chinese soup – crab and sweetcorn – so that we could use her Chinese 'Dragon' soup bowls and porcelain spoons.

In July 43 she went on to write of her own mother.

> "My mother is getting on very well, & persevering on her crutches, she walks up & down the long ward daily. She is now getting interested in her fine needlework again, which is a very good sign & I am sure it will be a great thing for her to have this interest. Dick went down to see her last week, after a visit to Guildford on

duty, & found her looking much better. She gets outdoors in a wheelchair every day weather permits. There seems every hope she will be able to leave hospital in September."

Thinking of genetic inheritance, I wonder if my grandmother had shallow hip joints, which in the case of my mother, my sister and I myself, led to the early onset of osteoarthritis in the ball and socket joint. My mother was one of the first in the country to be given an artificial hip. She never had the second hip replaced and never again walked without pain and difficulty. By the time Jane, and then I, had the operation on both hips, the technique and materials used had improved, and goes on improving. 'Poor Mop', as I called her in November 1942 on hearing of her accident, had broken her hip which left her with one leg shorter than the other. Perhaps she had osteoarthritis in the joint as well; it was clear she struggled with pain. We knew better than to voice any sympathy. That was one thing Mop would not expect or accept. She'd been knocked down in November 1942, suffered an attack of gastro-enteritis in December, and was still in hospital when my mother wrote for July's Chronicle, with the hope she might be allowed home in September. Very nearly a year ...

Mop, christened Anna-Maria Hilda Josephine, was born into the Mellersh family of Holloway Hill House in November 1868, so at the time of the accident she was 74. She went on to live until June 1971, still alert in her mind if not her body. My other grandmother, Louisa Withington, nee Becker, was born in 1854. She also lived to a great age. She died in Montreal, marooned there by the war. At the time of the Chronicle, she was still alive, happily living with her daughter and three grandsons, doing her needlework, crosswords and playing bridge. This is how she wrote to Cousin Alice on February 14th 1942.

<u>From Louisa Withington, February 1942</u>
"We are, as usual, in deep snow & temp. often way below zero! I don't get out at all, but have plenty to do indoors. I keep pretty well, 88 this year! A terrible age. Ted takes his degree in May & will either go into the army or be put to munitions work. Bob wants to go into the Air Force. Moll very busy now, no maid & 6 people to cook & wash up for. 8 at present as we have for two weeks, Fred McVicar & his little niece! Her mother is in hospital.

I do all the family mending & clean the silver, make my own bed, & dust my room & do any odd jobs I am able for, but Moll is the main spring of the establishment. We are rationed in sugar, but the ration is ample, more than we need. Petrol is going to be rationed soon, but the real trouble with cars is the tyres, as no new ones will be procurable. Ours are good but when they give out we must put the car up."

Several things strike me in this letter from my grandmother. I hadn't realised that Canada had any rationing at all. But of course imports of everything Canada could not produce were as affected by the U-boats in the Atlantic as ours were. Then the mention of bed-making reminds me of the business this was before the days of briefly shaking a duvet. Three blankets and an eiderdown above the top sheet used to take far longer to straighten out and tuck in, especially if 'hospital corners' were required. Most chilling in retrospect is her happily-related news of the two elder of her three grandsons.

Returning to the July 1943 folder, Irene was the only other cousin to write a newsletter. Her contribution is, as usual, full of journeys and meetings with family members.

From Irene Becker, August 1943
"13/8/43
We have just arrived at Glossop, after most of us meeting for the first week-end of August at the Gilbey's at York.
I spent most of July at Bournemouth with my Mother and returned for the last week of the month to Epsom to meet Cecily who came for her quarterly 9 days' leave from her lonely Battery Station. She first travelled up to Manchester and Glossop for a night for Juliet's birthday on the 29th and returned to London by the midnight train from Manchester on the 30th. I met her at Aunt Loo's flat, where she had called in for breakfast, and we spent a gruelling day chasing round shops, with one cool break at the lunch hour concert at the National Gallery. After that was the Bank holiday week-end, so we all spent a peaceful few days at home, Cecily resting after her three months' hard work and broken nights on duty. It was lovely weather and we enjoyed the countryside on bicycles.
We went up on the Tuesday evening to see the Tempest at the open air theatre at Regents' Park – a very pleasant evening after a hot day. I was interested to see so many Londoners and holiday makers enjoying the Park and the flowers in the Queens' Gardens. Cecily had an Oxford friend to stay with her for two nights, and we gave them an extra camp bed in the sitting room, for want of a spare bedroom!

On the Wednesday evening they went up to the Promenade Concert at the Albert Hall but failed to get seats so, after spending an hour or more on their camp stools outside, managed to get standing room inside for the concert. But they said it was well worth it! I listened at home to such part of it which was broadcast.

The Thursday we spent in London shopping and took Aunt Loo to the International ballet in the evening, which was very good as they had a new one on – Twelfth Night – adapted from Shakespeare. This was very interesting, particularly the very excellent miming. During the day we received a telephone message from Trevor to say Wilfred had been granted a week's leave, and as we were (Juliet, myself & Dorothy Hallan) to meet next day at Mollie Gilbey's[86] at York, he suggested going there at once, as his leave started that evening. So I left Epsom at 8 o'clock next morning, en route for York, and had to desert Cecily before she left in the afternoon on her return to duty and camp life. She wrote to me to say she missed my usual assistance in packing her off as she had rather a lot of luggage, and some old unwanted books from No. 70 Eccleston Square to collect, which she thought would be useful for the A.T.S. library at her camp site, for the Winter evenings.

Trevor had lent her an old ammunition box he had in the garage at Epsom to take them in, but it had to be packed and screwed up in London with the books, and she had, needless to say, a date with a friend to go to the mid-day concert at the National Gallery again as a last fling before catching her train.

She writes "I've caught the 3.55 train from Paddington, though I can hardly believe it, as I had the dickens of a job fixing all the badges on to my cleaned uniform this morning, and had a rush to catch my train up to Waterloo in time to meet Iona Simon at the National Gallery as you know. After the concert I had an amusing time with the Ammunition box. I returned to Waterloo after getting quite a good lunch in the War Workers' Canteen next door to the National Gallery. The first Taxi-driver I saw, said he was married when I asked him whether or not he was engaged! However I told him I had a coffin to collect besides my other luggage from the left luggage office and he hailed me a Taxi round the back of the Station where the Taxis enter. I got to No. 70 about 3.15, and the taxi driver said he had had a "job with the ammunition" in the last war, and he wielded the screwdrivers with skill, if not speed. The books I had picked out fitted into the box exactly and at Paddington I was just about to mention to the luggage label man what the package was, when the porter winked at me, and I kept my mouth shut for a change! I haven't had to pay anything extra so far, though books are not officially counted as personal luggage. The taxi fare across London was sufficient though! I felt I must give

---

[86] Mollie Gilbey and her family were often mentioned in my childhood. They had a yacht anchored in the Dart, as far as I remember. Their children (older than Jane and me) were Geoffrey, Rosemary and Veronica.

the driver a bit more than the usual tip as he had certainly helped me to catch my train."

At York I met Juliet and Dorothy who arrived there in the afternoon from Glossop and we all met Wilfred at Greengates, Mollie's house. Trevor came up the next afternoon for two nights and both Mollie's girls, Rosemary and Veronica, were there on leave at the week-end. Veronica is in the A.T.S. mechanical transport and usually drives an Ambulance about in her neighbourhood and manages to get home quite often, though she lives in Barracks. Rosemary does clerical work, also in the A.T.S.

Geoffrey came home on Sunday from his camp, so we saw the whole family. Wilf wanted to spend a few days of his 7 days of leave at Glossop, so we four came back here on Monday and Trevor returned to London. Wilf enjoyed his holiday and the rest and change; he hasn't been well for ages and has been depressed and feeling what he calls "thoroughly browned off" for some time now. However, I hope he was better for the break and will be able to cope with his rather strenuous course from now on. The time went all too fast unfortunately!

Julie & I missed him very much when he went, so we have been vigorously gardening and clearing the weeds out of the allotment garden as hard as we can since yesterday afternoon. Julie has a tremendous lot of poultry to look after now, until the cockerels and drakes have been killed off. We have some two year old hens too, to kill off when they have finished laying, but at the moment we still have eggs from these 9 hens which are now our only source of supply, until the pullets begin which I hope will be well before Xmas. …

I saw quite a nice bit of Aunt Ciss and Lettice while I was at Bournemouth last month. Aunt Ciss was, I am glad to say, looking much better than I have seen her for some time and was wonderfully active. Lettice was very busy with her Red Cross work and is still allowed to use her car for collecting all the parcels of work from the different farmers' wives in the neighbourhood. Aunt Ciss is thus able to enjoy an occasional drive as the passenger, which is always a pleasure to her."

Alice writes a note below Irene's contribution:

<u>From Alice Crompton, August 1943</u>
"It was Juliet's birthday on 29th July: she was 12 years old. I append part of a letter she wrote me, on 31st July."

Part of Juliet's letter to Cousin Alice is attached to the page. Reading this, it's amazing to think that Juliet, the poultry-keeper and letter-writer, was only 12.

Letter from Juliet, 31.7.43
"We have been having a heat wave here lately and we have just had a thunder storm which was preceded by a dust storm, and all the litter in the town seems to blow in through our windows which were open because it was too hot all day.

We have seventeen four-month-old chicks which we bought when they were only a day old, seven three month old ones which we have hatched from our own eggs laid by the Wallamers (or however you spell it as they are a Dutch breed). Besides these we have eleven ducks whose day's programme seems to be eat (about a pound of food in three minutes and only nine weeks old), drink, eat, drink (until they finish the food), sleep, have a bath, sleep, have a bath (until some more food comes), then they start the programme again, until the day is over, then they start it again the next day. We have already had an offer to exchange a drake.

I made an elephant (out of an old pair of daddies trousers) for a bring and buy sale in aid of Tintwhistle church missionary fund, and it sold for seven and six. It had red ears and tail and black eyes and looked very much like "Dumbo" by the time it was finished. I also made a rabbit out of a green duster which sold for three and six."

After carefully writing out Juliet's letter on August 12th, Alice finished her contribution, the last remaining one of the year 1943, with news of her plan to stay with Cissie and Lettice in Ringwood after leaving Irene's mother at Barnston in Bournemouth. I wonder if cousins kept a pair of sheets labelled 'Cousin Alice' to save laundry bills inbetween her visits.

*

FOURTEEN

The Little Blitz – 1944

*"The air seems tense with future happenings and
all the sorrow that is in store for so many."*

1944 was another thin year for contributions to the Chronicle, no doubt caused by a combination of circumstances. Only the folders for February, March and May exist. The cover for May is missing, and the flimsy sheets of paper inside are badly torn. Perhaps Alice's Tony or one of the kittens got at the folder. Paper mites may have feasted on pages in later years when the Chronicle was stored in John Werner's suitcase from the year of Alice's death until Jane and I began the task of typing. Folders may have been taken from the suitcase and lent to friends and relations, never to be returned. Most likely, folders went astray in the inland post or to the bottom of the Atlantic while doing the rounds of the cousins.

Alice starts the first folder of the year with a heartfelt plea:

"EDITORIAL NOTE
I have waited & waited, but the last contribution for Feb. reached me only on 20 March.
In future I propose to post the C.F.C. on 5th of each month whether or not the full tally of pages has come in.
Will recipients please not keep each number more than 3 (or 4) nights before posting on? Otherwise it will all be intolerably stale by the time it reaches Aunt Loo.
A.C. 21 Mar. 1944"

This is followed by a contribution which Alice headed 'Becker (Cecilia) A.T.S.' obviously proud that a young, female Becker cousin was playing her part in the war.

From Cecily Becker, February 1944
"Our anti-aircraft mixed battery has been on the move a good deal recently and we have not yet returned to our own site. We are living in the meantime in a large country house at the foot of a hill covered

with elm woods. We have no operational duties and provided sufficient vegetables are prepared for the next few hours, we can go out for recreational training or so-called physical training in the woods. The A.T.S. are supposed to take roughly three periods of P.T. a week in the form of exercises which are conducted by an instructress who is usually an N.C.O. who has been sent on a course of training. We have practically none available at the moment under present conditions and hill-climbing seems quite as pleasant and probably as beneficial as most exercises. If we stay there a little longer there will be flowers to pick as well.

For the rest of the time, we have educational discussions on world and home affairs which are considered a very important item in military training nowadays, in view of post-war plans. When I say educational, I should explain that in many senses an outsider in the audience would probably disagree that they were so. A discussion group is led either by an officer, which in the case of the A.T.S. usually means myself, or in theory by anyone who has sufficient ideas on the subject in hand such as "Housing After the War". Usually I find that no-one is willing to volunteer for the job of discussion leader from amongst the girls, so that the opening questions thrown out to the audience have to be made by me. However, I'm getting quite used to this now and though I rarely know more than the briefest outline of the topic for discussion, I find this is no disadvantage in getting a discussion going, as most people are willing to open their mouths willingly if the person in the chair doesn't take on the attitude of lecturer. We rarely come to any conclusions on the more abstruse subjects, though it's surprising how much interest people do take in them. Occasionally you get the complaints "What can we personally do about helping to rule the country?" etc., which is rather difficult to counter; but as discussion groups become a regular part of the weekly training programme and everyone feels there is a definite organization and aim in them, they are accepted by men and women alike. Mixed discussions are the most valuable, but the A.T.S. are inclined to hold their silence during these unless encouraged by a question.

I have just spent seven of my nine days leave in London, seeing the shows and what friends are there, and am now visiting Juliet at Glossop. We took a trip to Buxton yesterday, visiting Poole's Cavern of which I'd never heard until we passed the gate."

The next two contributions come from Jack and Alice, both reporting illness. Epidemics and ill health run through the Chronicle with a regularity that wouldn't exist today.

From Jack Crompton, February 1944
"There is no news here, but Ivy is laid up with an unpleasant attack of boils under the arm which compels her to keep quiet, a thing she doesn't find easy. She was going up to London to help Gladys[87] into

the unfurnished flat she has just taken, but a stopper has been put on that for the time being. She hopes however to get up ere long. Not very good to be going up to London just now, but it seems "really necessary" as the sisters & nieces there are all working. We have had sharp frosts nightly but the days have been fine & generally sunny & the ground is in good shape for working. I am well on with the cottage garden, but the house garden is at a stand-still & looks like remaining so. A great pity that this ideal weather is being missed. Ivy of course is more or less in bed so I am going out again with the canteen.

Mrs Bowes-Lyon returned to Altham a few days ago from London, driven away by the Blitz so I expect she will take over the canteen again when she has recovered from her severe operation. We had quite a successful salvage drive for books & rubber, but bottles & tins are a drag in the market. We are getting 3 – 5 eggs daily from our few hens, which are parked on the tennis court; as the court hasn't been used for about 2 years it's the best thing we can do with it.

Sowings here are going strong. I have put in shallots & 2 rows of broad beans, but nothing else yet. This is not an early place, but I shall try a few peas in a sheltered spot. Anyone trying to read this will probably be surprised by the lack of margin on the front page. Sorry about that.

Ivy's niece Elizabeth Brenchley is to marry a Czech baron sometime this month. I don't fancy any of the cousins have met her, but I hope he is the right sort. I regret that I still have a prejudice against foreigners, quite unreasoning & one of the things we must get rid of, together with national boundaries and restrictions . But it doesn't look like happening in my time.

I've gone wrong again on the matter of a margin. I shall leave it to the editor.

We can't say how thankful we are to hear the news of Roger. It is splendid & the relief to Grace must be unspeakable. "

Jack's contribution prompts several responses. The Mrs Bowes Lyons who has been mentioned by the Cromptons several times is likely to have been a relation of the Queen. She had inside knowledge of the Palace as recounted by Ivy earlier. She had now been "driven back to Altham by the Blitz". Bombing had continued every year of the Chronicle but not at the intensity of the two Blitzes, the first between September 1940 and May 1941, and the Little Blitz, from 21st January 1944 until 19th April 1944. The years inbetween the two blitzes were known as the Lull, although bombs had continued to fall.

---

[87] Gladys – either Ivy's sister or the wife of Joey Henderson

When Jack was writing, the Little Blitz was at its height. In four months of raids, principally on London, Bristol, Hull and Cardiff, about 1,500 people were killed and around 3,000 seriously injured. The raids were said to be in retaliation for the British saturation-bombing of Berlin and other major German cities. Once more I'm reminded of playground fights. "He started it. He picked on me first."

Both Cecily and Jack in their newsletters allude to the future. Cecily talks of the discussions she leads with groups of ATS on post-war plans. Jack thinks ahead to a world without national boundaries and restrictions. (The borderless European Union's ambivalence in the treatment of migrants comes to mind.) In 1944 there must have been enough good news to encourage hopes for an imminent peace. The Allies were moving up the long leg of Italy, having captured Sicily at its toe. The previous autumn, Mussolini had been deposed by the titular head of the government, King Victor Emanuel, and replaced by a military government led by Marshal Pietro Badoglio who was not disposed to continue fighting in what he saw was an unwinnable war. He signed an unconditional surrender to General Eisenhower of the US the day before the Allies landed at Salerno on the Italian mainland. Italy was no longer our enemy. This sounds like good news. In fact, it was bad, particularly for the Italians. The Germans moved in on Rome, imposed military law, rescued Mussolini to head a puppet regime in the north, and the King and Badoglio fled. Partisans in a particular area of Rome were rounded up and massacred in reprisal for an attack on German troops. A total of 335 Italians were shot in the back of the head in a cave called Fosse Ardeatine which was then blown up with explosives to hide the evidence of the atrocity. The recapture of Italy became much harder now that German troops were on the ground in numbers. It was German troops who defeated the American invaders at Anzio.

Where was Roger in all this? We last heard of him in the letter he wrote home in February 1943, included in Grace's contribution of June 1943. Jack Crompton's news of February 1944 holds the first mention of Roger since then. The cousins would all have been feeling for Henry and Grace, and Roger's brothers Paul and John, throughout these eight months of silence. They'd already lost one son. With our ease of instant communication with every part of the world, it is hard to imagine the agony of daily hope and disappointment over such a long period.

By the time Alice visited the Werners in Wilmslow in March, the news of Roger's safety had made conversation about him possible once again. He could be talked of in the present tense with confidence. Alice reports that shed heard 'much about Roger' and his gift for languages.

> From Alice Crompton
> "February I spent very quietly in Oldham the one event being a jaunt to the excellent Pantomime in Manchester, "Jack & the Beanstalk." Mrs Sutherland (here for the duration) & I took our hostess to the Matinee, lunching first in the good dining room at Victoria Station. It really was a first rate show and keeping closely to the fairy story, with a quite terrifying Fee-Fi-Fo-Fum giant, & a Jack as superior to the old-fashioned Principal Boy as Dame Trot, his mother, was to the earlier Dames. On 1st Feb. I had a great treat in spending the day at Glossop, with Irene & Juliet, who is growing quick & tall like Jack's beanstalk! Wonderfully clever she is with her hands, & will soon be a rival to Ivy & Grace in soft toy making. On 28 Feb. I went to Wilmslow for a week's visit to Grace. Next day I collapsed with what the Dr. says is a strained tired heart.
> It was most deplorable to be giving Grace the trouble of nursing me, but the Dr. wd. not let me leave my bed for some days, & said I shd. have to be "a jolly sight worse" before any Nursing Home wd. take me in. Grace looked after me in the most efficient kind & tactful way possible. I heard much abt. Roger, which. I didn't know before, e.g. how good he is at languages, & has been studying German & Italian. He also learnt some difficult Indian dialect wh. helped him to get into Command of Gurkhas.
> A.C. 21 Mar."

Grace's own contribution gives more details although it doesn't answer all the questions present day readers may have. Was Roger released from the Italian prisoner of war camp after the Italians surrendered, only to be recaptured by the Germans? Or had he escaped?

> From Grace Werner
> "I think all the cousins will find it stale news that Roger is now in Germany – we heard by telephone from Ewen Kerr's Mother. She had a letter from Ewen written on Jan. 27th saying "Roger & the

Colonel came here today." Since that we have heard from Mrs O'Bree that Peter had seen Roger come in with his Colonel – so it's nice anyway that they are all together. I gather that Roger is now most likely under detention & that we may not hear from him for some months – until then we may not write as we have not got his prisoner of war number – the name of the Camp is Oflag VIII F. I have written to Roger under cover of Ewen Kerr but don't want to do this often as it may hold up Ewen's mail. Anyway, knowing Roger is safe matters most & we shall look forward to hearing from him when he is able to write. Ewen said both Roger & the Col. looked fit & well, so that's a blessing too. I feel rather like a pricked bubble since I heard Roger was safe. I have held myself in check so long & kept a stiff upper lip – now I feel I can relax. I know just how much these months have taken out of me.

Poor Alice has not had a very nice visit here, she went down the day after her arrival & has been in bed ever since. She is better now, I am glad to say - & will soon be about again. John has been in bed, too, with Pharyngitis. He still looks rather white but hopes to go back to his farm work next week. Father has been back for a couple of weeks & looks well & able to have his daily walk each day. Henry has no more boils so hope he has finished with them – he seems better in spite of a cold in his head.

We – Henry & I – had an amusing evening at the beginning of this month. The Works where Henry is got up a Pantomime party & Henry thought we ought to go. We managed to get out of the knife & fork tea at the Kardomah & met at the Pantomime. I thoroughly enjoyed the whole evening. The people were nice & seemed on very good terms with Henry. He says they all call him Mr Werner, except the girls who sometimes call him "love" !!! a very matey factory, I think.

Roy has just been home on leave, looking a picture of health – he's a dear boy. Josephine is getting home two weeks earlier than usual as the school has had a good many cases of scarlet fever. So far she has escaped . I have had a friend's child here for her half term. She left the day Alice arrived. Aunt Loo & Leigh will remember her Mother – Elfie Wick. She's a terribly clever child & always makes me feel about four years old.

I was so glad to get a letter from Helen (Leigh's wife). It's good to feel how happy they are – Alice is putting the letter in the C.F.C.

We are still waiting to see Bob Easton, he hopes to get leave the end of March. He has moved along the South coast to the West – but is not near enough I should think to visit his Aunt Molly on a day's leave.

Since writing about Roger, I have heard from the Red Cross that I ought to hear from him any day now. The delay will only be that he has not received his prisoner of war number not due to any punishment."

Why did they expect he would be given detention or punished in some way? Was it because he and the Colonel might be treated as escapees? Grace still had to wait for direct news. My mother was also keen to hear more.

From Molly Withington
"It is indeed good to know that Grace has had news of Roger at long last, a <u>great</u> relief to her & her family, though it is very disappointing for him to be once more a P.O.W. poor fellow. We shall hear further details before long, no doubt. …
I hear Bobby is now at Sidmouth, but I haven't heard from him direct – I hope he'll be able to get over to see us."

The missing folders would have told us the news of Bob Easton's arrival in England from Montreal. Both Grace and the two Molly's (Easton and Withington) wondered if he would visit the family in Tavistock and meet Dick's family for the first time. I wonder, too, scrabbling for a scrap of memory of this first cousin. Out of all the cousins in the pages of the Chronicle and beyond, Ted, Bob and Dickie Easton were the only first cousins Jane and I had. My mother's only surviving brother never had children, and Molly Easton, the boys' mother, was my father's only sibling. The appearance of John Werner as the father of the potter we met in our local village re-introduced into my memory a host of second cousins. John was the nearest in age to us. Here he is, that February 1944.

From John Werner, February 1944
"At the moment I'm recovering from pharyngitis which sounds very serious but is actually only inflammation of the throat. However I'm not doing this in order to give an account of my state of health but to give a brief idea of what I've been doing during the last month on the farm.
The farm itself is by most standards very small, only about 40 acres. We keep about 20 cattle, (mostly shorthorns and Friesians), and the main job in the fields is to produce food for the cattle. My first job was the pulling & carting of turnips: they are ground up & added to the cattle food. The kale came next for me, although they've been using it since before Christmas. This is fed separately to the cows each morning. When it has been carted, it is stacked standing up against the walls of the "shippen" (cattle house). After the kale had all been cut & carted we were faced with rather a problem as the hard bottom stalks were left in the ground & it was necessary to have them cleared before the hired tractor-plough arrived. So it was decided that

I should dig them out (aided occasionally by a part-time labourer). I reckon I dug about two miles of the darned things going up & down the rows.

Every now & then one of the drains would get blocked in one of the meadows down by the river, & I would dessert my Kale & go off with the labourer Duncan & clear there.

Occasionally I worked with the farmer who's called Price. He's very amusing. He had a young man working on the farm - who cut all the hedges - whom he had the greatest admiration for, not because he was clever at his job but because he could curse!

I shall be glad when I'm better & will be able to get back to work again."

Grace, who had no doubt been reading over his shoulder, added to John's news:

From Grace Werner
"Since writing my notes, we have had a P.C. from Roger – mostly printed, but anyway it was a joy to see any of his writing – written on Feb. 16th. His prisoner of war no. is 1913/VIII F. Oflag VIII F, Germany."

Wikipedia has produced the information that Oflag VIII-F was a camp at Mahrisch-Trubau in the south east of Germany. 2,000 officers were held there, mostly British captured in North Africa and the Greek Islands. The camp was closed after the prisoners were transferred to Oflag 79 near Braunschweig. That was in April 1944.

So another move ahead for Roger. In the next month's folder, Grace writes:-

From Grace Werner, March 1944
"Beyond the P.C. from Roger received the first week of the month, we have no more news of him. I expect now the Air Mail Letter Cards have been stopped letters will take longer to get to him & from him. I sent off a parcel I had half got ready when Italy fell – last Friday week - & have already heard from the Red Cross that it is on its way. They have sent me another book of 20 clothes coupons – so I may get another parcel off as soon as I can get it ready. I had hoped to have heard again from Roger with some ideas for the things he needs. In the Prisoner of War Magazine they gave several good accounts of the Camp where Roger is – a swimming pool & football field - & room for other sports. I think Roger will have caught up with a lot of Gurkha Officers that he knew & had lost touch with – he was moved so many times."

Kathleen writes of her hope of seeing Bob. I want to include the whole of her contribution, for the sake of her simple and touching style. Her writing voice I would describe with a line from Twelfth Night: *'it had a dying fall'*.

> From Kathleen Smithells, March 1944
>
> "Archie & I have been up North for a week (Swan Hotel, Newby Bridge, Windermere). The weather was not very good. However, it did not rain but it was rather cold & windy. The spring flowers were waiting for the sun. I did find some small wild daffodils, but they were not out. It was lovely to get the fresh air & change. The river was very low. I should think today has filled it up for it has poured all day here.
> Father is coming back on Monday. I fear he will feel the loss of his old friend the backgammon player, he was very seedy when Father was last here, & had not really pulled round. He passed away 2 weeks ago. I am so sorry, for it was such a happy friendship.
> The allotment is going on slowly. 2 rows of potatoes in, 1 row of peas, 2 rows of shallots. I hope it will not be the last we shall see of them, time will show.
> I have not heard from Bobby Easton again, perhaps he is spending his leave with Dick & Molly. I am looking forward to seeing him. I hope it will be soon."

To this Cousin Alice added a note: *"Later – Bob Easton is on his way to India. Ed."*

The final contribution for March comes from my mother. As I was rising six by this time, I have some clear memories of what she writes about.

> From Molly Withington, March 1944
>
> "Dick has just returned to H.Q. after his 9 days leave, he had splendid weather, until the last two days, but as rain is so badly wanted (most unusual for Tavistock!) in the gardens & for pastureland, one could not complain! He got a good deal of golf & did many useful jobs, including cutting down a tree (by permission of the Landlord!) & bushes on the hedge, trimming the hen run, & distempering the day nursery & the downstairs cloakroom! Jane & Susie break up on the 7th. We had a last trip to Plymouth last week (as we are now outside the "Banned Area") to see the International Ballet from Sadler's Wells; we saw "Carnival – (Schumann's music), "Endymion" – a Spanish ballet, & "Enigma", which I enjoyed the most, but was rather above the children's heads, of course, being based on a Medieval morality play. We had been in one afternoon early in the month to

Plymouth to see a film about a lovely collie "Lassie Come Home" – it was very good indeed, but very affecting – Susie & I wept nearly all the time!! However, after many adventures, Lassie did eventually arrive home, I am glad to say!
I have had a cable from Bob Easton who has evidently left England, presumably for India, as he volunteered for that Command. The cable merely said goodbye & good luck, & no date. I wish we could have seen him again. I fancy he may have left Sidmouth at short notice. The last letter from Mother is dated 27th Feb. – Ted has got his commission & was hoping for leave, & then going on a course at Prince Edward Island.
My father has been up to Moorfields Hospital for treatment, & the specialist still seems satisfied, though there is as yet no improvement in the sight, but he has not got his glasses yet & has to return to Moorfields after Easter to have them fitted. I had a present of 3 Seville oranges &, with 1 lemon, Bessie made 5½ lbs. of very good marmalade, quite a treat. We have had several dishes of rhubarb out of the garden; there has been none in the shops yet."

The rhubarb patch in Markham's garden held for me the talismanic power of a treasure island. I drew a plan for a three-level house that I would build on the site. I reckoned the earth would be soft enough to dig, even if John Vicary down the road couldn't be persuaded to help in the venture. The ground floor was the topmost level. From there one went down two floors, stopping before reaching Australia. Recalling the pencilled plan now, I realise it was modelled on the bracken houses we often built on the moor, simply by bending the dried bracken over to form floors and walls. The earth was not so amenable to building. In fact, it didn't work. But the underground house existed most beautifully in my imagination and I spent much time haunting its levels.

Then Lassie – oh dear! The next time I was so heartbroken was when I was sent away to boarding school.

The next surviving month's collection of newsletters, the one for May, has no cover and has been given a modern metal fastener for the pages' punched holes. Irene's handwriting is on the first page. She ends her long contribution *"I have been full up with various other activities to do with other people, not concerned with the Family so it would be inappropriate to describe them but life is very hectic still in many ways and I seem to spend very little of my time in my own home – not nearly as much as I should like."*

Despite this, she covered a number of pages for the Chronicle describing time spent with her scattered children and visits to cousins around the country. There are some holes in the paper but here is the bulk of her contribution. How long can it have taken her to write?

<u>From Irene Becker, May 1944</u>
"May has been an unusually busy month for us all. I started off at Glossop where, late one night about 12.30 a.m., Cecily arrived by taxi from Hyde, the nearest place to Glossop to which she could find a train running at 11 p.m. - where she had just arrived from South Wales on a week's sick leave, as she had just got up from her bed and German Measles. She had had the usual Army inoculation to cope with as well, so felt quite ill at the time, though was more than compensated by the prospect of a week at home.
We stayed, she & I, a few days with Juliet and - on the 6[th,] when she had quite recovered -we sallied forth at 6. a.m. to Darlington with a view to seeing Wilfred at the week-end. He, too, had been inoculated so was having an easy two days on the Saturday afternoon and all day on Sunday. We arrived at Darlington at 11 o'clock and Cecily sallied forth to hunt a bedroom for the night, while I held the fort and our bags in the Station tea room as we hadn't much hope of finding anything nearer to Wilfred's billet. We were justified in so thinking, as we found out later on. However Cecily returned triumphant in about half an hour having visited several places. She said "I hope it will do, it isn't much of an hotel but they have a double bed for to-night and it is just outside the station." So we deposited our bags and took the next train over to see Wilfred in Darlington, where we met him at the King's Arms. We all had a great afternoon and evening and an excellent dinner at the so called King's Arms, and the two young things were thrilled to meet at last after having been separated for over a year on end. They had always been the greatest of friends, these two and very little separated except at school since their childhood days.
We returned, Cecily and I, to Darlington to sleep - and back to see Wilfred next day until 2.30, when we had to leave to catch the afternoon express from Darlington to London. In the morning we had explored the glorious old castle with its magnificent Norman keep at the top of the town with Wilfred, had a walk in the bluebell woods and sat for some time chatting on a tree trunk by the river's edge. We had an excellent journey until we arrived back at Waterloo at 9.50 p.m. to catch our train for Epsom, when we found everyone in the World returning home from a happy day out. Soldiers and civilians, mothers, fathers and children - all in enormous queues at the booking offices, so that even after half an hour's wait in the queue we were

unable to get our train at 10.7 and would have had to wait until almost midnight for the next. So we decided to proceed by underground to Victoria, as no taxis were then to be had at Waterloo and the newly installed inter-station 'bus was going the wrong way for us. It was very hot and our bags, eggs from Glossop & sundry parcels were very heavy. A nuisance, too, to have to do all the long moving stairway twice over! However we got to Victoria and found a late Sunday night train at 11.15 and we arrived at Epsom just before midnight. Trevor was on the platform to meet us and such a joy! He truly saved our lives by helping to carry our bags.

Cecily had to return from her leave the next afternoon, but she enjoyed an hour and a half's revel in 'Bumpas' book shop before catching her train back.

We have had a glorious spell of weather: though it was cold during the early part of the month, it improved tremendously about the 16th and has been really summery and warm since. But no rain at all in London or at Epsom and we certainly need it for the gardens & vegetables.

I went down to Bournemouth on the 21st to see my Mother and Aunt Loo Watts[88] who are living to-gether for the time-being at Barnston there. They seemed to be enjoying the sunshine and were very busy tidying up the garden, which had become rather a wilderness since Offer, the gardener, had been transferred last autumn in his Special police job from Westbourne to another district. Mother seemed to be spending all the mornings on her knees in an old blue apron, weeding and planting, whilst Aunt Loo Watts trotted up to the shops at Westbourne to collect food and rations. It is nearly a mile away and a bit of a problem for elderly folks these days as no food stuffs at all are delivered now except milk. Aunt Loo has her two middle aged maids there & Miss Laing who lives with her in London, so between them they manage quite *(piece missing)*

the sea was a *(piece missing)*

sunshine and the flowers *(piece missing)*

the gardens, and the rhododendrons *(piece missing)*

beautiful and prolific then ever *(piece missing)*

I don't think I have ever seen such masses of flowers on them as there are this year. I went up one afternoon on a surprise visit to Aunt Ciss & Lettice. The latter was out on her round with the delivery van for soldiers' teas and comforts and did not return until 6 o'clock, so they asked me to stay on a bit and join them at their evening meal. I had five hours with them altogether, which was a great joy as we don't meet very often these days and had a great deal to say to each other.

Trevor had been down on the Monday night before and had spent the Sunday at Barnston seeing Aunt Loo & Mother.

---

[88] Irene's mother's sister Louisa, not my grandmother.

Aunt Ciss was very busy with the garden, which was looking lovely, and the vegetable garden over the railway crossing was most flourishing and prolific. They have now six hens in their coal run - a cross between red leghorns and light Sussex breed. Aunt Ciss is unfortunately suffering from neuritis in her hip and thigh which is very painful and cramps her style rather as regards her activities, poor dear. And she will never take any rest at all during the day time, but no one can make her do otherwise unfortunately. She is entirely a law unto herself in this way.

Lettice, too, has been over-working with all her war-time activities, the secretaryship of the Red Cross depot where she is responsible for cutting out & delivering the work to the farmer's wives & various many folk round the countryside who sew the garments & put them to-gether for the men in hospital. She also does two whole days a week on the van with Miss Wavell (the Viceroy's sister)[89], and a night's fire watch into the bargain.

She has rheumatism in her joints also and the Dr. has ordered her some special kind of electrical baths, which treatment she is having this month and she has to knock off her two days in the van during June. We had a great gossip about everything and the 5 hours I spent at the Homestead went very quickly.

Trevor is very busy with many irons in the fire and really has no time to take it easy at all. I only hope this stress may ease off before long as I fear he is wearing himself out and he goes to bed later and later. It is never before 2 A.M. now-a-days and he is confined to his reading hours when dinner is over round about 9 o'clock or often later and most other people are quiet. However in other ways I think his health has been rather better lately than it used to be. I think that is all the family news for the moment....

Juliet has just sent me an account of the Glossop flood which happened on Whit Monday evening May 29th and I thought it might be of interest for the C.F.C.

Extract from Juliet's letter, June 3rd 1944

"We have been very busy putting back what we can find of the garden and its produce after the storm last Monday evening. People say it was the worst storm they have had in Glossop that they can remember.

I think it was fifteen hundred tons of logs that were washed down from the Turn Lee Mill to just below Dinting Arches, and they knocked the wall down and went into the river, and are still being collected. I heard yesterday that some have been found at Liverpool!! All the houses down the town were flooded and two of the rooms of one house have gone; Harrison's (the large Grocer's shop where we deal) were also flooded, as the river just a little higher up came over

---

[89] Field Marshall Archibald Percival Wavell, (1883 – 1950), Viceroy of India from June 1943 until India's independence in 1947.

the wall and down the road. A woman was drowned and her body was not found until two days later at Compstall. It thundered a bit throughout Tuesday and we had another storm almost as heavy as the first storm, on Wednesday morning, at about half past six. Rus Tallis spent the Monday night at our flat here, as the Works was flooded.

The park (surrounding the school) is in an awful mess, two of the bridges having gone, rhododendrons uprooted, the paths, turned into pits two or three feet deep, and lots of walls are gone; the result being that the school is not allowed in the Park and there are no games. I believe Old Glossop is in an awful mess, though we have not been to see.

It washed up lots of beans and peas out of the garden and even potatoes too. Lots of our neighbours' hens were drowned. Mr Eyre lost one, Mr Hall another and Mr Hurst lost twelve pullets. A piglet was drowned at the Works piggery and I believe the sow saved herself by standing on her hind legs. Our hens are alright."

In the 1960s Juliet, the writer of that letter, became our solicitor. When we moved from London and Greece to bring up our children in my home county, we would meet Juliet when she came to stay in Shaldon with her brother Wilfred's widow Pat. In the 60s the Becker yacht was moored in the Dart estuary. Dark green, as I remember, with polished brass fittings. This must have been the yacht which had been moored in Poole and which Irene talked of in the early part of the Chronicle. Was it requisitioned? One of the Dunkirk rescuers? There are many questions that I could ask but who is there left to answer? Wilf Becker's widow, Pat, lives in Shaldon and can dredge up some clues from the depths of memory. I intend to discover if my cousin Dickie Easton in New York is all right – by which I mean still alive.

John Werner could have answered some of my present questions, but my questions were formulated too late. Born in 1926, he died, aged 87, in 2013 before I had got to grips with the Chronicle. Like the holes in its pages, death leaves unfillable gaps in the lives of the living.

His mother's contribution for May 1944 looks as though a mouse had found it. Fragments remain.

From Grace Werner, May 1944
… (John has been) …helping a man with a market garden – long hours but so far he seems to like it. He was dreadfully fed up for a few days at not being sent for, but has settled down now as he sees

there is nothing he can do about it - He will be eighteen on June 4th so there is time enough for him yet. Paul is hoping for a short holiday any day now but will not be surprised if he does not get it. I think he, like all of us, does not feel it is a time for holidaying. The air seems tense with future happenings & all the sorrow that is in store for so many.

Ivy very kindly asked us "one & all" to Ford but we feel we should not travel just for pleasure – Also Henry won't get a holiday before September – when he will have been almost a year at his present job. Mrs Hobson (my help) has lost her Father, so has only come in fits & starts all this month. She is off for a holiday – to a sister in the lakes – then I hope she will return. Gladys is away for Josephine's half term so I have Joey & Gordon here for a few days – so we are a full house. Father [Joe Henderson] has been here all this month & has enjoyed the warm spell which seems to have gone from the north once more & it's dull & wet. Dick came up for a couple of nights during the month. He got endless teasing – Molly had given him a book of poems which he was carrying about with him. I expect we were wrong & that it is the "done thing" to do in the army as it was Lord Wavell's edition."

I feel for my father being teased by the family for carrying around a book of poetry. This was 'Other Men's Flowers'. He knew most of the poems by heart. The collection was a best-seller. Poetry like music speaks the unspeakable.

Members of a family run the gamut of personalities. Even siblings can be remarkably unalike. Grace, I know from memories, was a dear - but maybe not a reader. Her "I expect we were wrong" shows her magnanimous spirit. But to balance the family books after Grace's teasing approach to poetry, I'll include Alice's contribution for May.

From Alice Crompton, May 1944
"During the whole of May I have more or less led an invalid's life, for a week or two entirely in bed, & then up only from about 11.30 to 9 p.m. It sounds dull, but really I almost enjoyed it! I had no aches or pains, & I appreciated the complete rest, & any amount of time for reading. Marjory Lees & her household were kindness itself & never let me feel for a moment that I was a burden. There were heaps of books in their house, & the Manchester Guardian daily! Friends brought me the Sunday Times & Times Literary Supp't, & by post came "Spectator" & the E. Sussex Express. I had lots of letters. Marjory & I played backgammon every evening, but only a few games – very different from my long bouts with Aunt Essie & of late with Joe.

Never having left the house during May, save for one walk round the garden, & one afternoon sitting out, I have nearly nothing to relate! I write now from Tavistock where Molly has most kindly invited me. I managed the journey via Bristol (where Ivy met me & we spent the night) quite comfortably on 7 – 8 June, & was none the worse for it."

The month's folder ends with my mother's news.

From Molly Withington, May 1944
"Another dry sunny month here, though not very warm , & we had a good deal of cold north wind. Rain is still needed for the gardens. Jane had her 8th birthday this month & we had the birthday party on the 13th - a Saturday, & it was more convenient than the 11th. Unfortunately, it drizzled all day & so we had to have indoor games & treasure hunt. We were 16 altogether, quite enough to provide for now-a-days, as things get more scarce. We had our very last jelly packet & last tin of Mandarin orange slices, which are such a favourite with children – of course, no crackers or balloons like the old days, but Jane had her 8 candles on the cake & quite a good spread. All sorts of games were played afterwards, & no one seemed in a hurry to go. Jane & Susie always enjoy wearing pretty party frocks, the former can still wear a very nice turquoise blue one passed on from Juliet, it is in such good condition it will do Susie next year & several more, I hope! Susie wore a white & pink flowered chiffon that I got Jane for Susie's christening party, so it has certainly done well!! It was let down by putting in 2 rows of lace insertion at the waist line to match the narrow lace edging.
I have had 2 Airgraphs and 1 letter this month from Bob[90], who has been in a Jungle Training School, & wrote last from a Low Flying school, he says he hopes to be shooting up Japs on the Chindwin soon. He seems to like India very well, & enjoying his experiences. I also had a lovely photo of Ted from Molly in his Air Force uniform, he is very like his father, I think. Mother seems pretty well & writes her usual good hand - the letters seem to take a good month or 5 weeks now-a-days. She actually got to church on Easter Day which was a great event, after being shut in the house all winter.
My father's sight is improving wonderfully, he has taken up bicycling again & enjoys reading & the crossword. We haven't seen Dick since he was down on duty for a couple of days at the end of April."

---

[90] This paragraph refers to the Montreal branch of the family: Bob and Ted Easton, their mother Molly Easton and my father's mother, Louisa Withington.

FIFTEEN

The Last Year of the War – 1944 – 45

"All our hearts are full again with love for all at Montreal."

The contribution written by Molly Withington in May is the last that survives for 1944. After this, the Chronicle goes silent for over half a year. We next hear from the cousins in February 1945. Much happened in the interval. The first big event that affected everyone was D-Day. Many cousins would have alluded to it in those missing pages for June 1944. My mother surely described the picnic we had in early June, sitting on a river bank on grass so short-cropped it was like pale green baize, by what we called the Humpy Bridge. This place we knew as Halfway House. There may have been a café with this name on the road from Tavistock to Yelverton and Plymouth.

On this particular picnic we heard a tremendous rumbling sound which we decided was not thunder. It was coming from the direction of Tavistock, growing gradually louder. Then something large appeared crossing the bridge, grinding up its steep slope and then down the near side, followed by another, and another, and another. "Ducks!" cried by mother in a very excited way. On and on they came, up and over the bridge, round the corner and away. Cumbersome metal ducks, out of all proportion to the hump-backed bridge which was a familiar old friend to me. I hoped it could bear the weight and number of these heavy vehicles which weren't ducks at all but army tanks. That much I knew.

Later I realised that we had witnessed the mustering of amphibious tanks for the Allied landings in France. *D-Day*! I can recall the excited trepidation that spilled from the word. Like Happy Birthday except D-day was for all of us, not just for the person having the birthday. How much the cousins knew about the Normandy landings at the time is concealed in the missing pages of the Chronicle.

Today, November 2nd 2015, I have hunted for the bridge on the internet. It might have been called Grenofen Bridge. As I regularly travelled to prep school in Yelverton before I went away to boarding school, the name is probably right for the picnic place. I've found a website that features it and spent rather too long staring at photographs of wet-geared ramblers walking through woods on manicured paths, helped by the kind of walking sticks that could be used to roast pigs on spits. I try to match the website's information with my memories. It tells me a time capsule was set into a lump of cement in the year of Queen Elizabeth's Diamond Jubilee. That was 2012. The capsule's contents were put together by the children of Whitchurch, to mark the completion of Gem Bridge. There's a new picnic spot near this bridge, which replaced Brunel's railway bridge built in 1859 for the South Devon and Tavistock Railway. I used to cross Brunel's bridge in the train on my way to Plymouth when I spent a year at Plymouth's technical college. The railway line was closed in 1962. So Gem Bridge is not Grenofen Bridge. That lies near a car park. It looks as though the main Tavistock-Plymouth road no longer crosses it.

Jane and I were once Whitchurch school children, crossing the moor to Miss Attridge-Smith's kindergarten. The Chronicle is our time capsule. We are the only survivors from its pages, bar Cousin Dickie Easton in New York. The last time Dickie and I exchanged emails, just after last Christmas, he'd been in hospital with something called blank mind syndrome. Since then, and especially while working on the Chronicle, I have thought of him frequently but was hesitant to contact, for fear of what I might learn. Today I must break this silly, self-induced silence. I will telephone him.

Some hours later, here's the result:

Email from Richard Easton
"02.11.2015
Today at 4:01 PM
How extremely pleasant to speak to you this morning! I greatly look forward to reading your pieces. I have so far lost contact with so many people - even some people who live nearby! - that it was wonderfully calming to remember the days when one was more active and jollier than I am now. Thank you over and over! xx Cousin Dickie."

On the phone, there was no sign of a blank mind. He is even still working, aged 83. No stage parts, but recordings.

The hospital occurrence last January was through overwork; a very frightening episode of finding himself a prisoner in his own mind as well as in the hospital. I told him about the wartime Chronicle and how it included regular news from Montreal. We talked of our feeling of affinity, despite very rarely meeting. Dickie put it down to our both being a younger child; in Dickie's case, the youngest of three. Older siblings and parents, he said, don't pay much attention to younger members of the family, and so we younger ones can get on with own lives in our own way. He elaborated on this thought. He'd felt overlooked. Ted and Bob were a pair: Dickie an afterthought. Ted had been Molly's boy; Bob was Len's. Dickie said he was more in tune with his English mother than his West Canadian father. For myself, I felt more in tune with my father than with my mother. We decided the Becker inheritance was strong in both of us and had created an emotional tie.

We both agreed we didn't like the phone and put off using it. We can't see the person's face, so we cannot gauge their response. At this we both began to imagine absurd scenes, describing the expressions on the faces of our invisible respondents while they grew bored with our stories.

The Beckers loved stories. They were continually fascinated by the odd things people say, and would write them down and repeat them ad infinitum. There is a collection of 'Aunt L.A's sayings' in the pages of a ledger that was passed on to me by my father. Aunt L.A. – an aunt, I think, of Hannibal Leigh Becker - sat at the long dining table, part of the establishment at mealtimes though at other times in the company of servants for she was simple and needed looking after. She didn't like visitors. On a September 30th she addressed a German cousin who'd come to stay. "When do you leave? First of Ock, ow would that do?" She liked her glass of wine. "Rain it on, Ashton, there's a Dutchman." I have a mid-19th century photograph of Aunt L.A, a tiny sharp-faced woman with Ashton, the embodiment of a butler, in attendance behind her chair. Aunt L.A. took exception to anyone playing the piano. My grandmother was a good player, and studied in Leipzig. Aunt L.A. was not impressed. "Can't you stop? Aren't your 'ands tired?" The ledger recorded other family sayings. If ever anyone was late to appear for breakfast, the excuse once given by a German cousin was trotted out. "Ze soap ee got com-plete-ly in." Into the plug hole? Into his beard? Into his ears? We'd feel the laughter welling up the second someone began with "ze soap".

Such things are family cement, almost a secret language that excludes other people even if explanations are given. Cohesion depends on exclusion, the heart of the division between them and us in families and in nations. This law of nature works on the level of the individual within a family too, as Dickie experienced.

I have gone through the typescript of the CFC and extracted all the various mentions of the Eastons. The collection runs to 12 pages. It will make a poignant mixture of pleasure and sadness for Dickie to read about his childhood and his two elder brothers. At the beginning of the Chronicle, Dickie was 8. Bob was 16 and a half and *"growing out of all his clothes with lightning and disastrous rapidity",* wrote his mother. Ted, the eldest, was at university with two more years to go. *"He loves his home and his Elsie and weekends in the Laurentians and what he calls binges."* He'd passed his Officer Training Corps exams, his mother reported, but *"now nothing more is to be done until he is through college ... I pray that he will never have to go to war."*

In July 1940 Ted was working in a gold mine. In a letter home, he wrote: *"I have now been down in the mine 3 times and still get a kick out of it. The cage is so quick, it's just like falling out of an aeroplane. When it stops you bounce up and down like a ball on an elastic. Great fun!"*

Great fun! The remark holds a sickening chill, knowing what is to happen to Ted. Four and half years later, he had arrived in India, as reported by my mother in the first surviving folder for the year 1945.

<u>From Molly Withington, February 1945</u>
"Paper shortage still acute, & this seems to be more in the nature of blotting paper! Ted arrived safely in India about the beginning of the month & I have had several letters from him, one took only a week. He was in excellent sprits & enjoying all his new experiences. I should say he was in a Transit camp near Bombay, but he couldn't

divulge. He was getting some English mail & was very glad of it. He was getting some tennis at a nearby Club, followed by swimming & tea on the lawn afterwards – which reminded me of our happy times in India - 20 years ago! He says he is looking forward to 'getting cracking. Life on a squadron out here must be really fun.'"

Kathleen Smithells had received a letter, too. *"So glad to have had a letter from Ted, he sounds very happy."*

Excellent, fun, glad, happy … the positive words mount up. Yet the cousins in 1945 would have been acutely aware that Ted was following in his brother Bob's footsteps. The last mention of Bob in the surviving folders of the Chronicle was in May 1944 when my mother wrote that he was in Jungle School in India. The missing folders of the Chronicle would have held the news that Bob had crashed into the Indian Ocean and been killed. We can imagine the dread with which the family followed news of Ted.

By the time the cousins were writing news for the following month's folder, Ted had been posted missing. The March folder contains their concern, anxiety and grief. Irene and Alice assumed he'd been killed, while Kathleen still refers to him in the present tense.

From Irene Becker, March 1945
"I should like to say how very much we cousins all feel, of love and sympathy to Molly and dear Aunt Loo in this last blow with the loss of the gallant Ted. Where ever he went they all seemed to love him, and I hear great praise of his lovable personality from every one of the family I meet. It is too devastating to think of, and I only hope that our very sorrowing sympathy may be at least a small comfort to Mollie."

From Alice Crompton, March 1945
"Like all the other cousins I am deeply grieved by the sad news from Canada. Ted seems to have won the hearts of all who saw him. We can realize what a comfort dear Aunt Loo is to poor Molly."

From Kathleen Smithells, March 1945
"We have all been knocked out, by the news of dear Ted being posted missing. Our hearts are full for Moll, Len, & Aunt Loo. These anxious days of waiting for news. It is hard to describe how much we feel for them. He is such a darling, we all love him here. It is just what Grace went through with Roger until she heard he was a prisoner of war. Now we are waiting for news of him again."

From Grace Werner, March 1945

239

"All our hearts are full again with love for all at Montreal in their new anxiety & we wait with them for more news. We had such a brave letter from Molly a few days ago - & she says how thankful she is to have Aunt Loo with her – I am sure she will be a tower of strength to Molly & them all – She has known sorrow herself to such a great extent ."

My mother's contribution was, as always with her W surname, the last in the folder. She wrote:

From Molly Withington, March 1945
"All the cousins will have heard before this of the sad news from India that dear Ted is posted missing, the date was 11th March & we got the telegram from R.C.A.F. H.Q. in London on the 15th. One's thoughts are all the time with his parents & grandmother. It seems so hard they should have to go through this again so soon after Bob's death. I had had a letter from Ted, such a happy one, only the day before, posted 7th March. He had just joined an R.A.F. Squadron near Calcutta, attached to S.E.A.C. H.Q. Both letters from L.W. this month were written before the bad news reached them at Montreal, but I have had an Air Mail letter from poor Moll dated 24th March, they had had no news since, nor any more details except that Ted's bomber was on a mission against enemy shipping and failed to return. Our thoughts are much with Grace, too, at this anxious time, wondering how things are with Roger in Germany. I do hope & pray there may soon be news of him."

How long was it before every member of the family gave up hope of Ted's survival? When I sent Dickie extracts from the Chronicle, I asked him for the dates of his brothers' deaths. This is his emailed reply.

Email from Richard Easton, New York, 2015
"How wonderful! What a work you've chosen to do!
Many thanks - I'm reading it very slowly as I keep being led off on a path of memory from something you've written. Wondrous!!
For your questions:-
I don't remember Cousin Alice - but that proves nothing I fear - I must have met her though.
For my brothers - Bob went first on August 18 1944 and Ted followed on March 11 1945.
Also my parents went at a similar space between - My father first (Bob was his favourite) and then my Mother (Ted was hers).
As for me: My memory is not much better! In my teens I used to go to the local Montreal Art Gallery for classes every Saturday - until one day we were set to draw Stained Glass windows - 3 students per

window. I wasn't about to work with two others so I stayed home and, listening to the radio, I heard 'Calling All Children' - a weekly program of the local Childrens' Theatre and they announced a free entrance into their School of Acting for the best 'I want to be an actor because ...' letter. I didn't but I figured I could write the letter and did - and of course - as I was probably the only applicant! - I won. They had a weekly radio program Saturday mornings – 'Calling All Children' - and I quickly became the regular male voice and then began to work in the grown-up programs. And hence into the local Amateur Montreal Repertory Theatre and became a protege of the great actress, Eleanor Stewart. And so it went, until I finished school (staying on for an extra year at the big central school to play Hamlet directed by an important local star, Charles Rittenhouse.) I used to leave home and take the train into the city and go straight to the MRT and build sets etc. until time to rehearse at Montreal High School - the principal finally had me in to his office to say that this production was so expensive - and so important to the school -that he could not throw me out - but made me promise that once the play opened he would never see me there again. "Certainly, sir!" I said - and honored my promise.

By then I had turned professional and was doing real radio and work at the MRT and The Childrens' Theatre and the local Summer Stock - Brae Manor Theatre.

Then I moved to Toronto for radio shows and then weekly repertory at Canadian Repertory Theatre in Ottawa and then the first season at Stratford Ontario with Tyrone Guthrie directing and Alec Guinness starring. At the end of the season Alec offered a scholarship to the Central School in London - Guthrie did not approve his choice so he came into the scheme and put me in. And the rest is history!

Phew! More anon."

A precious, living voice for the present Chronicle. It is all too easy to let people slip through our fingers. We can find a whole host of reasons for failing to make contact. This is especially shaming today when communication is so easy. We can plead busy-ness, laziness, diffidence, depression, illness, but there's only one explanation that is justified: the loss of self through dementia or death. *Carpe diem*! The pages of the Chronicle have made me more aware of the Roman poet's message. Better to seize the day than trust the future.

The cousins, while writing their newsletters every month for Cousin Alice, were as ignorant of their future as we are of ours. Could they foresee, at the start of 1945, that the war would end that summer? The fighting was growing more desperate on all sides. On January 1st 1945, 60 German prisoners of war had been shot by US guards. This massacre was said to be in retaliation for the massacre of 80 American prisoners by German SS troops. Did the cousins hear of this, or was the news suppressed?

The news of the Japanese retreat across the Irrawaddy River in Burma was surely announced and my mother would have heard it with her brother in mind. Grace Werner gave news, in February 1945, various members of her family who were serving.

> From Grace Werner, February 1945
> Roy is - as far as we know - still in the Mediterranean & Graham, up to now, has not got his hoped-for leave from India. A letter from Roger dated 14.12.44 in which he says he is trying to make a Christmas Cake – but good ingredients are hard to come by. A postcard dated 11.1.45 on which he says –'I fear the shooting season will be over before I return.'"

Roger, languishing in a prisoner of war camp in Germany, had doubted the war would end before the shooting season did in February. How much about the war's progress would be known in the camps? The embargo on giving away information, even in personal letters, was deeply ingrained and obeyed. The cousins refrained from writing about the war's battles, invasions, retreats, victories and losses in any specific terms. There's no mention in the Chronicle of the hot pace of events taking place in the first half of 1945 in Europe and the Pacific. Soviet Russian troops were advancing in Eastern Europe. Warsaw was entered by the Red Army in January and a communist regime installed. The Allies won what was known as the Battle of the Bulge as US and British troops completed a pincer movement towards the German borders. Hitler retreated to his bunker with his loyal lover Eva Braun.

In Burma, General Wingate's troops succeeded in taking over control of the Ledo Road linking China and India from the Japanese. The Japanese were retreating from the Philippines, massacring and raping civilians as they did so. The Americans were firebombing Japanese cities; we and the Americans were blanket-bombing German cities, while V2 rockets were exploding in England and Belgium. On February 14th, American planes bombed Prague *by mistake*. But – to our shame - the later bombing of Dresden was intended. In March the Allies crossed the Rhine into Germany but slowed their advance to allow the Soviet army to take Berlin. The share-out of Europe agreed between Roosevelt, Churchill and Stalin at the Yalta Conference of February 4th was in train. The Red Army entered Austria at the end of March, the Allies took Frankfurt, the Soviets took Danzig. Concentration camps were liberated and the horrors within revealed. On April 9th a group of Germans who'd been plotting against Hitler were hanged by the Nazis.

Weirdly, and echoing playground rules, a chain of countries had declared war on Germany in favour of the Allies. You can almost hear the explanations: *"we've actually wanted to be on your side all along."*

Here's the timetable:

February 4th, Ecuador declared war on Germany and Japan.

February 8th, Paraguay declared war on Germany and Japan.

February 15th, Venezuela declared war on Germany and Japan.

February 24th, Egypt declared war on Germany and Japan.

February 25th, Turkey declared war on Germany and Japan.

Februay 26th, Syria declared war on Germany and Japan.

March 4th, Finland declared war on Germany and Japan.

March 28th, Argentina declared war on Germany and Japan.

What sort of war, and where, were these countries going to fight? Germany was on the point of collapse, even if Japan was determined to fight on to the last breath of the last soldier. Himmler wanted to surrender to Allies but was shot by the Nazis for such a betrayal. On April 29th, Hitler married Eva Braun and the next day they committed suicide. On May 1st Goebbels and his wife killed their children and then they too committed suicide.

On May 7th Germany surrendered. May 8th was declared Victory in Europe Day, and bells rang throughout the country. But we were still at war with Japan.

On July 6th, Norway declared war on Japan.

On July 14th, Italy declared war on Japan.

On August 6th, a US B-29 bomber dropped an atomic bomb on Hiroshima.

On August 8th, the Soviet Union declared war on Japan.

On August 9th, a US B-29 bomber dropped the second atomic bomb - on Nagasaki.

On August 15th, the Japanese Emperor Hirohito prevailed against the military who wished to continue fighting, and surrendered to the Allies.

I'm scouring the Chronicle for mention of any of these events. After my mother's last contribution in March 1945, there is a gap until the July folder. I would have liked to read about the celebrations in Tavistock on V.E. Day. We went down to the Square to wave small Union Jacks on sticks in a big crowd in front of the Town Hall. Jane's birthday was celebrated on May 11th with a red, white and blue roll of crepe paper spread down the centre of the table over the best white damask tablecloth. The last tin of mandarin oranges had been opened for her birthday the year before. On Victory in Europe Day she was 9 and I was rising 7. The Americans had been around for some time before this. Their lorries careered up and down Down Road on their way to Plasterdown Camp, by Pew Tor. The soldiers stood in the open backs of the lorries. They laughed and called out as they threw us oranges and packets of chewing gum. *Cheerful* people, I thought, perhaps drawing a contrast to the general appearance of everyone around. So-and-so looks so thin, as one of the cousins wrote in the last months of the war. We are war-weary, wrote another.

We weren't starving, just hungry. In the cold, north-facing larder, beside the big, square, glass tank where the eggs were preserved in isinglass[91], the packet of beef stock cubes was kept. A treat was to unwrap a cube carefully, surreptitiously, while hiding behind the door, lick its exquisitely salty surface, then refold the wrapper and replace the cube in exactly the same position. I was also fond of hen food, taking a quick swipe at the contents of the aluminium bucket in the scullery as I ran past. Potato and carrot peelings and apple cores were the nuggets in a sawdusty mash.

---

[91] A preservative made from the dried swim bladders of fish.

Cousin Alice begins the next surviving folder with a typical blend of humility and stern purpose:

> "EDITORIAL NOTE
> It was entirely my fault that the June C.F.C. was so late. This July number is very late too because I <u>waited</u> for 2 contributions, one of which has not arrived.
> N.B. In future, I hope to despatch C.F.C. on 6th day of the month succeeding the month recorded in the number.[92]
> I shall <u>not</u> send reminders to Cousins, as after 5 ½ years they know that they are asked to send their notes on 3rd of month.
> A.C. Aug. 45"

Did the cousins quail? Even if they did feel like schoolchildren in disgrace, they still rallied to their editor's cry right up to the end of December 1945. The CFC still fulfilled its purpose of reassurance and mutual succour while the cousins' lives settled down after the upheaval and losses sustained since September 1939.

The July 1945 folder began its rounds in August. Alice, writing her own contribution in that month alluded to the greater freedom they would have in writing for the Chronicle.

> From Alice Crompton, July 1945
> "Dick has been home twice in August, & then came on the 31st to prepare for his new job as Chief Engineer at H.Q. (Nairobi) in British East Africa. Now that the War hush-hush is over, one hopes he will send a few notes occasionally to C.F.C. from B.E.A. Life in Tavistock has gone on at Markham in the usual cheerful way, people dropping in, & golf & bridge. Molly's Canteen & British Restaurant activities are now ended, but she has taken on District Visiting for the excellent Vicar Canon Bickersteth & I think is making a big success of it. She is a most popular member of society here & offerings of flowers, fruit & vegetables are for ever being brought to her.
> We all depart on 13 Sept. as at present planned, the Withingtons to Godalming & I to Doncombe.
> Jack has sent this interesting cutting from 'Times'. (*Cutting pasted in*)

---

[92] For example, the folder of newsletters with news of, say, May 1945 would start its circuit of the cousins on June 6th. Alice, I think, was wildly optimistic about timing throughout the Chronicle's wartime life.

> Sir, - As a footnote to the correspondence on the atomic bomb, may I offer this small coincidence?
> Groping in a darkened room on V night for something to read in bed, I found by chance a volume of Smollett's works. It almost opened itself at "Adventures of an Atom," in which the reader is addressed under the heading "The Atom Speaks": 'For the benefit of you miserable mortals I am determined to promulge the history of one period, during which I underwent some strange revolutions in the empire of Japan.'
> After that it was no great surprise to read: 'Fortune had not yet sufficiently humbled the pride of Japan."
> Yours, &tc, REGINALD POUND
> Rocmel, Sussex – Times 18/8/45.
> A.C."

I wonder if the cousins had any idea of the full scale of the horrors unleashed on the people living and working in the cities of Hiroshima and Nagasaki that August. The numbers of people killed by the two atomic bombs, both immediately and over time through the effects of radiation, are estimated to be anything from around 130,000 to 230,000. The first bomb had the nickname: Little Boy; the second, Fat Boy. The bombs were personalised while their effects were depersonalised. Whatever happened to those below had to be blanketed out of awareness. It was argued that the dropping of nuclear bombs was the only way to bring the war to an end and so save lives. The Japanese were the bad 'Them', faceless and guilty of heinous crimes. The Allies were the good 'Us', driven to retaliate against our better nature.

Lawrence LeShan in *The Psychology of War* contrasts two ways of seeing that we switch between, depending on the circumstances. When nothing threatens us as individuals or a group, we have nuanced views. We are able to perceive the reality around us in relatively rational terms; we can evaluate a situation in the mode of – his term - sensory reality. In times of war, there's a general shift in mind-set. We move from sensory into mythic reality. Everything is either good, if done by us, or evil if done by them. To avoid future war, LeShan proposes that we should understand the way this shift in thinking happens and call attention to it as it starts to happen. The idea that awareness is the first step towards change in individual behaviour is the mantra of humanistic psychotherapy. On a global scale – can it work? And have we time to change?

On Saturday October 31st 2015, a Russian plane with 242 people on board fell out of the sky over the Sinai Desert. The black box recorded an explosion at a height of 30,000 feet half an hour after take-off from Sharm el Sheikh airport on the Red Sea. It looks as though a bomb was smuggled on board in the tourists' luggage. IS – Islamic State – claims to have brought the plane down.

This is what war today looks like. IS is not a nation nor is it a place. It is a way of thinking. The Islamic fundamentalists live in mythic reality. The danger is that we slip into mythic thinking, too, and act accordingly, so perpetuating the battle.

If I were to ask the cousins the question that Koestler asked Freud[93], and why our country fought the war they had just lived through, they would reply in terms of mythic reality. Each believed that they were fighting an evil enemy. Not one of the cousins was a conscientious objector. Without doubt there was 'right on our side' in the Second World War – the concentration camps finally proved this - but we have no exclusive claim to goodness. And without our allies, we would not have won the war. Stalin's Red Army shot dissidents and deserters. America dropped two atomic bombs. We were partners in crime, as we are today. The last British prisoner was released from Guantanamo Bay on October 29th 2015, having been incarcerated there for 14 years without trial. It is thought that we were complicit in his torture. No nation, no human being, is ever entirely innocent.

*

---

[93] Why war?

SIXTEEN

The Aftermath - 1945

"Still muddling along. Oceans of repairs."

The folder labelled July, so late in being sent around due to the lateness of two contributions, contains news not just for that month but for the months until the end of November. The letters show the cousins gradually sorting themselves out after the hard graft of six years of war. Irene, the first as always in a folder, gives her customary fast and full account of what was going on in the Becker family while the whole country re-ordered itself to the conditions of peacetime.

From Irene Becker
"Trevor and I spent most of July at home at No. 70. Cecily came on 12 days leave on the 9th and we rushed about a certain amount and went to Bournemouth for a long week-end for her to see her two Grannies, whom she hadn't seen for four and five years respectively. It was lovely weather and we had two lovely sea bathes which we much enjoyed after a long lapse. What a joy it is to see all the crowds at the sea, enjoying themselves this summer. One used to think them a great nuisance in the old days, but this year the sight of them seems to add greatly to ones own enjoyment and pleasure. No wonder all the trains are crowded! On Saturdays the crowds here for the trains from Victoria down to the Coast are so large that the queues come right out of the station down the Buckingham Palace Rd. as far as St. George's Baths. I have never known such crowds at Victoria since the last War, when of course it was the fullest station ever. Now the leave trains all come in at roundabout 1.30 to 2 o'clock and the station is all packed on the Continental platforms side; the leave trains go back at about 11 p.m. so for some hours previously to that the stations is packed also, and you can barely get across inside without a great struggle. It will be interesting to see just how long it will go on for. Poor old Victoria, that was - all through the War, until last year and Paris was relieved - the very emptiest station in London!
Cecily is still working at Derby and doesn't know how long she will be in the A.T.S - but thinks almost certainly for about another year. Juliet came down with me from Glossop on the 25th to see her new headmistress at St. Paul's Girls' School, where she is going in the Autumn. She is due to go to Tavistock on Aug.15th so will wait here

now at No. 70 until then. We are expecting Wilfred on leave and it will not be worth the long journey back to Glossop for the short time available.

The workmen have not started to mend our broken house yet; the license has not yet been granted, though applied for – but things seem easier now in the way of getting a license – the chief difficulty is to find the workmen but Trevor is hoping they may be able to start by the end of next month (August).

We had the directors for the last Board Meeting at Vol-crepe Works at Glossop, for which we shall be in occupation of the Barclay's Bank Flat. In September Juliet and Dorothy are coming down to London to live, and most of the furniture as well. We shall only leave a few things such as arm chairs, tables & kitchen stuff - with beds from the Works for Trevor and the other directors to use when they go up. They will still need the flat, as hotels in Glossop are very indifferent and rooms to let practically non-existent at present. I shall go up and look after Trevor, when I can get out - with my household here, I may not have a great deal of spare time. We are hoping to get a local woman to look after the flat for us and keep it tidy and the moth out when no-one is there. The hens, chickens and ducks are all going to the original proprietor of the allotment, from whom Mike bought the hen houses four years ago. He is taking it all back again and is going to run the poultry and we hope sell us some eggs, when we are able to collect them and bring them to London.

Julie is rather sad at the idea of giving them all up, but in London we can't do anything about it. It would be too much of an undertaking and in any case our back area isn't large enough. Perhaps some date later in our lives we may have some down-settling in the country and be able to start again. Anyway, Juliet will be pretty well occupied going to school at Hammersmith every day and getting on with her education in earnest."

Alice's own contribution follows Irene's:

From Alice Crompton, July 1945
"On 1st July (Sunday) at Tavistock, I got to Church at 8 a.m. for the first time since end of Feb. 1944! I don't regard myself as an invalid now & am rejoicing in recovered energy! On 5 July I returned to Rye from Tavistock. Irene most kindly met me at Waterloo & saw me off from Cannon St. after tea. It was Polling Day & I had arranged to arrive in time to vote at Rye where I am a householder. However a friend discovered that I was not on the Rye Register & later my name was found on the Tavistock one. My Ration card 1944 -5, having been issued from the Tav: Food Office. I was not altogether sorry to be unable to vote as I wanted Churchill as P.M. but did not want a Conservative Govt. I had to content myself with my University vote wh. I gave with no uncertainty whatever to Eleanor Rathbone.

In Rye I had a hectic 3 ½ weeks. I had promised Molly to cook for her in the children's holidays, so thought I wd let my 26 Mermaid Cot for Aug & Sep. I put it in the Agent's hands & at once had 3 applications one of which I closed with. My tenant is a v. desirable one, a Mrs May, but she wanted the Cot for 6 months from 1 Aug. As she offered quite a satisfactory winter rent I closed with her. I can get a room if needed at a friend's in Rye, but I have various invitations too. I look forward to settling down in Rye again on 1 Feb/46, all being well.

It was a great pleasure to see my Rye friends again, & I had a v. kind welcome from them & from the tradespeople too. My friend Mrs Sutherland (Muriel who lives with Marjory Lees) came for a week's visit, during which I had 3 men to supper one evening and 8 women to tea next day. We also went out to coffee twice & to tea once. So we were not dull. Before Muriel came, I had Dick for a (very short) week-end, & Dicky Phillips, who was stationed at Lydd, cycled over to Sunday tea, & came again in the evening a few days after.

It was rather a terrific job getting the Cot ready for the tenant, who wanted as much space as possible. I had to store some suitcases full of things in order to empty cupboards & drawers. But Muriel & I got off by the 7.49 a.m. train on 1st Aug. she bound for Leamington and I for Tavistock."

In March my mother had reported that her brother Dicky had been in hospital near Calcutta with a broken arm. He was now home. Amazingly, a broken arm was the only mishap he'd suffered during the war, in contrast to Ivy Crompton's nephew, for example, who was captured and interned by the Japanese. By the time he was freed – as Ivy reported in September– he had lost four stone, and was suffering from ulcers and 'some kind of skin itch'. He'd met an Australian, just before the war. They'd only had six days together. However, said Ivy, they are together again now.

In the summer of 1945 there were many such reunions. My uncle Dicky was reunited with his wife Mary, the gentle teacher of sums when we stayed at Downderry. In September my mother wrote:

From Molly Withington, September 1945
"My brother has lately bought a house at Banstead & will be settling in as soon as he's demobilised. We should feel a great deal happier about him if his wife were in better health, as we can't think how she will manage as he will be at school nearly all day. They really want a thoroughly competent maid, but what a hope."

My Uncle Dicky was about to begin teaching economics and history at Sutton Grammar School for Boys, something he did with enthusiasm until his retirement. Mary, who had been so ill for some time, died soon after the end of the war. Dicky was on his own for years, closely monitored by my mother who was always hoping he'd find a new wife. He eventually married again. He and Elizabeth, who has only recently died, met at the Bridge table and were partners too on the golf course.

The end of the war in Europe meant Roger Werner was freed from his German prisoner of war camp and had come home. But he was not home for good. He was on his way back to a tea plantation in India when Grace wrote in August with news of her three surviving sons.

From Grace Werner, August 1945
"We have had lots of cheerful letters from John. After a short stay on Malta – which he did not like very much – he was moved to Sicily & he seems very happy there. He gets good bathing & has had several trips in a "whaler" or is it "Waler"- neither I expect – but the cousins will know what I mean, I hope.

I had a busy weekend about July 3rd week when Paul appeared with Norah Littlejohn – whom he has known for many years - & Roger with a girl called Audrey Norton. John had written to me soon after he left & said "If Roger asks to bring a girl called Audrey Norton home, I should encourage it. She's the right sort." She is quite a nice girl – but as far as I know they are not engaged. Roger wants the war in the East over & to start again with his Tea planters job, before he makes plans for his future.

By now Roger will be in India - he left here on Friday August 3rd. Henry & I came up to London on the 1st & Roger was then at his depot & was able to come out but had to report back every four hours. I stayed with Irene & Trevor & did so enjoy being with them again -& Henry put up in Paul's town flat. We had lunch with Roger Wed: & Thursday & then he said he would not get out again & expected to fly away in the early hours on the Friday. Henry then went off to Juliette Werner at Harrow & I came to Ford to stay with Jack & Ivy. Where I am thoroughly enjoying a lovely lazy holiday.

My Father went to Kathleen's & my good Mrs Hobson is looking after my animals for me. I shall be relieved when I hear from Roger & know what he has to do. The house will be terribly empty with no boys coming & going. Paul has left.M.A.P & is now on his peace time job once more – so will be hard at it & won't get home much from now on, I fear.

We hope to see Harold, Leigh's son, again before he goes back home – which he seems to think will be before Christmas."

Kathleen follows on from Grace with her typically brief contribution. The least sophisticated of the cousins, she's the one most able to touch the heart through sheer simplicity of expression. Her short message of sympathy to the Eastons on the loss of Ted was an instance of this. In the July folder, she is in her Eeyore mode.

From Kathleen Smithells, July 1945
"The summer seems to be flying on & we do not have much summer weather here: today started well, but we always finish up with a howling wind. It would be nice to have a day without it.
Before the war we always went to the Malvern hills for the weekend - everything has changed now & we stay at home.
Archie is playing golf & doing gardening, so he will get the air.
Father takes his morning walk. I have got some bridge for him over the weekend - we are able to take him out to bridge now as we can use the car. It is a change for him to get about.
Sunnyside is on holiday I am glad to say.
It is horrid saying goodbye to Roger again & for Grace not to know if he will be in the war again – just all going & coming. We seem to have seen so little of him.
We have all been very interested in the book about Ancoats Settlement there is much about Cousin Alice in it.
I am glad to think of Aunt Loo & Molly away having a break, it has been so nice for Gordon Henderson to have seen them & been with them – very lucky for him."

Kathleen often sounds lonely. My mother went to great lengths not to be.

From Molly Withington, July 1945
"Rather a quiet month here, after the gaieties of June, with Silver wedding & Birthday parties & lots of visitors. Alice left on 5th & Dick's leave finished on 4th & we were alone except for my F.A.N.Y officer billet, till the 18th when my Father came down for a visit of two weeks which was a great pleasure. I felt rather shy about my cooking efforts, but he was very kind & appreciative of my modest productions – the great thing was that I made the porridge to his satisfaction, as it is the most important thing on the breakfast menu as far as he is concerned! Luckily I got the car back on the road the very day he arrived after innumerable delays on the part of the local garage, which had it since the middle of May! So this was a great joy

& we had several picnics, & one Sunday packed lunch and tea & went down to Downderry on S. Cornish coast, about 30 miles away. It was a warm windless day though not particularly sunny, we could see the little town of Looe in the distance. Jane & Susie spent the time in & out of the sea & Daddy & I paddled. When I went to move the car from the Parking Place after tea I found it had got quite sunk into the sand & had great difficulty in getting it onto the road again, luckily several men came & helped push. So this will be a lesson to me not to drive off the road onto a sandy place again.

We had quite a lot of Bridge while Daddy was here & he got out for walks every day & thought nothing of going down town & back which was a great improvement on his last visit in December. Daddy left on 1st August & Alice returned from Rye, most kindly to help during children's holidays & Dick came down on 2nd his birthday, for Bank Holiday weekend when we had real summery weather."

Dick, my father, was born in 1893, so he would have been 52 on that August 2nd. My mother was rising 45. She still called her father 'Daddy' when writing for the Chronicle. I remember being puzzled when I first heard someone referring to Mummy. It took me a while to work out that she was not referring to the person who belonged solely to Jane and me. I had probably just joined Miss Atridge-Smith's nursery school, having reached the age when it's possible to imagine that other people have other, equally valid experiences to our own; the age of dawning empathy.

Sadly, I have no memories of Alice on picnics though she obviously enjoyed them. She pasted into the Chronicle a postcard of Dartmoor.

From Alice Crompton, August 1945

"The card above (kindly given to me by Jane) shows the sort of scene in which, during August, the household of Markham has been enjoying frequent picnics, 8 or 9 (I think) in the month! Having the car on the road again is an immense pleasure. I can't think why I have never heard more about the beauties of Dartmoor – a magnificent huge tract of quite unspoiled loveliness. The rivers vie with those of Scotland & Yorkshire & Lakeland with their rock pools & waterfalls. Jane & Susan are indeed fortunate in spending their childhood in such a glorious countryside.

I came back to Tavistock from Rye, on 1st August, perilously near the Bank Holiday travel crowds! Waterloo, where I had to wait some time was packed with people – soldiers, sailors, airmen, civilians & dogs. It would have amused me greatly, had I not been terribly sleepy, & in great fear of dozing past the hour of my trains departure!

> I had got up at 3 a.m. to finish getting 26 Mermaid St ready for the excellent tenant (Mrs May) who has taken it till the end of January. I expect to be in Rye again 20 – 25 October, at the George Hotel, where Marjory Lees and I will be together."

I expect to be in Rye on November 25th – 26th, bringing Cousin Alice closer with a visit to her home. I've booked us in, not at the George, but at the Mermaid Hotel.

Cousin Alice continued her contribution with a nostalgic description of Plymouth, renowned since its reconstruction for its lack of beauty.

> "In addition to the picnics, we have had two delightful days in Plymouth, which always seems to me one of the most beautiful & interesting towns in Gt. Britain. Of course the devastation of the blitz is terrible – the fine old Church in the heart of the town, the Guildhall & shopping centre are ruins. However, fine schemes for re-construction are being planned & meanwhile the Hoe with its glorious outlook on sea & woods is as enchanting as ever. We saw the wonderful colour film, Henry V, with Laurence Olivier in the title part. It was extraordinarily interesting to see the long bow archers in the Battle of Agincourt a day or two after we had heard of the Atomic Bomb in Japan – ancient & modern warfare!"

Like most of the population, Alice and the cousins cannot have had any idea of the scale and type of devastation the atomic bombs caused. There is only one more mention in the Chronicle's pages of the way the war was brought to an end. The cousins were absorbed in the aftermath of their own wartime experience. Trevor wrote to Alice on August 28th and she copied out his letter:

> From Trevor Becker, August 1945 (his first contribution)
> "We are still in a "muck" here & look like getting worse before we get better... this aftermath of Blitz coupled with V [*victory*] holidays & others, & now with the problems of re-conversion of industry, looks like providing me with mental indigestion for an indefinite period to come, but it will be better when it is possible to re-organize one's domestic affairs on slightly more normal lines. I don't think that anyone who hasn't been afflicted can realize what a pest it is to unscramble eggs, especially when one happens to have suffered from rather a surfeit of eggs in the first instance! I am expecting before long to get a licence for £800 of repairs (about half the total) after which we shall commence pulling down the ceilings & partitions of the three upper floors. Presumably we shall sit in gas masks in the

two below & towards Xmas adjourn to the upper stories while the fun continues below us. By that time I imagine that there will be sufficient coal to dry out the new plaster."

It is heart-rending to learn from Grace's contribution, which follows Trevor's letter, the family was still hoping that Ted might have survived. This was five months after he was reported missing.

<u>From Grace Werner, August 1945</u>
"Now that V.J. day has passed all of us will be thinking praying & hoping that Molly & Len may have some news. They are all seldom out of my thoughts just now.
Roger had a rather disjointed journey by air to India. He was taken ill when in the train between Karachi & Baklok suffering from violent pains in the tummy & bouts of sickness. He was travelling with a Major from the regiment who looked after him. He got him off the train at the next stop – by which time Roger was unable to walk & was practically unconscious – he was taken to a hospital & had been there three days when he last wrote. He felt quite all right again & expected to be released in a couple of days time. He did not seem to know the cause of the trouble but thought it was probably food poisoning. He most likely ate a lot of rich food in Karachi, which his tummy still can't stand after these years of prison food.
Henry had his seventieth birthday today. His cousin & his wife came for dinner last night & today we have had all the family & an old friend & his wife to tea – by all the family I mean Kaa & Archie, Joey, Gladys & Josephine & of course Father. John as usual was clever & timed his letter to his Father to the day. Paul too remembered & of course Henry's sister Juliette never forgets."

She included a letter from John, written on August 26th.

<u>Letter from John, 26.8.45</u>
"We had rather a good trip yesterday. Ten of us managed to squeeze ourselves into a small truck & go over to Milazzo a small town about 30 miles away over the mountains. I've never seen quite such amazing scenery. The mountains rise almost sheer from behind Messina & the road climbs up in almost unending spirals up the mountainsides. The ride is quite an adventure too because you are liable to meet a cart in the middle of the road – driven by an Italian who is probably asleep. When you get right to the top, the harbour at Messina looks like something out of a child's story book. It's rather a shock when you get down there to find it rather sordid & bombed & inhabited by a lot of savages – half of them have no idea of personal cleanliness whatsoever. We found a very pleasant beach & had a

bathe in almost hot water. We then took a run round the town & partook of spaghetti eggs & chips. Any good you get out of barracks you have to pay through the nose for. 10/- is very cheap for any kind of a meal – as it all comes from the 'Black Market'. The food we get in Barracks is dehydrated meat potatoes & the vegetables. I've had enough of it to last a life time.

The only daily paper we get out here is the 'Union Jack' – it's printed by the Army in Italy & gets to us a day late. We have all here made some very unpleasant remarks about an article that had appeared in the M/c Guardian the other day. The correspondent, apparently a woman, gets the idea that everyone out here can eat drink & be merry for about a quarter of the money you can in England. Of course it's absolute rot. The actual rate of exchange is 400 lira to the £1. So that laps up two, not too good, meals."

In these last months of the Chronicle, the cousins' contributions read like reports of the state of play in a feverish game where everyone changes position simultaneously. At children's parties we used to play a game like this called 'General Post'. Irene had spent the war shunting backwards and forwards, dealing with the conflicting demands of her husband and four children, so peace brought the hope of rebuilding the London home where all the family could meet. Home once again in Eccleston Square, she apologised for being late with her contribution:

From Irene Becker, Septembers 1945
"My notes for September are late again, I fear, and I know I shall get into hot water with our editor, especially after her emphatic footnote last month! But I do apologise and regret I wasn't able to help it, short of neglecting other jobs I have had to do at home, and in connection with our removal from Glossop to Eccleston Squre – or staying up a complete night. I often can't get to bed before 2 a.m. as it is, and when my tea comes at 7.30 a.m. I must confess it is rather a grind to feel suddenly that it is getting up time! But I am learning to move about much quicker than I used to do, and these brisk Autumn days are quite conducive to hurrying up. I often find myself breaking into a run as I proceed from shop to shop, or elsewhere on the daily rounds, and I can walk well faster than most of the pedestrians I overtake in the streets or in the underground approaches."

Overtake? I remember Aunt Irene as a slow and stately woman with a quiet, measured, almost languid, way of talking and moving around. Now that I've heard her voice in the Chronicle's pages, it's easier to imagine her breaking into a run as she heads for Victoria Station. Still, she did get a cup of early morning tea brought to her, to start her long day.

"Juliet and I permanently moved down from Glossop on the 15th so as to be ready for her to begin school at St. Paul's Girls' School, Hammersmith, on the 19th. We packed up everyone's clothes & belongings which were stored either at the flat or at the room up the High Street we have rented for the last three years for our surplus luggage. There were Mike's, Wilf's, Juliet's and Dorothy's things which had been stored there since 1940; Trevor's and mine and Cecily's also, which we had taken up there from time to time in many consignments to avoid its being blitzed; and a very good thing we did too – considering all that has happened to us. But it took a whole fortnight to pack it up, and us all working hard at that and doing little else. Dorothy cooked for us & looked after the hens in the meantime. However we got it all packed up, with Trevor helping with his things for a week of the time; got our various good-byes said, and saw Bishop's Van (the usual removal people from High St, Eccleston Sq. S.W.1,. who are beginning to know us quite well by now, since we have had eight removals all told since the War began) arrive and load it all up; it took them most of the day to do it; down the two flights of stairs above the Bank – then the lot above the tailor's shop in the High St; lastly Trevor's desk and Mike's from Vol-crepe Works, and his books etc. Somehow a wardrobe got left behind at Vol-Crepe Works but the firm managed to collect it later on and we had it delivered at No. 70 last week – much to our joy as we are so short of chests of drawers & receptacles now at No. 70 to put anything away in.

We are all living just how we can in the few rooms available at the bottom of the house. Nine of us all told, with the extra family and staff. The rooms are really quite comfortable considering, as long as the Weather isn't too cold, but the rooms are dark with the black stuff still over where the glass panes used to be, and we have to use a lot of artificial light. It is a bit gloomy, especially to the ones who have been living in the country, but one gets used to it and, after all, we are very lucky to have a roof over us really, considering what has happened – and plenty of space to sort out our belongings, repair & get cleaned damaged carpets and furniture. We have luckily found a very competent firm near by who still have a first class craftsman left in repairing furniture and he has promised to do it all in time. No sign of the licence to mend the War damage to the house coming through yet. But we are living in hopes and are meanwhile reasonably comfortable, even if our home looks somewhat chaotic.

Cecily and Wilfred have been backwards and forwards from time to time; she from Matlock and he from Folkstone - as a rule just for a few hours, and occasionally for a night thrown in. Wilfred has exchanged his old motor bicycle for a new one, which he has had just over a month and has managed to do 1600 miles on it, backwards and forwards to London & round about. He seems well now, though he is still rather thin. Julie is thrilled to see them both when they arrive often quite unexpectedly at any time of the day.

Wilfred came up last week after spending a few days apple picking in Kent. He brought a haversack full of the most lovely apples, glorious to cook & to eat. But he said they were not going to market at all, owing to the price control. The farmers were just selling privately in the 'black market'.

Cecily, by chance, turned up in the afternoon of the same day so we had quite a gathering for a short spell. Penelope Rees[94], my niece, is living with us now and going daily to Queen's College in Harley St, a "preparatory to University" educational establishment. She & Julie sleep in Lettice's bedroom for the time being and they enjoy being together. It is great fun for Julie, and makes all the difference for her in her London life after the country.

We were all quite sad to say good-bye to the chickens and ducks and the garden at Glossop, and Dorothy feels quite lost without them. Julie is, of course, very busy at school and with her preparation work in the evenings. I had to go down to Bournemouth towards the end of the month to see my Mother and help Edna, my youngest sister, with her whilst she collected her Winter clothes to take back to Tavistock. We had all our chores to do this time as we are unable to get any domestic help at all. But it was quite fun really; I enjoyed the cooking and the house was very comfortable - and so tidy and ornamental after our barracks at home! We were quite busy tidying up and disposing of the moth in some of the carpets and gathering the apples; she went up the trees with a pair of steps, and I fetched and handed up the baskets and picked the lower ones: the only drawback to this quite entertaining occupation was that we were bitten by swarms of mosquitoes; Edna on her legs & I on my arms, which proved they were swarming just about 4 feet above the ground – over the decaying apples.

I am on my way by train to Glossop now, with Trevor, to initiate the new housekeeper into looking after him and the other directors of Vol-Crepe Works when they stay at the little flat we all used to occupy. Hence the bad writing for which I apologize to the Cousins and hope they will be able to read the scrawl. We nearly missed our train being held up in Hyde Park by a procession of 30,000 strong – members of the War Damage Repairs Building trades on strike because the change over to Greenwich Mean time again had docked them of some of their pay - by losing the working hour in the afternoon, I think. We were stopped and jammed in a queue in the car, and were quite unable to move for over 20 minutes. However we just made it at Mary-le-bone with 5 minutes to walk up the length of

---

[94] Penelope was the daughter of Edna, Irene's sister, and Alan Rees who lived near the Golf Club at the top of our road in Tavistock. When Penny married a Tavistock neighbour, I was her bridesmaid.

the platform & get our luggage aboard. With our stay at Glossop, Trevor and I ended the month."

Up and down the country, north to south and back again, east to west and back again, the cousins reflect - on the scale of a nation small in geographic area which was never occupied by the enemy - the vast upheavals of global war evident elsewhere. In the present day, thousands upon thousands of men, women and children struggle to reach the safety of Europe in what is described as the biggest migration since the end of the Second World War. Even though we thought we had discovered the ultimate deterrent to war, that deterrent is useless in the face of the various kinds of war that are being waged today. No army can line up and fight the individuals who will strap explosives round their waists and walk into shopping malls in any city of the world.

It is estimated that a minimum of 60 million people perished in the Second World War.[95] The Last Post is sounded for them in annual November 11th ceremonies around the world. In 2015 I failed to join in any ceremony to honour all those who died in the 'War to end all Wars' of 1914 – 1918, and in all the many, many wars since then. I wasn't always so unfaithful to the people who fought the war against Hitler – the only war I knew from personal experience, however minor. I willingly joined in the quiet services of remembrance when my grandfather, a career soldier and stalwart supporter of the Royal British Legion, was still alive, as was my father who fought in both world wars and survived. I used to stand up proudly for the silent minute and think of the cousins I never met, plunging to their deaths in flaming planes over the Indian Ocean. But now – no longer. Remembrance Sunday has been inflated into a huge public display, where people can feel satisfyingly emotional even if they have no personal connection to a fallen soldier. It holds for me the same grotesque unreality as did all those mountains of polythene-wrapped bouquets for Princess Di outside Kensington Palace. Perhaps that was the moment when public displays of grief became addictive. The black-dressed politicians and officials laying wreaths at the Cenotaph, the

---

[95] Max Hastings, Ibid, p.669

phalanxes of parading troops, the mass production and sale of poppies, all the Last Posts and the nationwide minutes of silence – these occasions demonstrate grief rather than arise from it. Even though I know poppy sale money goes to support ex-service men and women, I put money into the Red Cross coffers instead.

Lest we forget is of course the argument in favour of elaborate November 11th ceremonies. But despite the ceremonies we *do* forget. The annual reminders do not shine light on the brutal realities of war. We see instead its fatal attraction. War brings excitement and romance into people's lives. Seventy thousand British women became GI brides. Nine thousand babies were born to the women who never became the brides of the GI fathers. Uniform combined with a cause can act like a pheromone, whatever the century.

This is Ivy reporting in September 1945 about the engagement of her son, Bobby Errington:

From Ivy Crompton, September 1945
"This has been a very happy month for us as Bobby has become engaged to a girl we like very much indeed. She is only 22, very unsophisticated & sweet. I am afraid they will have to wait a very long time as Bobby must get a job & work his way. I very much hope he may get some help about a job, but is not likely to be demobilised until the summer, I fear, & she probably later still. They are both in the Air Force & met up in Doncaster where there is a remount depot & they can go riding together. Horse riding is always fatal as well I know having watched & taken part in many a cross country romance. Riding home in the gloaming very tired, well I know it- ! Bobby hoped he might help to whip in a private pack of hounds on his off days but is not sure now if it will come off. Pamela Hebblethwaite is the girl and her home is at Fleet. I went down there last week & found everything so very nice, just as I would have ordered it. We feel Bobby is very lucky[96]...We have tenants in our small cottage now so are fully populated – a man & wife &"baby" which we swore never to have but they are most quiet & orderly, so we don't regret it yet. Jack & I went to visit George & Peggy last month: we found them all well & the children most charming & well behaved, yet quite full of fun & high spirits, not in the least suppressed – it speaks well

---

[96] Bobby and Pamela Errington took over the house at Doncombe Mill. I think this was after Jack's death when Ivy moved back into one of the cottages. The Erringtons sold Doncombe to the present owners in 1961.

for their school I think, but I shall be on my hobby horse again (i.e. nursery schools) if I don't look out

I had a short letter from Aunt Loo written on or near her 91st birthday; truly she is a marvel. I wish we might all grow old like her but of course it's far too much to hope."

Aunt Loo, my grandmother (and Jane's and Dickie Easton's), went on for a fair number of years. She died aged 98 in 1952, not quite the 102, rising 103, reached by my mother's mother. Grace and Kathleen's father, Joe Henderson, was in his 80s. Grace wrote in September.

From Grace Werner, September 1945
"Father has gone to Kathleen's after being here since I returned from Ford in early August. He's wonderfully well except for his legs which won't always get him far on his daily walk. It's difficult for him to get his hair cut out here, so he will be able to get that done in Didbury. We had hoped for news of Harold[97] – hope he has not gone off to Canada yet. Graham may be back any time now from India. Roy's Aircraft Carrier HMS "Skylark" is due in Southampton today but he did not feel at all sure that he would be on it. He thought he would be put off at Colombo. Gordon we expect daily. He has not been writing for some weeks. Josephine has gone off to school – we all miss her – she's a very happy-natured person & well loved by us all."

Grace also reported on the movements of her other menfolk.

"Paul has had to go for a medical for the Army which seems somewhat farcical when he has tried so hard all through the war to do his best to get into the R.N. or the Army – after he was turned out of the R.A.F with asthma. Anyway I don't really expect he will have to go – for one thing, he is over 30 years of age.
John seems very happy in Sicily & gets a lot of nice sea trips. I don't expect he will be there very much longer – but he won't be home for leave when he does move, more's the pity. Roger seems to think he may be out much sooner than he expected - & may even be back for Christmas which would be marvellous. He hasn't been at home for Christmas since 1936.
Henry expects to be looking for a new job at the end of the month. So goodness knows where we may move to within the next few months. We could easily let our half of this house & Mrs. Holtham says they want the Flat for another year. Winter approaches & with it

---

[97] Harold was Leigh and Helen Henderson's son from Kelowna, British Columbia.

comes my rheumatism again – I expect dashing out without bothering with an extra wrap to the hens does not help. What a bore it is, getting old."

Age and hens keep cropping up in these final contributions. My mother wrote:

> From Molly Withington, October 1945
> "I hope this won't be too late for the October issue of our Chronicle.
> Dick, as all the cousins know, has gone abroad, to H.Q. E. Africa at NAIROBI. He got back to Markham from London on 1st Sept & was very busy packing up his heavy kit to go by sea, sorting out things etc. having inoculations. He himself was to go by air about 17th. So we all went up to Godalming by train on the 13th – leaving Cousin Alice in charge of the house, Sammy & the hens! – and spent his last weekend at Beryl's[98]. Daddy kindly gave us the use of his car (he provided the petrol!) which was a great boon, as Dick had business to do in Guildford & had to go to Aldershot for a final inoculation. We spent one afternoon at Guildford with the George Mellershes in their new house.
> Dick went down to Bournemouth on the evening of the 17th. He called in at No. 70 on his way from Godalming and luckily found Trevor just back from his office. Trevor regaled him with sherry & went & saw him off. Dick flew by B.O.A.C. line, leaving the airport near Bournemouth on 18th morning. Aunt Ciss & Lettice made a great effort to speed him on his way, but unfortunately, he was not able to speak to them, as all the passengers were hustled into the plane. He spent a night at Cairo, & another at Khartoum, eventually arriving at Nairobi on 22nd Sept. I am now getting Airmail letters, but they are not at all speedy. Today's took 12 days. He says he will write an account of his journey for the C.F.C. He writes very enthusiastically of the place, climate, & his surroundings & is thoroughly enjoying himself."

My father's first and only contribution was pasted into the Chronicle by Alice. It is also the first and only typewritten contribution. The way it has been neatly set out makes me wonder if he typed it himself or had it typed by a secretary in the Nairobi headquarters. Both are equally possible. My father liked machines and the challenge of learning how things

---

[98] Cousin Beryl was my mother's first cousin. They grew up together in Holloway Hill House, Godalming, during the years Pop and Mop were abroad. Beryl was a V.A.D. in the First World War, and Red Cross nurse in the Second.

worked. He was methodical, and would have made, during the long journey, precise notes as neatly formatted as the final, typewritten pages. I can see him reaching into a jacket pocket for the stub of a pencil he always kept there. The journey took three and a half days, according to his diary but a day longer than this, according to my mother. The time difference may account for the discrepancy. She continued her account for September:

> From Molly Withington
> "It is rather lonely for me, after a good deal of coming & going all the summer, & no F.A.N.Y billet now, or maid in the house, but I have plenty to do & that's the main thing."

Cousin Alice included in the Chronicle a letter written by Aunt Ciss on September 20th.

> From A.E.I. Becker, Aunt Ciss, September 1945...
> "We went to see Dick off, but it was a damp squib, and we never met! Lettice just saw Dick's face in the plane as they took off, but the police won't let you have the run of the drome at all! & they said we were v.lucky to be allowed inside, escorted by a policeman. Dick came in a bus & must have been put straight in the plane & off, for we followed from the gate of the drome. Dick gave over the phone the no. of the plane he was to go in & the police escort enquired if the No. of the plane he was evidently in was that same no. It wasn't, so we were off the scent. We had breakfast at ¼ to 8, and got to Hove (?) ½ an hour before the plane was due to take off. They are always afraid of smuggling & the police at the Enquiries said we would never be allowed on the drome. They got through to the HEAD on the phone, & we were to be allowed only under police escort! …..
> I had inflammation of the gall bladder & jaundice recently in addition to my other troubles, & lost about 1 stone. Lettice was so worn out with the public work & the extra that involved on her through my being ill and unable for my own work that had WAR not ceased she felt she would have had to give up the Red X. My teeth seem to be cracking off these days & I have had to have teeth & stumps out. I had a wisdom tooth out on Monday …..
> The food problem increases, as our hens don't lay much. Last year we always had endless EGGS, & were never at a loss for a stranger's food. Our tomatoes have been late in ripening. We have had more peas than I ever had in the garden, but the drought came at the wrong time for the phlox, & they were frizzled – such a pity!
> I am going to write to Louie. I think she had a complete cure for her arthritis, either in England or in Canada. I want to hear more about it!

I feel so ***terribly*** sorry for the Eastons & Louie about those two – dear boys ……
We go out getting wood for winter. Blackberries have hung like grapes & we have had lots of mushrooms. We make marrow jam & add 1 lb of 3/6 honey! When we find we have 3 lbs of jam, I add 1 lb of honey, which makes 4 lbs of what we call 'Honey' even though it is mostly jam! We are v. thrilled about this!!"

In October the Beckers were still waiting for the builders and the licence to repair war damage to no. 70.

From Irene Becker, October 1945
"We are still all muddling along in our semi-underground and dark quarters awaiting the arrival of the workmen to set the upper part of the house in order here at No. 70 Eccleston Sq. We seem to have shaken down now in quite a tolerably comfortable groove. We have collected enough fuel for half the winter at any rate and are able to have the hot water on every evening from 4 o'clock onwards though it has to go out and cool off by morning in order to conserve stocks of coke, for more urgent weather than now progresses. It has been very kind to us all this wonderfully mild autumn, without wind, or scarcely any, and no frost. We are in Winter now and one would never know it in London, except that the days are very grey and we have our artificial light on practically all day now except in the flat where Trevor, Mike and I sleep. It already gets quite dark outside in the streets by 4.30 – quite like old pre-war days from the appearance of everything. London is ugly now so perhaps it is a good thing.
We have now completed Aunt Ciss' bathroom into quite a useful & roomy dining-room. Our own oak gate-legged table is now back from the repairer's shop after its upheaval in the Epsom Blitz and we have a small mahogany chest of drawers for the silver and cloth mats etc. with a good old former door (from Ashley Court, Epsom) as a table top to it. The lift[99] is a great boon, though the rope broke last week and wasted a pint of milk unexpectedly. Quite a blow this but forgotten in the intense relief that no one was hurt and curiously no crockery broken. Trevor was away but we were able to find a man to mend it in the course of a few days - fortunately, as it was an awful grind carrying all our meals up and down the stone stairs to the kitchen. However all the young folks, four of them, were at home, and they wore their shoes out on it (if they went) and not me! They were all very cheery over it.
I have Mike, Juliet and Penny Rees[100], my sister's girl, always with us now and Wilfred is home on a fortnight's embarkation leave; last time

---

[99] I described this lift in Chapter Three.
[100] Penny, the daughter of Edna and Alan Rees who lived near the Golf Club at the top of Down Road. She was studying in London. When she married

he never went; owing to V.J. day, things got a bit disorganised I think. Anyway something happened to him and he did not go. This time he is really off - in the middle of November, I think - to the Central Med: Forces. He does not know where of course. He is quite interested to be going at last, though rather sad he won't be home for Xmas after all; he is so near London now at Gravesend and Cecily has moved to Frensham, Surrey, so they both thought they might get a time off at Xmas. However it isn't to be; he has had a nice spell near home and we have been luckier than most.

Cecily is hoping to get home tomorrow for her leave to see Wilf before he does. I suppose Wilf will be away at least a year as he is in Group 48 for getting released, some time away in any case.

I have got quite accustomed to London once more and really feel at home now, especially for the Winter and I think the children are growing used to it. The girls play ping pong up in the top kitchen with great gusto, in spite of the holes & falling plaster in the ceiling and have certainly upheaved the pigeons whose home is up there."

Cousin Alice stayed the night with them in the middle of the month.

From Alice Crompton, October 1945

"During this beautiful month, I've enjoyed much variety, staying in 8 delightful places one after another, including a week's sojourn in my own cottage at Rye, 5 days of which Marjory Lees was with me. When Oct. began, I was just finishing my visit to Jack & Ivy. Ivy had had 2 nights before I left with Mrs. Hebblethwaite (the mother of Bobby's fiancée Pamela), whom she & Jack like very much. She has a nice house at Fleet, nr.Reading. Jack drove me to Bath on 4 Oct. & I had a good journey to an old friend, a retired Hospital Matron (once one of my Settlement girls) who lives in her own nice bungalow in North Bournemouth. Bournemouth was very full with happy holiday makers & looked most bright & cheerful with lovely flowers in the Gardens. I had hoped to see Mrs Watts & her daughters at Barnston, but they had left just before I arrived.

From 6th – 8th I was at Ringwood most glad to see Cissie & Lettice again, after 2 years. They were neither of them in very good form, but one is thankful to know that Lettice is much less busy now that War work is over & Cissie will profit by cessation from heavy garden work. Lettice took us a lovely drive in the New Forest on Sun. aft. wh. both her mother and I much enjoyed. The car was loaded up with wood whilst we stopped near a clearing. Next day I proceeded to Wycombe & had 8 happy days with the Ensors. Helen R. & I went into London on 13th for a meeting of the Manchester High School Old Girls Association (London branch). It was startling to see there a

---

Peter Fox, the son of Tavistock neighbours, I was her bridesmaid.

Miss Harrison, Fanny, who taught in the Preparatory School when I was in the Vth form, & who was present as a pupil on the day the school opened. She must be a good deal over 80 but made an excellent speech at this London gathering.

On 16th Oct. I went to Guildford to see Dr, Jobson, and then dined – (2 roast fowls!) & slept at 70 Eccleston Sq. It was indeed a joy to see Trevor & Irene in their own real home again, tho' the house & furnishing is bereft of much of its beauty. But it won't be very long now before things are more as they used to be. Anyway a visitor has all the welcoming kindness which always characterized that house. Next day I went off to see D. J.J. Mallon at the Reform Club. I asked him if he was there to quicken the Liberal Party but I gathered he thinks that can't be done! That night I slept at Violet Dale's (63 Eccleston Square) & next day returned to Rye, after visiting at Westfield Coll: Mrs. Stocks, who wrote the v.g. history of "50 Years in Evry St" to celebrate the Jubilee of the M/c University Settlement. It was nice to get to my own little house on 18th & the various tenants had left it in fairly good care.

Marjory Lees came on 20th, after attending the London Meetings of the National Council of Women. The weather was very windy during her stay, with deluges of rain at night, & the day before she left there were great gales and floods at Hastings (only 1/2 hr by rail from here) where we had intended to have an outing! We were both quite glad of a quiet time, & had a good deal of backgammon, & twice people came in for evening coffee and we went out to tea. Nearly every day we dined at one of the 3 pretty little restaurants here, where one gets excellent food at very reasonable terms. On 25th, Marjory left to stay with her niece, Mrs Macaulay at Shamley Green nr. Guildford. And I went to Sutton in W. Sussex to stay with Archie's aunt Alice Cohen, an old friend at the M/c High School. After seeing so much of the beauty of Devonshire, Wiltshire, Hampshire & Bucks as I have recently been lucky enough to do, I was glad to find that Sussex, my county by adoption, quite holds its own with any of them. The hanging woods on the S. Downs & the bracken covered commons with masses of silver birches & frequent huge oaks & beeches were looking at their best in the autumn gold & brown. But high winds were bringing the leaves down too fast. We had a couple of lovely drives to Pulborough & Petworth, but this time did not get so far as Chichester, 12 miles away. Alice's garden was full of chrysanths & roses, & tight buds of Iris stylosa unfolded their beauty in the house."

Meanwhile her brother Jack was working hard to bring order back to Doncombe Mill.

From Jack Crompton, October 1945
"During the wonderful spell of fine weather which must have lasted for a month, we have concentrated on the dry dam (Aunt Loo will

know what it is) digging up, clearing & replanting the herbaceous stuff. It hasn't been touched since we let the house in 1940 & was in an appalling state, but our old gardener has stuck at it & 2/3 is now in fair order, tho bind weed dock & dandelions will no doubt come up merrily. Half our roses have gone, so we are abolishing some beds & seeing what we can find to fill the gaps in the rose garden proper. We shall pretty well have to remake the grass at the bottom of the dam, but that will have to go on during the winter months & sow where necessary in the spring. Now the weather has broken & outdoor work is at a standstill we have turned our old man on to decorating inside and he has done both bathrooms & made a very good job of them. There has also been an accumulation of wet weather jobs for me. At the moment I am just completing a new sluice gate for the lake sluice. The old one had pretty well collapsed & let all the water out. There is also a job on the central heating boiler - not that we are thinking of using it at present but it needs attention. We had our Saving Week last week. I put a target of £200 for the village but only got £152 most of which was window dressing. I find people sticky about it now & that is generally the case in this part of the world. Pay packets are of course much smaller now & a lot of people have left & generally the direct stimulus of the war has gone, tho' saving is naturally as urgent as ever. However in the absence of a complete change of heart & the presence of the atomic bomb a pessimist might fairly say that it doesn't matter greatly what we plan now as mankind will be wiped out in a few years. I wonder?"

Grace and Henry Werner were coming to terms with the end of the war although in many respects the war hadn't ended for them. Charles would never come home. Roger was still serving in India, and John in Sicily. It looked as though neither would get leave for Christmas. In any case, Roger might only come back to see the family briefly before taking up tea-planting again in India. Yet the war *had* ended, which meant Henry was out of work.

From Grace Werner, October 1945
"The thing that is on my mind most is the fact that Henry's job of war work finished at the month end. He has advertised in the M/c Guardian, without any result - & has one going in the Times when they have room for it. I expect a rest will be good for him & there are oceans of repairs needing doing in the house & garden. Yesterday we had a "go" at the hen house & run – but the rest will be pretty awful if it goes on for too long. Paul has had a nasty attack of Asthma – which has left him limp, more so than usual he says. He always seems to get it at this time of the year. I had hoped to have him for this weekend but work has kept him south – We still have Alan Littler

here – he has been with us now as a P.G. for seven weeks & seems no nearer finding somewhere to live in M/c – which is where he has to be for his work. Rooms of any kind seem impossible.
Roger is now a Major & seems to have settled down to a more or less office job at the Gurkha headquarters in Bakloh, N. Punjab. Most of the other officers who were P.O.W's with him are back there now. He said in his letter that John had sent him a letter addressed to 4th P.O.W. Gurkha Rifles, instead of 4th P.W.O (Prince of Wales Own) & it had cost him several drinks in the Mess. He does not mention getting demobilised. Anyway, I have had a feeling all along he would not get out before March – but wish he had been able to be home for Christmas. He says he & a friend have bought a gun at Lahore, just as expensive as at home – they mean to join for a bit. Also he is getting plenty of riding & some fishing so life does not seem too bad, take it all round.
John is in Sicily still, & rather sad as his friend is leaving this week for England and won't be coming back again. He says they have had some quite cold weather but lovely weather on the whole but bathing has stopped – & sailing on off days has not been so nice without the warm sunshine. He says he & some of the others clubbed together & bought a wireless set - & have had great fun getting various programmes & all feel it has been money well spent. He tells me he has ordered a parcel of dried fruits & Christmas goods sent off through South Africa. Very welcome. I think - judging by the ships now – things will be very thin this winter."

The end of the war didn't yet bring much joy for my mother. Dick was far away in East Africa. The series of FANY billets who had provided company during his wartime absences had come to an end. Nanny Guerini had left in 1942, and the live-in cook Bessie no longer needed to live-in and cook. She returned to her home in London. My mother had to learn how to get meals on the table. She used to ring up a friend, receiver in one hand, a saucepan in the other. "What do I do after adding the flour?" She wore a cross-over-the bosom overall (perhaps left by Bessie) and sometimes a frilly apron. The sight of her at the stove was surprising. We knew we had better keep out of the way.

There's an undercurrent of depression in her October letter. The liberal use of exclamation marks are inadequate cover.

From Molly Withington, October 1945

"Very sorry I am without any notepaper of a suitable size, blocks seem always to be of small size nowadays. We had splendid weather all October except for the week or so of bad gales & storm that swept the whole country. The children were able to wear summer dresses till nearly the end of the month, but now it is beginning to be rather cold in the early mornings & Jane leaves the house at 8.25. I must say I rather miss the "Summertime" hours, now the evenings are getting so dark.

I get two or three letters a week from Dick, they take about 12 days as a rule. He is in good form & enjoying himself, getting good golf at weekends with a friend of Hong Kong days, who is also stationed at Nairobi, Major "Paddy" Wren. He has seen elephant, zebra, rhino, & other strange beasts in their native haunts & wishes he had his cine camera with him. He did one tour to Mombasa by car & got some sea-bathing there – altogether it seems a great deal more pleasant than life in London, with its crowds & queues."

So pleasant did my father find life in Kenya that he wanted my mother to join him. The family would settle there. My mother's refusal to budge from Tavistock was afterwards said to have saved our bacon. Otherwise, everyone opined, we'd have been "murdered in our beds by the Mau Mau."

The end of the war brought the beginning of the end of the British Empire. Independence was achieved in most cases by violence. At last, after enjoying a life of privilege on the backs of others, we were faced with reality. The Romans went through a much longer period of superiority over the people they called the *Brittunculi,* the little Brits, and their empire disintegrated more slowly. Here's an extract from a review in The London Review of Books, November 2015.[101]

"It has been suggested that what happened in the later fourth century is that when small farmers were bankrupted by the heavy taxes needed to pay for the soldiers, the richest members of society bought them out at knockdown prices and built their enormous estates and palatial villas in the Cotswolds and along the south coast. The poor got poorer, the rich got richer, and in the end the whole society collapsed."

This sounds familiar.

Since May when I started weaving the present chronicle around the cousins' chronicle, far greater numbers of migrants,

---

[101] LRB, 19 November 2015 issue. Tom Shippey's review of '*The Real Lives of Roman Britain*', by Guy de la Bedoyere.

forced by poverty, violence and war to flee their homes, are attempting to enter safer countries. Mexicans have been streaming into the US for decades, legally and illegally. Fourteen million migrants entered the US in the first decade of the 21st century. It's estimated that this year 800,000 migrants will enter Europe. The number of terrorist attacks is also increasing. On the internet there's a list of incidents that have occurred this year, giving the location and numbers of dead, wounded or kidnapped, and the ideological group of the perpetrators. The list goes on and on. It's far longer than I'd foreseen. People while going about their normal routines have been murdered by Islamic militants in Nigeria, Somalia, Chad, the Cameroons, Tunisia, Mali, Lebanon, Libya, Afghanistan, Pakistan, the Philippines, Saudi Arabia, Kuwait, Iraq, the Yemen, Turkey... .

To record in these pages just two of these massacres: in April in Kenya 148 students were murdered by four adherents of Al-Shabaab, and in Ankara suicide bombers left 102 dead, and 508 injured at a peace rally.

There's now a third.

Two days ago, on November 13th 2015, three teams of terrorists opened fire on people enjoying an evening out in three different locations in central Paris, leaving 129 dead and many more critically injured. The front line is anywhere and everywhere, shifting all the time.

More candles, more flowers, and another minute's silence. Nothing ersatz about these displays of shock and grief.

*

SEVENTEEN

The End of the Chronicle - 1945

"Everyone *once, once* only. Just o*nce* and no more." Rainer Maria Rilke

I woke to the sound of splashing water and quarrelling gulls. For a moment I thought I was in the waterside cottage we used to own in Port Isaac. Then I remembered. We were in Rye, staying at the Mermaid Inn. Near the bottom of the cobbled street, we'd found number 26, Cousin Alice's cottage. Its windows were veiled; darkness within. Someone closing the shop on the corner didn't know who owned the cottage. She suggested I knock. "We are all very friendly here," she said. I climbed the three steep steps to the cottage's black front door and lifted the knocker. I knew it was useless to be summoning Alice up in this way. I tried the house next door and listened to the same absence of response. Second or holiday homes, we reckoned, and November one of the quietest, emptiest months of the year in places like this.
   The sound of water came from the fountain playing in the small courtyard below our bedroom window. The gulls were squabbling around chimney pots on sagging, reddish-brown tiled roofs. A few leaves remained on a rampant Virginia creeper, crimson against black-and-white half-timbering. Inside, everything sloped and creaked. Our bedroom was number 2. No ghosts visited in the night. A fellow guest had told us the evening before of the hotel's reputation as one of the most haunted places in England. Six ghosts are said to share the hotel with present-day visitors. We didn't pursue this conversation, not wanting to spend a wakeful night misinterpreting every creak. Next morning, sitting up in bed with a cup of tea and the hotel's brochure, I learnt that a lady in grey sits by the fireplace in bedroom number 1. I don't believe in ghosts until I'm spending the night with them.
   I understand now why Cousin Alice liked the ancient little town of Rye so much. The town clusters on a rounded hill, drawing in its skirts against the water at its feet – the tidal river in which boats are moored. The sea has long since departed to

a distant point two miles away. The town has the air of proud retirement from its maritime history, rather than dismal redundancy.

In the silvery light of the morning we set off up Mermaid Street[102] to find our way to Lamb House. The cobbles glistened after rain. Did Cousin Alice use a stick? As I carefully placed each foot, I reminded myself of Alice's age at the time of the Cousins' Chronicle. She was 77 in 1940, the same age as I am in 2015. On August 18th 1940 an air raid destroyed the Garden Room of Lamb House. A plaque in the high red brick wall at right angles to the Georgian house records the event. This is where Henry James lived from 1897 and wrote three of his novels. 'Ways of the Dove', 'The Ambassadors', and 'The Golden Bowl'. Two other writers who lived at different times in Lamb House were Rumer Godden in 1968 – 1973 and in the 1930s E.F. Benson, a prolific writer best known for a series of satirical novels featuring two characters called Mapp and Lucia in the town of Tilling, his fictional version of Rye. The Garden Room was re-created for the filming of the series for television.

Benson is buried in the churchyard of St. Mary's Church just along the road. I cast a cursory eye around for a gravestone with the name Crompton on it, not knowing if Alice had died in Rye or elsewhere. Later on the way back to Devon via Godalming, I learnt from Jane that Alice had ended her days in a nursing home in Tooting, brought there from Rye by Uncle Trevor Becker. Jane went to visit Alice in Tooting several times in the mid-1950s. At the time, Jane was a student at the London School of Economics and living with Uncle Dicky in Sutton. She remembers Alice's very sweet smile and of course her deafness. We wondered how the Dr Jobson, her 'aurist' in Guildford, helped her. Hearing aids that were small and light enough to wear were only just becoming available in the mid-20th century. Perhaps her home-made, cardboard ear trumpet was more efficient than anything Dr Jobson could offer; maybe even more efficient than the fiddly miniaturised aids that help – and frustrate – today's hard of hearing.

---

[102] I've recently learnt that Ivy as a widow lived in the cottage next door to number 26. Grace, also widowed, would stay at number 26 for an occasional holiday and to spend time with Ivy.

Apart from mentioning her regular visits to Dr. Jobson, Alice only twice draws attention in the Chronicle to the difficulties of deafness. The first occasion was when she described my Hunt the Thimble invitation. The second time was in December 1945, in her final contribution.

> From Alice Crompton, December 1945
> "My chief interest in the earlier part of December was the Re-union Dr J J Mallon & I arranged for friends of the Manchester University Settlement. It was held at Toynbee Hall which is the Mother of Settlements all over the world). In 1937 we had a similar gathering & this present one was smaller, only about 37 being present. But we are all 8 years older! We had lovely flowers & very good refreshments, provided by Dr. Mallon's housekeeper & everyone seemed to be having a good time. Some of my early friends & helpers could not come, because of failing health e.g. Sir Sydney Chapman & Sir Gerald Hurst. But we had Prof. and Mrs Weiss, Sir Philip & Lady Hartog. And Lady Woolton was with us, but her husband was performing some function at Manchester Infirmary. They both used to help at Ancoats Hall in their undergraduate days. We had speeches from Mrs. Stocks whose History of the Settlement (excellently written) has been published in this its Jubilee year; from Dr Mallon who as usual was most amusing, & from R.C.K. Sensor (Scrutator of Sun.Times) who I am told was the best of the three.
> It was a very great pleasure to me that Trevor, Irene & Mike were with us. Characteristically Trevor did a wonderfully kind thing for me, & did it very cleverly too. He took full notes of the speeches in long hand and gave each page to me when full, so that I could grasp the best part of what was said. He used when a schoolboy to come to our Ancoats Xmas parties to help. I remember his being worried because the tarlatan sweet bags for the Xmas Tree might not be filled equally. So next day he came with a neat little scoop wh. he had made from a cocoa tin. Just like his thoroughness!"

Alice would have gone up to London for the reunion by train. I could imagine her setting forth from her white clapboard cottage in Mermaid Street to make her way down the narrow streets to the railway station, a pinkish-orange and ochre four-square building that reminded me of a slice of Battenburg cake. From here – sometimes with her cat Tony in a wicker basket, once with the family silver to save it from potentially invading Germans – she sat in trains which chuffed and puffed around the wartime countryside to stations in the north, the west and south: to London and Manchester, Wiltshire and Surrey and

Devon. She used her journeys and her Chronicle like the shuttle of a loom, weaving together for mutual support and encouragement throughout the war the separate strands of the Becker family and her many friends from her Settlement days.

Her Editorial Notes at the beginning of this last folder noted that, being number 72, it completed the Chronicle's 6th year of issue. She asked if anyone would like to take over the "not unpleasant task of Editorship." She was willing to hand over the job, but was ready to carry on if need be. She obviously expected to carry on for she goes on to say:

> *"Will the Kelowna Cousins please post to Rye each number when read and not let them accumulate? Otherwise I am sometimes without any of Len's invaluable cardboard covers. A.C. 1.1.46."*

Len Easton in Canada must have contributed the cardboard covers with a printed grid pattern that held the monthly newsletters in the Chronicle's last year. No-one came forward to continue Alice's work, and Alice clearly decided not to carry on. Maybe the cousins intimated to her that it was time to end the Chronicle, now that life was returning to normal. I think she would have missed the regularity of contact with all the members of the family. She would have missed hearing the family news every month, from Cissie Becker and Lettice Williams, and Ivy and Jack Crompton, and Grace Werner and Molly Easton and Molly Withington, and Irene and her brood of Beckers. She would have missed the business of garnering contributions in time each month, written - if the cousins managed it - on the right size of paper and with the right size of margin. She would have missed the business of punching holes, threading the pages together with scraps of wool, and sending the folders on their way from Rye's Post Office. She would have missed receiving so many letters all the time. From 1946 onwards the postman would have delivered far fewer envelopes to number 26. Without the Chronicle, I am afraid Cousin Alice would have slipped down the list of the family's priorities.

When, on our way home from Rye to Devon we called in for lunch with my sister in Godalming, I stood for a moment on Jane and Peter's patio, looking towards Downderry just visible through the trees at the end of their garden. I was waylaid by thoughts of the past and the odd juxtaposition of places and times in the life of an individual. I am still the one who sat on the lead-covered balcony outside the room where I slept in Mop's house, and who was photographed in the act of putting on a buckled shoe, looking up at the camera, 'being sweet'. I am still the one who climbed into the red pedal car and careered around the sandy paths between the apple trees in the garden where I stood on Jane's patio last week. I am the one who was called Susan and Susie and Sue, and am still called by these separate names depending on who is doing the calling. Am I a different person according to the name I'm called? How different am I today from the child in the Chronicle's pages? Apart from the harrowing effects of ageing, I feel we stay essentially the same all through our lifetimes.

Today, December 4th 2015, I am drawing near the end of this past and present chronicle. There's been a day-long debate in the House of Commons on what headline writers call war. It is a neat three-letter word, even if the thing that is described is far from neat, far too complex to be bound within three letters. Prime Minister Cameron put the case for extending the present bombing of IS targets in Iraq to bombing IS targets in Syria. Labour's leader Corbyn opposed this. He gave his Labour MPs a free vote, a principled decision which risked losing the debate. Many Labour MPs would vote on the government's side, and did so. The government won and immediately Tornado jets were on their way to supplement those based at Akrotiri airport, the Cyprus jumping-off point for bombing missions. Within hours, four British Tornados hit six targets in the Omar oil field in eastern Syria.

These British war planes and their bombing raids, according to Cameron and the majority of MPs, will help to bring about a political settlement in Syria. This is LeShan's mythical reality at work. It's been called magical thinking, a way of thought far removed from practicalities. *We must bomb this evil out of the world.* But IS is not a bombable target. It exists in minds which then act in the physical world to horrifying effect. The alternative to bombing a shifting target is to hold back in the physical world and battle instead for the minds of fundamental religionists on all sides. This is a far more difficult and long-term option.

Peter has just come into my study to report that Labour has won the Oldham by-election with a 10,000-odd majority. I feel a surge of hope. I interpret the result for a moment as a marvellous demonstration that the people of Oldham are on Corbyn's side, the side that does not want to respond to violence with violence. Wonderful, enlightened Oldham!

But then I understand that this is not the case. Most of the people who voted Labour are the ones who, naturally enough, think in terms of their own well-being. The vote was anti-austerity, not anti-war.

I am able to hold pacifist principles because I am fortunate enough to live in comfort and security. I'm not excluded in any way. I can stay in the country where I was born, speaking the language I was brought up to speak. I live in a democracy, not a dictatorship. For all its failings, our system aims to be fair and has held those aims for a very long time. I hear again Cousin Dickie's voice on the record he sent me in 1947: *"And it's by that there Magna Carta, as was signed by the barrons of old, that in England today we can do what we like – so long as we do what we're told."*

Recently I came across a book by a Californian called, coincidentally, Ernest Becker. The title is *Escape from Evil*. It's a neat coincidence that someone with the same name as the progenitor of the Manchester family of cousins should have written a book dealing with the question: why war? The book was published by his widow in 1975[103]. A reviewer described it as an exploration of the natural history of evil, a synthesis of post-Freudian, post-Marxian thought. I cant paraphrase an entire book but I can quote again a poem from Rainer Maria Rilke which Marie Becker included in the first pages.

> Why, if it's possible to spend this span
> Of existence as laurel, a little darker than all
> Other greens, with little waves on every
> Leaf-edge (like the smile of a breeze), why, then,
> must we be human and, shunning destiny,

---

[103] *Escape from Evil,* by Ernest Becker, (1924 – 1974), published by his widow with the Free Press, USA, 1975

Long for it? ...
    Oh, not because happiness,
That over-hasty profit of loss impending, *exists*.
Not from curiosity, or to practise the heart,
That would also be in the laurel ...
But because to be here is much, and the transient Here
Seems to need and concern us strangely. Us, the most
    transient.
Everyone *once, once* only. Just o*nce* and no more.
And we also *once*. Never again. But this having been
Once, although only o*nce*, to have been of the earth,
Seems irrevocable.

And so we drive ourselves and want to achieve it,
Want to hold it in our simple hands,
In the surfeited gaze and in the speechless heart.
Want to become it. Give it to whom? Rather,
Keep all forever ... but to the other realm,
Alas, what can be taken? Not the power of seeing,
Learned here so slowly, and nothing that's happened
    Here.
Nothing.

Nothing can be taken, but much can be left. I will end my commentary on the Cousins' Chronicle by including the whole of the last folder as written by the cousins. They must have the last word.

<u>From A.E.I Becker, Aunt Cissie, December 1945</u>
"I can't write at length as I have a sore thumb and it hurts me to write. I trapped it badly – such a nuisance as I want to write a lot of Xmas letters. We have so enjoyed the autumn tints this year and the weather was the best of the year. I don't know that I ever saw the atmosphere so blue & mauve & indigo as we saw it on different days, and the bracken and beech leaves looked so perfect in the sunshine. We have gathered abt. 1 ½ tons of logs by degrees so we revel in a very good fire when our work is done and we gather round it in the evening ... We may go to Barnston to see Mrs. Watts & Irene tomorrow (no date on letter) if Lett. can get the car to start, but it has been drained of all its water for safety in the frost & it's a job to get it all started again. It ought to be in Salisbury to be repainted but the coach builder hasn't got the paint, tho' he ordered it a month ago or more ...

I don't think I shall be back in London before the end of next summer. If we are here for the winter, I wd. prefer to stay till the end of summer, & then wind up here for good. I shall be very sad to leave the country, & this autumn I have simply loved the forest in all its wonderful beauty, something not to ever forget. Lettice has still got housemaid's knee in her elbow, she's had it about a month. It's better but not gone: She has had it twice before ...Trevor has introduced us to a new edible fungus & took an endless quantity back to London with him. They grow by hundreds on a dead tree in the forest. I have been taking Kruschen salts for the last month & feel all the better. I find if I do very little I am better than if I do a lot but it's difficult not to do things if they need attention. I am knitting Lettice a Cardigan but have had to stop till my thumb improves.

We have been enjoying Wartime 'Scotch Woodcock' lately & find it a very filling & quick meal. A round of hot marged toast spread with fish paste, anchovy sauce or anything savoury. Then make a thinnish white sauce, chop up a raw shallot & some parsley; add to sauce, bring to the boil, & pour over the savoury toast. The dish is open to endless variations of both 'spread' & sauce. If <u>very</u> hungry, 2 rounds of toast go down nicely!"

From Irene Becker, December 1945
"December has flown by with great rapidity. Trevor and I started off with a farewell visit to Monmouthshire on the 1st. My sister Winnie and her husband have just sold their home of many years and bought another much smaller one at Shaldon, near Teignmouth, Devon.[104]. They have struggled on through the war with their large house and garden, with inadequate staff throughout, and have now at last made up their minds to move where they can have more leisure and no longer the perpetual struggle of keeping a large place going, especially as they have no family, and only themselves to house. Their home is at Newport, which is my birth place and associated with all our earliest recollections and friends, and it was rather sad in a way to me to say good-bye. Winnie's home was always our last link with this long-ago, very happy past. Though we didn't go back there very often, especially during the War years, we did go on occasions, and I always loved going and meeting each time a certain number of old friends. Now that milestone is passed and the last link is about to end. The future for them will be different and I expect we shall all enjoy going to see them down in Devonshire, especially in the Summer at boating and fishing times. But we shall, all of us, including our children, always remember the jolly times we spent in that lovely countryside with picnics and parties, bathing in the river

---

[104] Pat Becker, the widow of Wilfred, lives in Ness Cottage, the house she built in the garden of Winnie's Shaldon house. It featured on TV's *Grand Designs*.

Usk, the tennis, the blackberrying, gathering mushrooms, and all we used to do.

We had quite a pleasant week-end and drove down to Cardiff and on to Taff's Well on the Monday afternoon, where we saw the building that had been on the site of part of our garden, where we used to live at Taff's Well, about 25 years ago. They have built a large bank on the part of the garden where the drive was and quite a number of houses on the lawn! Though the house itself is still much as before, with people living in it. I have no regrets about Taff's Well and felt quite glad we are not living there now, at any rate. Both Cecily and Wilfred were born there and christened in the Church and Mike used to hare about all over the garden on his tricycle, racing the trains arriving at the station at the end of the garden.

A week later I went down to Bournemouth to see how my mother was getting on with her temporary cook-housekeeper. Her memory is getting very bad and she didn't seem to know much about it in her not very frequent letters to me. I found, as I guessed might happen, that the housekeeper intended leaving for good on the 18th so I had to make arrangements to return later and take her to Tavistock for Xmas. My sister Edna said she would be very pleased to have her, and as it was impossible to make any other arrangements in the short time, we fixed it all up. There was a new maid coming on Jan 1st but until then Mother would have no-one at all to live in the house.

So I went down again on the 17th, stayed two nights at Barnston, and made the arrangements and we travelled on to Tavistock on the Wednesday the 19th. It wasn't too cold, which was pleasant, and though a number of other people were on the move, we managed to get seats in both trains, for which I was truly thankful. It was very pleasant at Tavistock. It has much softer air than London; it was sunshiny the next morning, though a bit showery between times, but there was a lovely feeling almost of spring in the air on the Moors. I went out for a walk on the downs, while Edna exercised her new horse and I called in to see Mollie and Jane and Susan, who were both full of fun and thrilled at the idea of their visit to Godalming for Xmas.

I returned home to London that afternoon, the 20th, as I did not want to fall into the Xmas traffic jam and I really had a very comfortable journey up to Waterloo, where Mike met me at the barrier. Trevor had been up to Glossop for three nights and he also returned the same day as I did. I wrote nearly all my Xmas letters in the train this year as with the three long trips I seemed to be spending such a time sitting that it was a golden opportunity to get something done: and I had very little time otherwise.

For Xmas itself we were all to-gether except for Wilfred who is now out in Italy. Juliet had a postcard from him on Xmas Eve stating he had found a niche for himself about 30 miles from Venice, which city he went down to explore on his day off the week before. He said it was certainly the most beautiful city he had ever seen. The shops were lovely and full of all the beautiful things which London lacks – at a price! He climbed the Campanili in the Piazza San Marco, which he had marked with an arrow on his picture card, and said he had a glorious view of the distant Dolomites and the Adriatic. This was interesting news to us, as Trevor and I spent a very happy few days in Venice twenty years ago when we stayed at the Hotel Continentale on the edge of the large lagoon near the sea coast. It was June then and the flowers in the gardens and on the stalls were glorious. It is such a joy to us to know Wilfred has had this good chance of seeing a bit of the World at its best. I imagine Venice has had no War damage and is as lovely as ever. He wrote on the 15th (Dec) soon after arrival and the card took 9 days to come. We have not heard since so perhaps other letters than Xmas ones will take longer.

Cecily came home on Friday the 21st and was able to be away until the 30th, as all the girls (except for a very few) at the Military School were away on holiday over Xmas. They had left a small skeleton staff on picket duty; but all the officers were away, so Cecily went down by the 9.27 a.m. from Waterloo on Xmas morning to superintend the Xmas dinner festivities there. She returned about 6.30 in time for our Xmas dinner here at No. 70. We had had quite a harassing time trying to find something appropriate for dinner beforehand, but we had no success with a turkey this year. We were unlucky in the butcher's draw and thought we should be rather short until, on the 21st, Nora the cook heard from her sister in Bucks whose husband has a market garden that she could get us a good one if we could collect it. So Nora went off post haste on the Saturday morning (the 22nd) and returned with a sumptuous bird on Sunday afternoon, which more than fed us all (in fact it made two meals) and we were ten all told: five of us - as we had no one except our own family this year; but the maids had two friends in, who have come back to London with their employers after the general war scattering. They played cards after dinner until midnight when Trevor took the visitors home in the car as they had to go as far as the Albert Hall neighbourhood, about two miles from here. It was fun having Cecily home and we enjoyed ourselves although we were only just the family. We drank Wilf's health and other absent friends, such as Roger, and I expect Grace was thinking of him too.

We couldn't ask anyone extra into dinner to begin with until we had secured something for our meal, also I was away taking Mother to Tavistock and not able to arrange it. Then at the last moment of course when we knew our goose was secured, everyone seemed to have their arrangements made up.

We went to tea at Aunt Loo Watts' flat down the square where she was entertaining Mollie and Geoffrey Gilby, Pat Reid and his wife and little girl Diana, for lunch & tea. Mollie & Geoffrey were missing their girls this year as they were both in Yorks and couldn't get home at Xmas-time.

Cecily returned on Sunday morning the 30th to her billet as she was changing her job and was leaving for Aldershot on the 1st.

Mike organised a party for the New Year's Eve dinner dance at the R.A.C. It was partly to celebrate the beginning of my birthday on the 1st and partly as a New Year's party for a small Xmas peace celebration. Trevor goes out on the spree very little and I think he quite enjoyed the evening. I know I did. We had three young couples and Trevor & myself. Two other young men, one who had just returned from five years with the R.A.F. in the Middle East and he was very gay and appeared to be really thrilled with his evening out. This one, John Burges, we knew as quite a small boy but had not seen him for years. There were three nice girls; a friend of Mike's, a friend of Cecily's and a little French girl, a friend of Veronica Gilby's. The young folks danced all the evening from 8.30 until 1.40 a.m. during dinner and all the time except of course during the cabaret at 11 o'clock. But Trevor and I required our dinner first to warm us up and it was latish before we got going. We were quite glad to find we hadn't got too rusty in spite of the fact we had not danced for at least six years!

What a relief this New Year came in to bid good-bye to all the fighting, doodlers and bombs. It is strange now to realize that only a year ago (at Xmas) we had a flying bomb over Glossop and several doing their worst over the Manchester area generally. Let us hope we may have a true Peace Conference this time and that they may be a real foundation for a World Settlement.

Strange to say, the news of the inauguration of the Conference at Westminster which is about to begin is being announced on the Wireless during the 6 o'clock news at this very moment. Let us hope & pray that it may be really successful this time."

From Alice Crompton, December 1945

"I stayed the night of the (reunion) party with Marjory Lees, at the very comfortable Kingsley Hotel, Bloomsbury Road. She came from Oldham on purpose for the party, returning there next day. Two other friends came from Bournemouth and one from Paynton (Ches.) not to mention others from Tonbridge, Guildford & Wycombe. The next two nights I stayed with the Hartogs in Kensington & did a little sightseeing. I had wanted to see Henry IV, but heard it wd. be impossible to get seats. So I contented myself one day with the Vict & Albert Museum where are the sculptures from Westminster Abbey, removed during the war and shortly to be returned to their home - those in the Triforium never to be seen again! After an hour or two with them the show of Picasso (& Matisse) pictures, also in the Museum, seemed more of a nightmare than ever. In all the controversy now raging in the Press about Picasso I am a strong anti. There was also a lovely little exhibition of Calligraphy by Edward Johnston wh. I greatly enjoyed. There I picked up some charming little verses about Blue Tits wh. I've sent to some of the Cousins.

Next day I refreshed my soul at the National Gallery, amongst the Old Masters. – The week-end I spent at High Wycome with Helen Ensor – very restful & peaceful!

Xmas preps. absorbed me on my return to Rye. However much I decide to do little or nothing, I never can resist being caught in the whirl of cards. I asked two friends, one after the other, to spend the fiesta with me here. However neither could come. But the two Miss Mannings kindly asked me to dinner & tea. At the risk of being thought silly, I copy here as much as I remember of their rhymed invitation (- MS unfortunately mislaid) – and my reply. (Ivy would have done the whole thing with much more wit).

"Alice dear when we asked you here
Our simple meal to share
We hoped to offer something nice
If nothing rich & rare.
But, spite of all our well laid plans
And all the butcher's talk
Instead of pheasant, fowl, or goose,
He sends a joint of PORK"

The next two verses apologize for the pork, and hope to see me all the same. My reply:

"What though of poultry, game & fish
The gourmands glibly talk
For me there is no better dish
Than a roast joint of pork.

Bring forth the apples, onions, sage
Which Mary* will combine
   * *the Mannings' excellent maid*
And tho the storms outside may rage
Indoors like Kings we'll dine.

The Chinamen their houses burnt
(So Elia tells at least)
And to the ruins gladly turned
To snatch the longed-for feast

For us no need such fires to see
Twas not done in the west
What luck for me to-day to be
Your very grateful guest."

I don't know if the Cousins are familiar with Charles Lamb's 'Dissertation on Roast Pork.' I remember Uncle Arthur reading it to me at Grandpapa's in Whally Range about 1876, & our chuckling over it together.

I had a very pleasant time at the Mannings: another guest was there (Miss Meredith) & a niece staying with them. Their drawing room, looking south to the Channel, was flooded with sunshine in the afternoon. After tea, I went back to Mermaid St. busily & happily occupied all evening with quantities of letters and cards. Altogether a very happy & peaceful Christmas, with time & leisure to think about the season more than is easy in the usual crowds & festivities.

A mysterious little happening has pleased me in Dec. Someone sent £3 to Dr Mallon asking him to buy a present for me, but on no account to divulge name of donor. Dr M. wisely sent a cheque to me so that I can choose the object myself. I'm contemplating an electric kettle for my bedroom, where I have a power plug. Or I may get something when in London in Jan. I haven't the least idea who is the donor!

A.C.

P.S. Is it a Lancashire or North Country custom to accompany roast pork with sage & onions? We had none in Rye on Xmas Day, & more than once that has been my experience in the South. A.C."

From Ivy Crompton, December 1945
"I write this on beautiful paper provided by Alice with margin duly turned down to forfend not against the likes of Shanks but the brains of hers which are far more prevalent[105] but I am duly grateful.

This month has been full of festivity (1) a party in London to celebrate Bobby and Pam's engagement (2) the father and mother of Xmas time parties for the village children & the New year's Day one we are having for a few local friends, the Bakers and the Harveys, Mr. Lucas who Alice knows, to drink a bottle of sherry I was given for Xmas.

The children's party was a great success & is of course always the nicest. We had a Xmas tree up to the ceiling and about 30 children making up to about 50 with parents. I contrived a toy for each child by making or painting up & generally resuscitating some very nice old toys of Caroline and Daphne's. We had 3 Xmas cakes made by the good baker and almond pasted and iced by Minnie. I stuck them full of tiny Union Jacks which Alice gave me ages ago & each child had a tiny flag with his slice and seemed delighted. Alice also kindly sent me a contribution of sweets which went with brightly coloured paper bags for each child.

We have rushing water everywhere here and are almost inundated, there is a rushing torrent all through the dam running down the steps and down the drive, it is a mercy we had it tarred and laid like a road in the spring otherwise we should be paddling in seas of mud. Jack

---

[105] Ivy's idiosyncratic way of thanking Alice for turning down the margin in advance for her, which Ivy thought was motivated by Alice's desire to protect her own clever competence against Ivy's incompetence. Well, I think that's what Ivy meant.

was up at 2.30 this morn, wakened by the rushing sound of water & had to go & lift the sluices which he had already done before retiring. The sun is shining brightly, the whole effect rather wild & bizarre but quite beautiful. It's a bit anxious for the cottages but Jack manages the water wonderfully. The so wet garden is the house's gem & we have now had the 2 bathrooms one lavatory & 2 bedrooms beautifully done up by our dear old gardener who is indeed a handy man & we count ourselves very lucky.

Bobby & Pam spent Xmas with her mother at Fleet & on Boxing Day had lunch with Lady Busham (Peggy's mother) where Peggy & George & Peggy's sister Betty, the 3 children, George & Peggy's 2 girls & Betty's little boy were gathered together. Then they came here for Boxing night & back to work next day. Pam has most beautiful manners & is very pleasant to have in the house, she is wonderfully appreciative of every small thing & is much more like we used to be in our youth than the moderns of today. That doesn't mean anything against the moderns now of which I take & keep my hat off to, but only an extra good mark for Pam. I hope she has enough "beans" to face life under modern and impecunious conditions; she is willowy & with the most lovely fair colouring but does not look awfully strong, but they tear about so I suppose she must be.

Jack paid a visit to Dolly Bramwell (his sister in law) & spent the night before our party there, he much enjoyed seeing them all again, except the boy David who is in Malaya. We hope to have some of them on a visit here. We slew 2 chickens for Xmas & I still have one cockerel & 2 female fowl for the pot. Eight hens and 6 ducks remaining. We are getting 1 duck's egg & 2 or 3 hens' eggs daily. It seems to me that the hens' moult has been very severe this year, perhaps to suit the mild weather & get it thoroughly done; they begin to look decent again now but it is at present a maddening matter for them, poor dears.

We haven't sent any Xmas cards this year but would like Kathleen & Archie to know how lovely we thought the card they sent us and here is sending our love & wishes all good to everyone in 1946 – and would it be out of place to say how nice we think everyone is?"[106]

From Jack Crompton, December 1945
"Two major incidents mark December's caper. A. Ivy's cocktail party in London. B. A burglary here early in the month. The party was to celebrate Bobby's engagement and was held in Gladys' flat in the Brompton Rd. Ivy and I drove up the day before laden with food, flowers etc from home & I dropped Ivy at the flat & after tea drove out to Surbiton & spent the night with Dolly Bramwell, my sister-in-law, whom I hadn't seen for years - also seeing there her husband, whom I had previously just met, and their other 2 daughters whom I

---

[106] Not out of place at all, Ivy. You could say nice things about nice people in the days before the birth of cynicism.

had never seen. It was a great pleasure to see them all. I left Surbiton after lunch & drove back in time for the party, which was a great success. There were about 45 people there. They began moving about 6.20 and some liked it so much that they were still there at 10. I fled away at 9 and got some food at a nearby restaurant & then retired to a bedroom in the same block. Nelly Alescher gave me breakfast and I returned here in the car leaving Ivy to do some jobs for her sisters & to go to a wedding later. She has now got back. Those at the party known to the CFC were Trevor, Irene, and Michael, Paul Werner, Nelly and Chas. Alescher, Elizabeth & Rolf Bick, Gladys and ? Simson.

The burglary was an odd affair. It happened just before we left for London. A pane was broken in the French window leading on to the loggia, the key was turned and the door opened. Ivy's desk & cupboard was smashed but nothing appeared taken tho there was £20 in an envelope in the desk. They did the same in my study, where there was £4 loose, emptied my wallet, left clothing & petrol coupons, but took Ivy and my identity cards. We miss nothing else except a mantelpiece clock from the drawing room. The police came very promptly with fingerprint experts, cameras, etc. but so far there are no developments. They might have taken silver, cash, clothing etc ad lib. We are lucky that the thing doesn't make sense so far.

Things outside are more or less at a standstill owing to the wet & our old gardener has been painting & decorating my bedroom & made a very good job of it. We shall do the rest bit by bit by ourselves. It hasn't been touched since it was built ages ago, but has stood up to things very well on the whole.""

From Grace Werner, December 1945

"A mild month in the North as far as we were concerned in these parts. Our Flat goes on slowly. Kathleen took Father in order that he should be out of the draughts & mess – but so far, beyond a mess, there is little of the Flat to be seen.

We had a very nice evening party at the beginning of the month. Sir William Milligan's daughter is back in Wilmslow. She married Denis Vernon. We used to play tennis with him at the Schneiders in the old days. They gave a very good "do" and Henry and I both enjoyed it - & we met many people we had not seen for a long time.

I managed a visit to the Mauldeth Incurable Hospital to see the Nurse who was with Mother when she died. She has been an inmate there since 1931 & beyond a few visits to the garden in a wheel chair has never been out of bed all these years. I always feel better when I have been there & realised that anyone who has their health & strength to get about should not complain ...

We had our usual Christmas Party & as there were no young people we had it in the evening – Kathleen, Father, Barbara Henderson & Archie along with Joey, Gladys, Josephine and Roy. All arrived in the time for the Kings Speech. Paul had a few friends in on Christmas morning for Drinks. He was here for five days. He and I went & helped with the Rodiers' Children's Party: thirty children none over the age of seven on Christmas Eve, a lovely sight. Mark Rodier was Charles's great friend & was killed a year after Charles. He was R.N. & lost his life during the Saint Nazaire raid. Alice will remember him - he came to see us the night we heard about Charles from the Air Ministry. He was a charming fellow & his parents will never get over his loss... The party was in honour of his niece's seventh birthday. Our two geese fed us well and were very tender. We were eleven in all. And once again Mrs Hobson took charge in the kitchen with a friend if hers so I had a restful day.

Roy is still at home, his arm had to be replastered. So it's a long business. Gordon is at Warrington & home for the New Year. Josephine, like a bright young flower, is dashing from party to party. It's lovely to see her so enjoying life & makes one feel young again. Harold, much to our sorrow but I am sure to his joy, sailed back to Canada on the 22nd. We had so hoped that he might be with us for Christmas. He crept into all our hearts & we shall miss not having his visits to look forward to. Father returned here on the 29th for a few nights. K & A with Barbara were off to a New Year's Eve party & as there is no maid living in did not like – of course – leaving him on his own. We were very sombre here."

From Molly Withington (a letter copied for the Chronicle by A.C.), December 1945
"Molly has had Jane ill in bed at Godalming with temperature & inflammation of the middle ear, & has naturally been anxious. Jane is improving now (8th Jan) but the Dr. won't let her travel back to Tavistock 'till about 11 Jan. So I am giving news for C.F.C. from Molly's letters. She & the 2 children went to her Cousin Beryl Lucas at Tuesley Corner, Godalming, for Xmas. She says:

"We've had a lovely Xmas – so many people about which. is v. refreshing for me. We were 8 for Xmas dinner at Downderry & 14 for tea here that day. The children go to a party at the George Mellersh's at Guildford on 29th Dec. On 28 Dec Beryl had a Children's party – about 20 for tea. It all went off very well and was such fun: charming children. I like a winter party – more cosy than a summer one, and the house looks so pretty with the Xmas decorations & Beryl & I decorated a lovely Xmas tree with electric lights on it.

Dicky & his wife have been at Downderry for 5 days, but (28 Dec) have gone back to Sutton today. Mary is a pitiful sight, so thin and distorted with this frightful rheumatism, really a perfect wreck. She is so good & uncomplaining. She isn't quite so stiff as she was, though her circulation is so bad. She is going to a Home again next week at Beckenham. I don't know how long for but she really needs nursing."

Molly had much enjoyed seeing Irene at Tavistock, when she (Irene) paid a flying visit there to take Mrs Watts to Mrs Rees."

The Cousins' Family Chronicle ends with a newspaper cutting pasted in, with a note written by Henry Werner.

From Henry Werner, December 1945
"This may be interesting to the cousins as it is written by a cousin of mine whose name is Rappard not Pappard as in the Daily Mail. I saw him in August when seeing Roger off to India and had an interesting chat with him. He was on a mission for the Swiss Government.

Cutting from Daily Mail:
LETTER TO LONDON
...But this is Britain's brightest hour.
Sir – After the war, Field-Marshal Jan Smuts once forecast, Great Britain will be poorer and weaker but more deeply admired and more generally beloved all over the world than ever before in her history.
But my English friends, only too convinced of the impoverishment and enfeeblement of their country, fail to realise that the latter part of the philosopher-statesmen's prophecy has come true at least as fully as the former.
What we in other lands admire most and love best in Britain is the quiet, unassuming heroism of her people; their steadfastness of purpose.
We admire their persistent will to see the right thing done not only to themselves but to all others, be it on the public forum of international conference or in food queues.
It is, in a word, the fundamental humanity of British virility.
Only a self-confident Britain can assume the moral and political leadership which we on the Continent have ever expected of her, and of which we stand in exceptionally dire need today.
There men and women in all countries – in those crushed by defeat after having been defiled by Nazism, and in those struggling out of the material ruin and moral morass of prolonged occupation and co-operation with the pestilential foe – who are impatient to reconstruct a better world. It is all these men and women who look to Britain for leadership.
They realise that outclassed as she is in manpower and in industrial resources by her two giant Allies to the east and west, she cannot restore and maintain the material supremacy to which the world in the 19th century owed its peace and its progress.
But they know also that she has lost none of the virtues which prevented that supremacy from ever becoming oppressive.
It is all these men and women in the destroyed homes, the wrecked factories, the disorganised and often demoralised

universities of devastated Europe that know they can count on the wisdom and the courage of Britain for guidance.

To the present generation of Englishmen, bereaved of some of their earthly belongings, crushed by taxation, rationed to the last hole in their belt, it may seem paradoxical, ironical even, to speak of this as Britain's brightest hour.

I do so because I sincerely feel that never before in the course of modern history has any country enjoyed the respect, affection, and confidence of the citizens of other nations as Great Britain does today. –

William E. Rappard, Rue de Lausanne, Geneva."

Cousin Alice added to this her own note that Professor William E. Rappard was a Director of the Graduate Institute of International Studies, Geneva, and former Director of the League of Nations Mandate Section.

The objective of the League of Nations, established at the end of the first world war, was to prevent wars by means of collective security and disarmament. With the outbreak of the Second World War, this optimistic aim had clearly failed. On October 24th 1945 the League was replaced by the United Nations. At first there were 51 member states, now there are 193. That should be a sign of progress.

Yet wars continue to be waged.

*

The Beckers, Wilfred, Trevor (sitting), Michael, Juliet, Cecily, Irene

Jack and Ivy Crompton either side of Pamela's parents
Mrs and Mr Hebblethwaite

Dick with his sister Molly Easton and Grace Werner, 1960s

Bobby Errington, Peggy and George Errington,
Caroline and Daphne as bridesmaids to Pamela
(nee Hebblethwaite) on her marriage to Bobby

Louisa Withington, 1993

My mother as a young women, Lake Windermere

My parents and Jane at a wedding, 1938
(I might be in a pram)

EIGHTEEN

Letter to the Cousins
Devon, December 31st 2015

Rain, rain and more rain. I've come in to my study to capture the tail end of the year. In the last twenty minutes, the view from my window has been masked by a sheet of rain which a strong wind is chucking against the window panes. I am remembering Juliet's description of a Glossop flood. There were floods in your day, Cousins. But in our day we don't just have the British climate, we have global climate change. There is no going back. The Arctic ice is melting. This year the Jet Stream has got stuck.

Yesterday, December 30th, the river Culm burst its banks and filled the low-lying fields from Hemyock to Culmstock and beyond, forging a wide watery sweep all the way down the Culm Valley, to swell even further the already overflowing river Exe. At the foot of our hill, the road, which usually crosses the Culm to lead into the village, disappeared beneath a raging torrent 100 yards wide. A mile downstream in the hamlet of Whitehall, the river swallowed another crossing. After a midday drinks party, we waded across the lane to Whitehall Mill where Lansi from Beijing looked out on her garden which had become an expanse of coffee-coloured water lapping at the walls of her house. Lansi was not worried. She trusted the pumping system put in by the previous owners. Two friends were staying with her, on a visit from Frankfurt. Rudi is an engineer and designer of alternative technology systems.

At the party on the 30th, we'd talked of climate change, migrants, terrorism - and porcelain. A Culm Davy neighbour mentioned a book he'd been reading about Meissen china. Meissen is in the province of Thuringia. The Germans of Thuringia discovered the way to make fine porcelain from a local clay, so challenging the Chinese monopoly. I have some blue and white Meissen china, which I've always understood came from the Hannibal Leigh Becker household. Perhaps it goes further back, to Ernest Becker who came from Thuringia. When Dickie Easton was living in London, he displayed some identical china on his mantelpiece. The blue and white Meissen plates emphasised our common inheritance.

Dresden, also in Thuringia, is another place name synonymous with fine porcelain. In four raids between 13 and 15 February 1945, 722 heavy bombers of the British Royal Air Force and 527 USAF bombers dropped more than 3,900 tons of high-explosive bombs and incendiary devices on Dresden. An estimated 23,000 or more people were killed.

There was no Christmas card from Dickie again this year. This thought prompted me to phone him. He sounded like someone bravely heaving himself up from a very low place. We plan to get ourselves set up on Skype. Family connections become more important as we get older. His 'blank mind syndrome', as they call it in the States, was slightly more evident. He again talked of the way he was the odd one out in the family, off on his own. His couple of elder brothers were close in age. He, the third son, was much younger, an afterthought, maybe even a surprising mistake. After they were killed, he was again the third of two. This time his parents made the exclusive couple. Len and Molly Easton were not unkind, they were just too full of grief to have much time for Dickie. The theatre became his home from an early age.

Peter and I were fortunate in our time and place of birth. Our only experience of war was as children growing up in a country which was not invaded. Peter's father, who had been an accountant with the Army and Navy Stores in India, was commandeered for work in the Ministry of Food which was moved to North Wales. Peter's uncle survived a Japanese prisoner of war camp. My uncle who served in Burma only suffered a broken arm. My father emerged from serving in both world wars without any physical or mental harm, as far as I can judge. Both Peter's parents and mine stayed together in long-lasting marriages with no apparent difficulty beyond an occasional, amiable bickering. The war did have its effects, though, on both of us. There were only a few years in my childhood when my father and I were continually together; from 1946 when he came home until I went away to school in 1949. In Peter's case there were frequent changes of location during the war. Like the cousins of the Chronicle, the Barrett family of four were constantly on the move – from London to Hever to

Deganwy to London again – and Peter kept changing schools. In the periods when the family was in the south east, the constant noise of planes overhead, the air raids, the bombing, and the threat of invasion had a lasting effect. He remains acutely sensitive to noise, particularly from aircraft. His earthly paradise was his studio in the house we built in the 1960s on the Greek island of Amorgos, where the only sounds were the occasional clinking of goat bells or the distant chug of a passing caique.

All in all, we've been lucky in our lives. I type this sentence with gratitude. A page from the Observer of December 27th lies on the desk beside me. The headline and lead-in reads:

"2015: A YEAR OF TERROR. AFTER PARIS, TUNISIA AND CALIFORNIA, CAN WE STOP IT SPREADING?

The sombre list of attacks across the globe has made this year one of the worst on record. Jason Burke analyses the background to the violence and its export from the Middle East to the west – and asks what hope there is for improvement in the year ahead."

I started writing this in May 2015. On June 26th, sunbathers on a beach in Tunisia were shot dead by an Islamic State gunman. Of the 38 killed, 30 were British, three Irish, one Belgian, one Portuguese and one Russian. I guess most of them were the sort of holiday-makers who have little idea of where they are. They got on a plane in their respective countries and got off at the airport local to their destination which would provide them with sun and sea and relaxation. They could have been anywhere else in the world that offers these things. As it turned out, the resort was the scene of their death.

On the last day of October a Russian airliner crashed in the Sinai Desert. The 224 passengers and crew were killed. The passengers had been holidaying in the Red Sea resort of Sharm el-Sheikh. Islamic State claimed that affiliates in Sinai had planted a homemade bomb on the plane, in retaliation for the Russian bombing campaign in Syria.

On the 12th day of November shoppers in a residential area of Beirut were targeted by two suicide bombers. 239 were injured and 44 killed.

The Californian event, mentioned in the headline, was reported as an act of terrorism. A young couple killed 14 people in San Bernadino, proclaiming they were acting on behalf of Islamic State. In a land where gun crime flourishes on a vast scale, and thousands of innocent people are killed every year, the number of dead made it seem a relatively puny atrocity.

We are now into January 2016. Channel Four News told us that in the first five days of the year there have been 452 shooting incidents in America. 280 people have been injured and 125 lost their lives. A Republican presidential candidate, Senator Ted Cruz, wearing a lumberjack's check shirt, gave his view on the right to bear arms, as enshrined in the Constitution. "You don't stop bad guys by taking away our guns. You stop bad guys by using our guns." How many 'bad guys' are mentally disturbed? How safe is it to sell a gun to someone suffering from borderline personality disorder? These are people who experience sudden, unprompted surges of uncontainable rage. They cannot help these 'explosions'. Recent research shows differences in brain structure of people with this disorder. Many gun crimes seem to come out of nowhere. What was the motivation of the person who shot 20 children dead at Sandyhook, Connecticut, two years ago? This mass killing, out of the many that happen all the time, particularly affected President Obama. "Every time I think about those kids," he said, turning sideways to the camera before he was able to continue. "It gets me mad." His eyes glistened; tears seeped down his cheeks. The measures for gun control, which he may not be able to get past Congress, are minimal.

What hope have we when mankind continues to add violence to violence, and sane leaders are seen as weak.

The question I quoted at the beginning of this chronicle was "why war?" The simple two-word question includes so many bigger ones. We are trying to make sense of the fiendishly complicated, interwoven pattern of violent events happening around the world, and come up with solutions, even when we as ordinary citizens can do little or nothing to point ourselves in a better direction.

There are many theories put forward to explain the existence of war: Freud's Death instinct, the 'oil and corn' arguments, man's territorial needs. There are lots of reasons for fighting. It is what most people agree is the right response when occasion demands such action. It is what all life forms do, from the lioness defending her cubs to the Senator Teds of this world. We shouldn't be surprised by any act of aggression or violent defence. We can be creative, though, in finding better, more nuanced ways of accommodating our differences and avoiding fights in the first place.

We come together when we are threatened. On a parochial level, Cousin Alice's Chronicle united the cousins. Once the war was over, the CFC came to an end and the cousins ceased to communicate regularly. On a global level, perhaps the only hope for peaceful co-existence is for us to be challenged by an outside force. I'm not thinking of alien invasions. Something more down-to-earth could fit the bill. The one that comes immediately to mind is climate change. We are seeing more frequent natural disasters that will, sooner or later, put our survival on the brink.

Dear cousins everywhere, let's be optimistic. The League of Nations evolved into the United Nations, which must now become something more effective. I believe it is possible for us to evolve over time into more rational beings who can unite to keep our global home in life-sustaining order. If time we have.

<u>January 6th 2016, the Twelfth Day of Christmas</u>
Rain, rain, and more rain! A local flood inspired the thoughts of this ordinary, non-expert, 77- year old as I end my version of the Cousins' Chronicle. I want to conclude with something which fell into my hands the other day. Written in December 1945, it neatly echoes the end of the C.F.C.

An old schoolfriend, Sally nee Hamilton, who lives not far away brought me a folder of photocopied material which had been compiled by someone unknown for the annual festival of Horningsham, a village on the Longleat estate. The folder's compiler had chosen as a theme for the village's festival in 2008 the sojourn of the Royal School at Longleat during the

Second World War. The photocopied article I reproduce below was written by the headmistress at the time. Miss Harding, known as Lottie, led the school during its evacuation to Longleat from Bath. My sister Jane joined the school while it still occupied the mansion. Aged 10 in 1947, she remembers hearing the creaks at night while listening to the story of the ghostly 'Grey Lady' related by older girls.

In the folder was a contribution from an Old Girl who recalled following a little old lady in black up a spiral staircase, holding a door open for her at the top, and finding that she had disappeared. I learnt from another enclosure in the folder that Lottie had previously been the headmistress of Sandecotes school in Bournemouth, where Irene Becker had been, and later Juliet. This is a coincidence but no surprise. The threads that form our human networks are constantly intertwined.

From the 2008 Horningsham festival folder of Royal School memorabilia
"General Notes (December 1945)
The first thought in all our hearts this Christmastide must be one of thankfulness that the war is over, even though the problems that lie before us all are more complex and difficult than the comparatively straightforward task of winning the war. As a School we have been singularly fortunate; the casualties, grievous though each was, have been far less than we thought might be in 1939; we have lived here in safety, well fed and with few epidemics, and the quiet constructive work of education has gone on undisturbed. It seems strange now to look back on those dangerous days of 1940 and 1941 and to recall the dread that weighed on our hearts. Some days stand out vividly. There was one when a parent, a distinguished general, came to say that his daughter was to go abroad as it seemed likely that we should be invaded at any moment, and if this country were to be a battle ground it would be no place for children. There was another day when two serious young officers came to look over the house as a suitable H.Q. for the Staff in charge of the battle that would be fought round Warminster. They told us that the tank-trap, that astonishing little ditch that stretched across England and passed just outside the gates of Longleat, was our second line of defence, and so Longleat would be in the thick of the fight. When asked if the School was to be evacuated once more, they said we must stay since the Government had decided at all costs to avoid the problem of refugees on the roads."

I must interrupt here with some statistics. At the end of the war, between 11 and 20 million people displaced by the war were moving about Europe in search of shelter. Two years after the end of the war, 850,000 people were living in camps for displaced persons. In 2015 more than a million refugees and migrants entered Europe. The number of people stuck in the Calais camp known as The Jungle has risen to 6,000.

Back to Lottie and the Royal School at Longleat.

"They chose a suitable place in the cellars for a wireless transmitter, arranged for officers to be quartered in the Great Hall, the cooking to be done in the kitchen, and the wounded to be cared for in the Gatehouse. The whole thing seemed like some fantastic nightmare, though it had its humorous side, when a few days later two other officers, ignorant of the previous visit, came to do exactly the same thing, and seemed slightly dashed when they heard of the earlier birds. There was yet another day when in brilliant sunshine large numbers of German bombers came over us on their way to attack Bristol. We stood out in break-time watching what seemed like an army of silver beetles moving relentlessly miles above us; then the fighters came out from Bristol and the German planes turned back only to meet another lot of fighters from Yeovil. The whole thing seemed so unreal and remote and yet so exciting that we had no sense of danger - the School was most upset at being sent to the cellars. There were the nights when German bombers went over us on their way to attack Bristol or South Wales or the West Midlands, and from the roof one could see the furious anti-aircraft fire from the Bristol defences and the long fingers of the searchlights silently probing the skies. The School had not returned from the holidays on the nights of the Bath raids, but for those members of the staff who were here it was a painful unforgettable experience. Some of us learnt to go to bed very late and to sleep very light so as to be ready should the School have to go to the cellars. The last vivid memory is of the night before D Day, when we lay listening to the endless roar of planes overhead and though 'This is It' as we prayed for the safety of all concerned.

Those days are over; the planes rarely fly near us now; the searchlights are gone; the Americans have left and their hospital in the park is empty; and fathers and brothers are coming back from prison camps and from Burma and from the Continent. Now we are asking when we are to return to Bath. The Admiralty, however, seem to stick to our buildings like barnacles, though they assure us they are doing their best to find alternative accommodation. Much will have to be done to our buildings when they go, so we cannot hope for a very early return. Till that day, in order that we may always remember them, we shall look at the lovely things we must leave behind and shall long for.

Our stay here, so far from the suffering, the homelessness and hungry misery of others, should make us realise that we have not been spared to lead selfish lives, but called to service the needs of the world: the greater our immunity from harm, the heavier our responsibility to be worthy of our calling."

Wars continue. Where's our answer?

Postscript and Acknowledgements
First of all, I want to say a heartfelt thank you to two people who have been my sounding boards throughout the production of this book. They are my husband Peter and my good friend and invaluable editor Christine Walker. Besides giving steady support, they have brought my attention to gaffes and corrected stupid errors. I claim responsibility for all that remains despite this help.

Thanks to Max Hastings for his kind permission to quote liberally from *All Hell Let Loose, The World at War 1939-1945*, a wonderful resource. Thanks, too, to my sister Jane and Lynn Guy, fellow typists and decoders of handwriting; to Nicola Werner who lent me the original Cousins' Family Chronicle and, with her sisters Frances and Catherine, have given me permission to publish the extracts in this book; and to the cousins who have provided support, information and photographs.

Among the known living descendants of the four 19th century Becker siblings are:
(descended from Mary Becker, born 1927, m. John Henderson)
Charlie, Roger and Diana, the children of the late Roger Werner, the Assam tea-planter, son of Grace
Charlotte and Alexander, children of the late Paul Werner, son of Grace
Frances, Nicola, Catherine, daughters of the late John Werner, youngest son of Grace
(descended from Wilfred Becker, born 1850, m.Alexandra)
Jacki, Pauline, Susie, Steven and Helen, the children of the late Wilfred Becker, son of Trevor
(descended from Louisa Becker, born 1854, m. Edmund Withington)
Richard Easton, son of Molly Easton
Jane and myself, daughters of Richard Withington

Cousin Alice, daughter of Victoria Becker, never married. Her brother Jack, married to Ivy, only had step-children so Victoria's genetic line died out. But I was lucky to meet, thanks to the present owners of Doncombe Mill, Daphne (now Lady Powell), the younger daughter of George and Peggy

Errington, Ivy's son by her first marriage and his wife. Thanks to Daphne for providing information and photographs.

Mary Becker's line proliferated down to today's Werners. Wilfred Becker's line faltered. Of his son Trevor's four children, Michael, Cecily and Juliet never married and died young. But the younger son, Wilfred, married. He and Pat had six children born between 1952 and 1966: Jacki, Pauline, Robert (who died in 1973), Susan, Steven and Helen.

Louisa Becker's line started many years after Mary's, as she was the youngest of the large family. Jane and I are of the generation above the Becker cousins listed here and two generations above the Werner cousins. Our single first cousin is Richard, living in New York[107]. He devoted his life to acting and remained single. Jane made up the numbers with her five sons. I have two children by adoption. So families multiply or shrink; genes are passed on down the line or meet an abrupt end. Some families stick together; others split asunder. A family is an organism like any other, owing allegiance to the laws of nature: the survival of the fittest. We are Us. Others are Them. It's not surprising that humans fight, especially when inspired by mentally unstable demagogues. Homo sapiens is a dangerous animal, but one capable of glorious acts of altruism and art. May we and our habitat survive, despite our nature.

I'm concluding this in the autumn of 2016. Seven thousand migrants are rescued in the Mediterranean. Large numbers continue to drown. In Syria, chlorine gas suffocates children, if they have not been maimed or killed by bombs. Atrocities abound, many of them never making our British news channels. We watch the approach of the American presidential election with foreboding. We have no idea what lies in the UK's future outside the European Union, having been manoeuvered out by the sleight of hand of two unprincipled politicians.

---

[107] It was wonderful to see Dickie in New York in June 2016. He gave us a wonderful meal at the Redeye Grill on Seventh Avenue. By virtue of his Tony award, unfailing charm and regular custom, he was greeted with great warmth by the staff.

At the same time, there have been the Rio Olympics, to take an instance of human brilliance. We watched the divers facing backwards, with just the toe-half of each foot on the edge of the high diving board... then held our breath for the moment of still, balanced, intense concentration ...witnessed the sudden gathering of will... and then the flash of twists, turns and somersaults before the diver entered the water like a knife. A human being can do that! And another instance, listening to the angelic voice of a soprano singing a Danish composer's watery Ophelia. Music from another realm, surely. Good and evil; destruction and creation, existing side by side. It was ever thus.

This book is like a net cast into time, catching moments of the present as well as England's wartime past. It's a personal perspective on the experiences of an English family of cousins, experiences shared by so many other families who lived through the Second World War.

In appreciation of Cousin Alice and all the cousins who contributed to her Cousins' Family Chronicle

Susan Barrett
Devon, 2016

The cover of the folder containing the newsletters written
between June 1943 and February 1945

OTHER WORK BY SUSAN BARRETT, 1968 to 2016

JAM TODAY Michael Joseph ISBN 7181 0664 4
'*Goes at a cracking pace.*' Robert Nye, Guardian
'*Pithy and to the point. Beautifully sustained.*' Sheffield Morning Telegraph
'*A jolly romp ... I found this hilarious.*' Daily Telegraph

MOSES Michael Joseph ISBN 7181 0760 8
'*One of the wittiest novels I have read recently.*' Derek Stanford, Scotsman
'*A delightful and amusing little comedy.*' John Whitley, Sunday Times

NOAH'S ARK Michael Joseph ISBN 7181 0892 2
'*A delightful comedy of manners, astringent enough not to be coy and thoughtful enough not to be frivolous.*' Francis King, Sunday Telegraph
'*Susan Barrett is extremely skilled at comic dialogues, especially in domestic scenes and inter-family conversations.*' Valerie Jenkins, Evening Standard

PRIVATE VIEW Michael Joseph ISBN 7181 1036 6
'*Highly professional and enjoyable.*' Times Literary Supplement
'*Attractively written and above all attractively shaped.*' Evening Standard

RUBBISH Michael Joseph ISBN 7181 1288 1
'*A jolly lark about a nicely complicated felony. ...Taking a few swipes at materialistic society on her way, Mrs Barrett contrives some marvellous muddles.*' Sunday Telegraph

THE BEACON Hamish Hamilton 0-312-07038-1
'*What lifts The Beacon on to a different plane is Susan Barrett's understanding of people.*' Martyn Goff, Daily Telegraph

STEPHEN AND VIOLET Collins ISBN 0-00-223337-1
'*Susan Barrett has a direct style. She writes plainly, without nonsense. Credibility... is stamped on the pages like a visa on a passport.*' Andrew Sinclair, The Times
'*Susan Barrett's poignant and pleasing novel weaves together the two strands of the journey home and the unfolding narrative of Violet's*

life with great economy. She develops her characters with sensitivity and humour.' Simon Rae, Times Literary Supplement
'*A psychological itinerary movingly traced with great insight and skill.*' Patrick Leigh Fermor

NON-FICTION

TRAVELS WITH A WILDLIFE ARTIST
The living landscape of Greece, by Peter and Susan Barrett
Harrap-Columbus ISBN 0-86287285-5
"*The sort of book you wish you had written yourself,*"
Gerald Durrell

INDEPENDENTLY PUBLISHED FICTION

MAKING A DIFFERENCE ISBN 1-4251-1004-5
Trafford Print on Demand
This novel was inspired by a visit to Kosovo before the break-up of Yugoslavia. Through the main character who is convinced she has failed people who trusted her, the story demonstrates how all our actions, however small or unintentional, can make a significant difference to other people's lives.

WHITE LIES ISBN 13-978-1536806847
CreateSpace, Amazon, 2016
The joys and hazards of adoption are seen from the perspectives of three women over half a century. At the novel's heart is a mystery designed to keep you guessing until the end.

A HOME FROM HOME ISBN – 10: 1537014838
CreateSpace, Amazon, 2016
Malpractice and mayhem – the events of a single day in a care home are described in a way that blends humour with compassion.
'*I enjoyed A Home from Home, and admired Susan Barrett's imaginative verve and technical skill. ...She brings off one of the best things that a novelist can do – the creation of a world – and writes about it both vividly and elegantly.*'
Michael Frayn

Also:
Children's books with Peter Barrett, published worldwide.
Television play 'The Portrait', London Weekend Television.

Printed in Great Britain
by Amazon